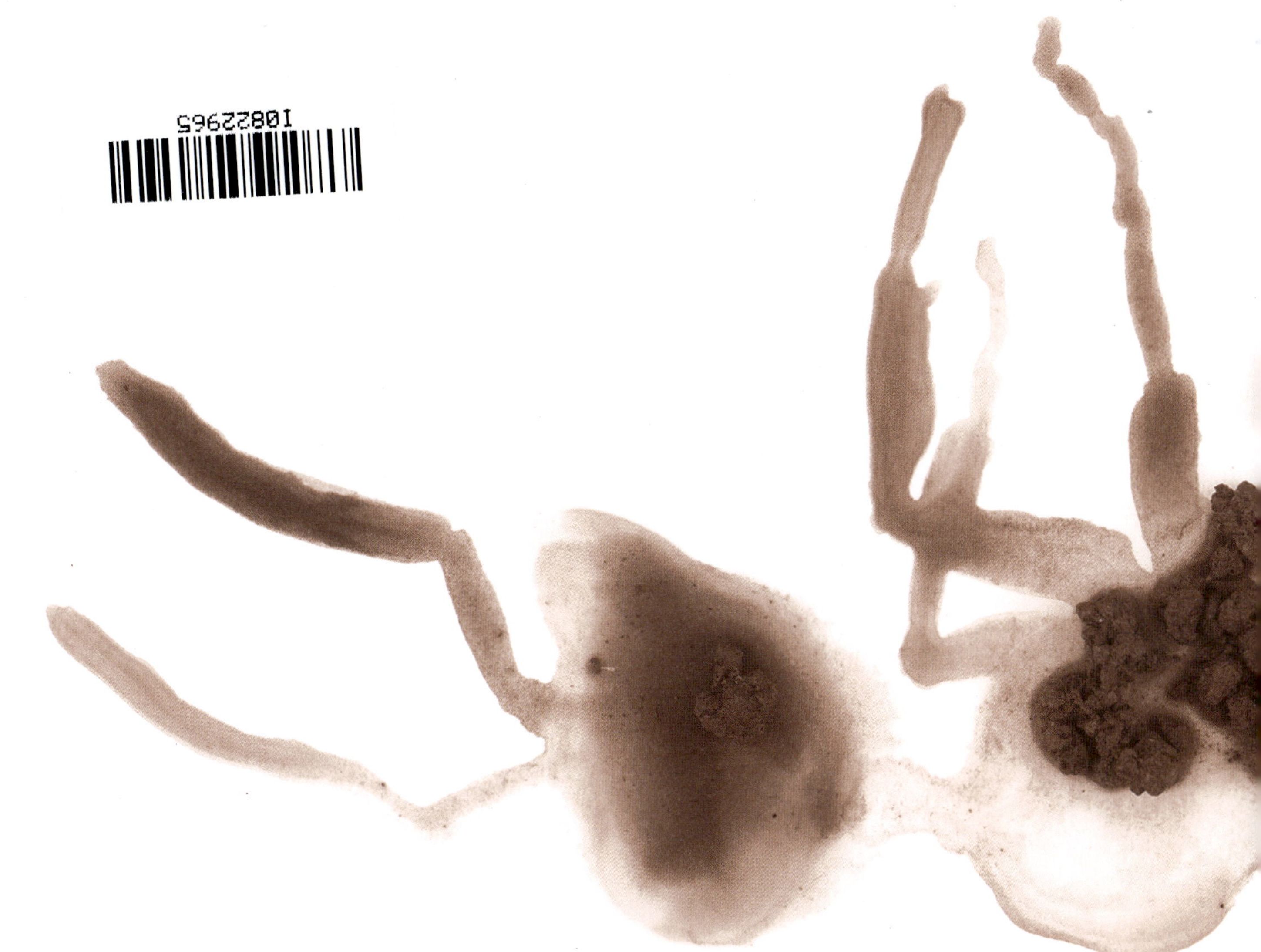

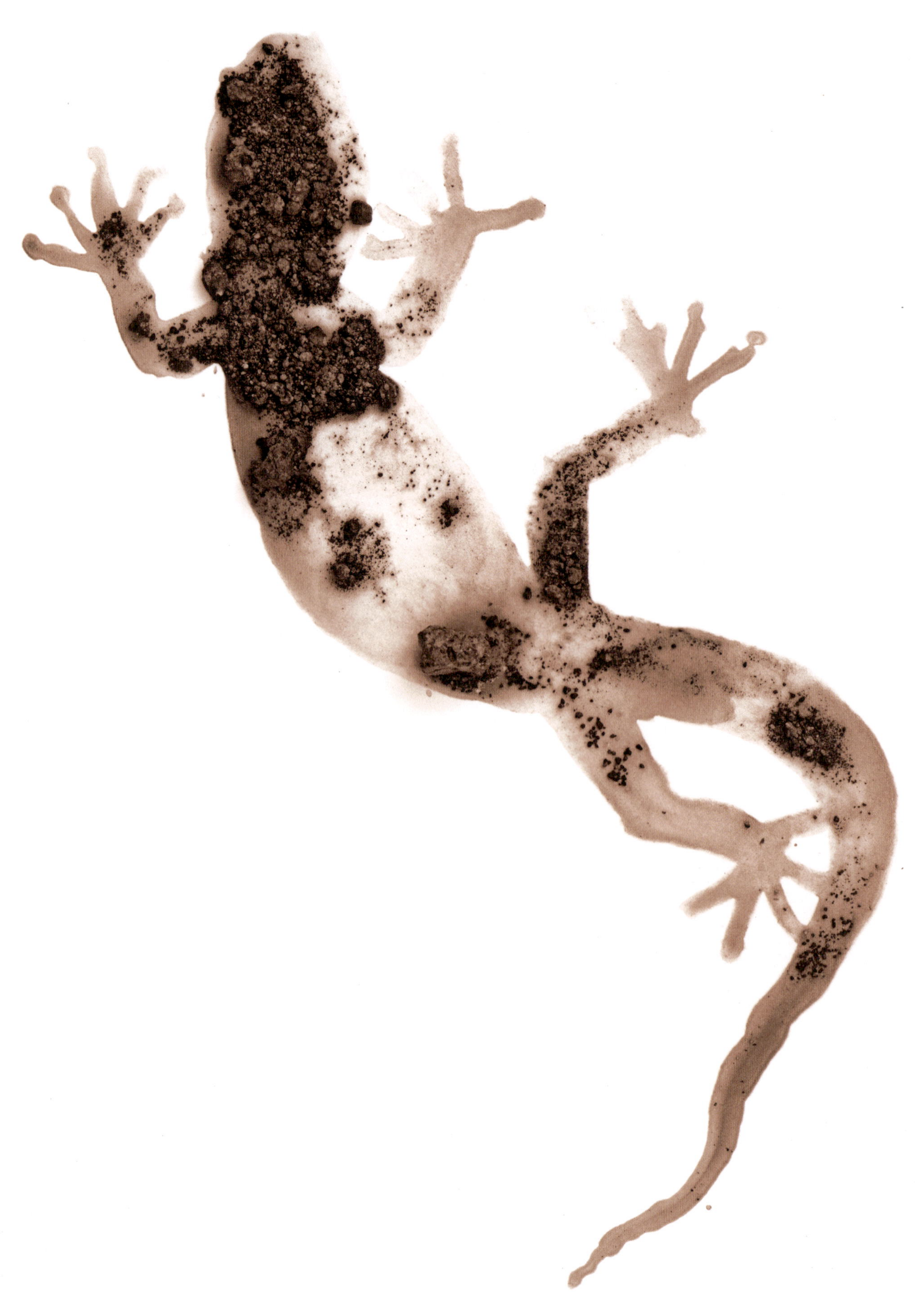

ALEXIS ROCKMAN

Naples: Course of Empire

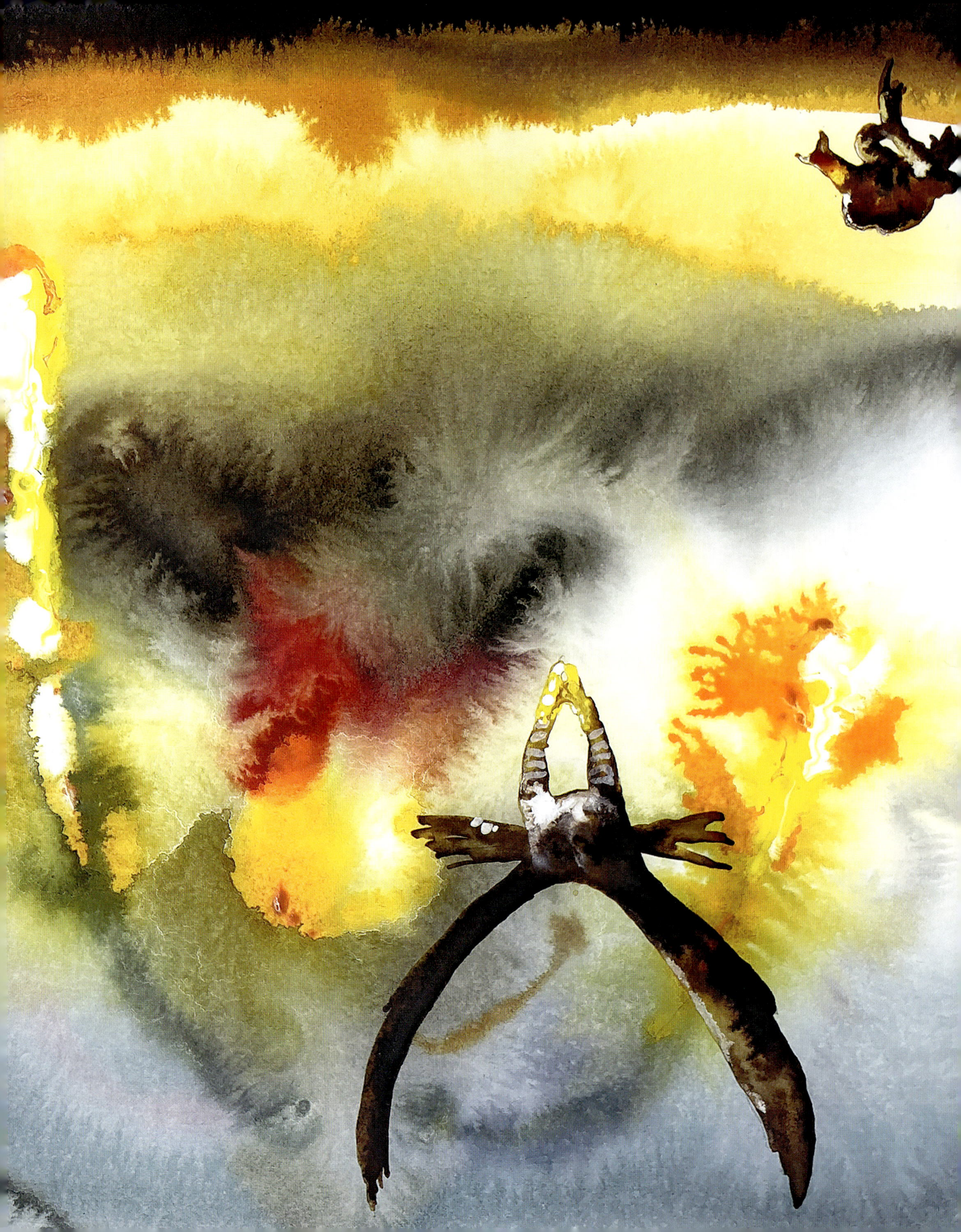

ALEXIS ROCKMAN

Naples: Course of Empire

Essay by

Dorothy Spears

MAGENTA PLAINS

HIRMER

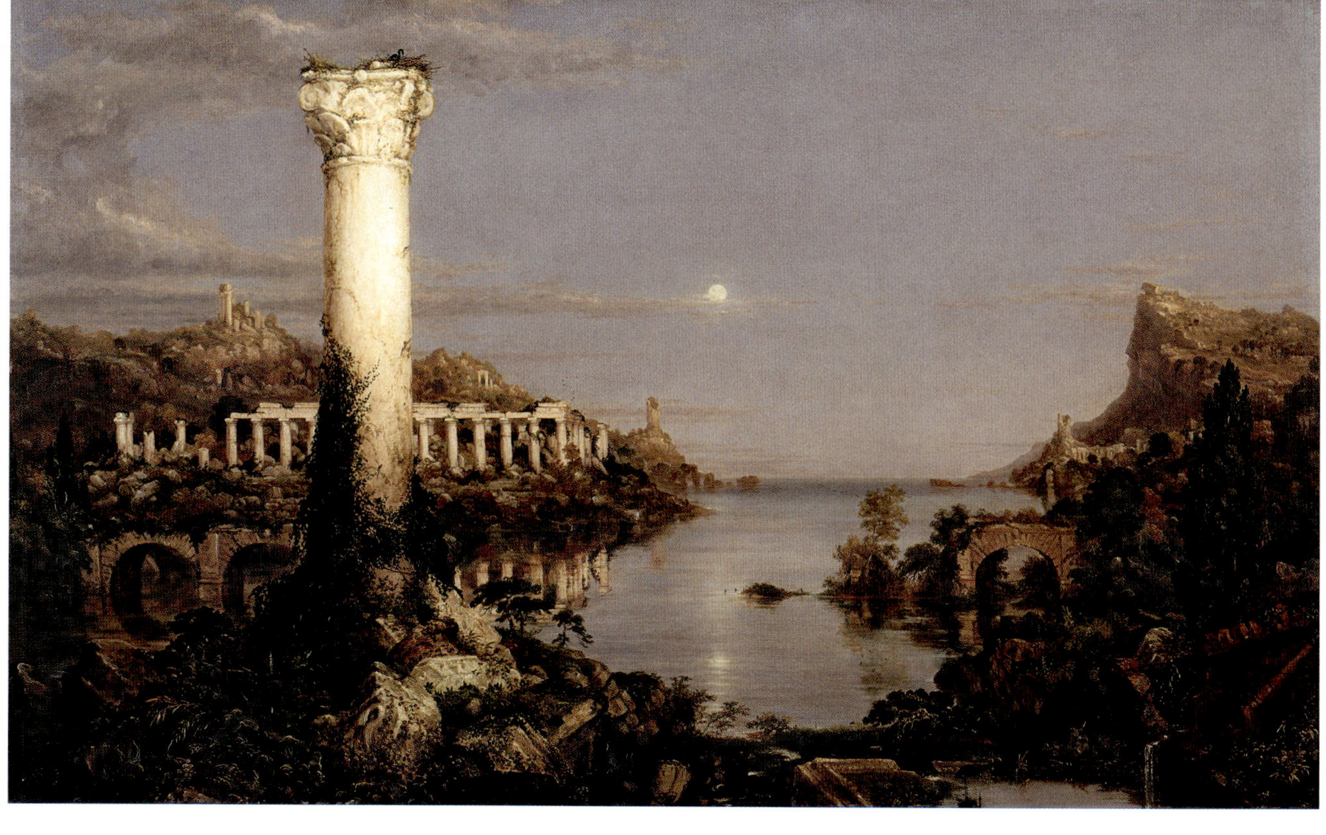

Thomas Cole (1801–1848), *The Course of Empire: Destruction*, 1834.
Oil on canvas, 39½ × 63½ inches (100.3 × 161.2 cm). The New York Historical, New York

Borrowed Time

by Dorothy Spears

Long ago, the landmass that would eventually become Naples sat below water, and much of Italy and Southern Europe were visible only as an archipelago of islands surrounded by the Tethys Sea. The global climate then was much warmer, and the sea, having reached some of its highest levels in history, was home to a seemingly boundless variety of colorful dinosaurs, marine reptiles, small early mammals, and flowering plants. "This was around 94 million years ago," Alexis told me. "During the late-Cretaceous period."

Alexis is my husband. He's also an artist who, having spent his forty-year career making paintings about life on our planet before and after humans came and destroyed so much of it, can sometimes sound like a walking pocket-guide to geological history. He and I had come to Naples to research a new body of work loosely based on Thomas Cole's famous series of five paintings, *The Course of Empire*. Alexis' new body of work would riff on the subject of empires come and gone in that uniquely spectacular — and precarious — place over time, and I planned to write an accompanying catalogue essay.

Alexis is passionate about natural history and dinosaurs. The more recent — *much* more recent, as he's quick to point out — appearance of human itinerant hunter and gatherers, who lived in caves and interbred with Neanderthals, is also a source of deep intrigue. So is the human introduction of domestic animals, and human engagement in activities such as ship-building and fishing. Add to that Naples' unrivaled trove of Western paintings and mosaics, from ancient Greek and Roman civilizations through the Renaissance, that have survived devastating natural disasters, crippling plagues, and blood-soaked struggles over the millennia. Then, taking all this into account, you'll understand why we've chosen this fabled, and multifaceted European city, perched atop the front ankle of the boot-shape peninsula known as Italy for our project.

Alexis is a planner. He was already considering his new body of work when we arrived that hot July. In keeping with his overarching passions, the empire he wished to privilege would encompass the overarching time-frame of nature's history, from the earliest known life forms in the area, and extending to its uncertain future when, perhaps, Nature would have her final say after the relatively brief indignity resulting from human occupation.

Alexis' proposed paintings, related watercolors, and drawings were originally intended for exhibit at the Fondazione Morra Greco, a former-palace boasting 2000-square meters of exhibition space. New sculptures, paintings, and ceramics by fellow artists Mark Dion and Dana Sherwood would be exhibited alongside Alexis' work in a three-person show that would reveal their many shared concerns regarding natural history and human impact on the environment, in this case Naples. The four of us are friends — Mark and Dana are also married. The prospect of spending nearly a week on a kind of protracted double date/research trip, touring the great museums and institutions of Naples, then sharing our experiences and ideas over sumptuous meals, as guests of the foundation's founder, Maurizio Morra Greco, felt like a dream come true.

To prepare for Mark and Dana's arrival the following day, the curator of the Fondazione, Giulia Pollicita took us on a tour of its stunning 16th-century space in the Palazzo Caracciolo di Avellino. Located in what is now considered the heart of Naples' historical center, the Fondazione's first floor recalled the building's earliest days as a convent, with the arching doorways and intriguing architectural details. The second floor seemed to owe a debt to the nobles who eventually took it over, with its soaring vaulted ceilings, classic columns, elaborately restored frescoed walls, and beautiful floor-to-ceiling windows framed by French doors. A staircase carved in volcanic rock led to a traditional white box space on the upper floor. There was also an underground space dating back some 800 years, its low curved ceiling carved out of bedrock and the remains of ancient Greek walls. Alexis' eyes glittered with possibilities after our visit. But the glories of Naples were only just beginning to unfold.

That evening, we toured the ancient catacombs, Ipogeo dei Cristallini, located below a private property adjacent to our hotel. The catacombs were first discovered in 1889 when, by sheer chance, the property's aristocratic owners blasted through their cellar and found a vast underground hollow, which they followed to this ancient burial ground, dating from the late 4th to the early 3rd century BCE.

Flashlights in hand, Alexis and I proceeded down a steep uneven staircase into darkness. Some sixty meters below ground, the air felt considerably cooler. We'd been advised to bring sweaters. Alexis, true to his Northern and Eastern European roots, wore a polo shirt and shorts. More Mediterranean-blooded me? I clutched my sweater around me, and we continued into catacombs that were said to be in use when Naples, still known by its name Neapolis, served as a major trade port for the ancient Greeks.

A series of separate burial chambers revealed well-preserved stone tombs shaped like bathtubs carved into the rock, hollow and dark. There were plastic trays piled high with skulls, femurs, tibia, and other smaller human bones, apparently in the process of being sorted, alongside architectural fragments — a head of a goddess; a carved capital of an ancient Corinthian column. Through a door in the final chamber, we saw the carved head of a Medusa, her face painted in flesh tones, her greenish hair

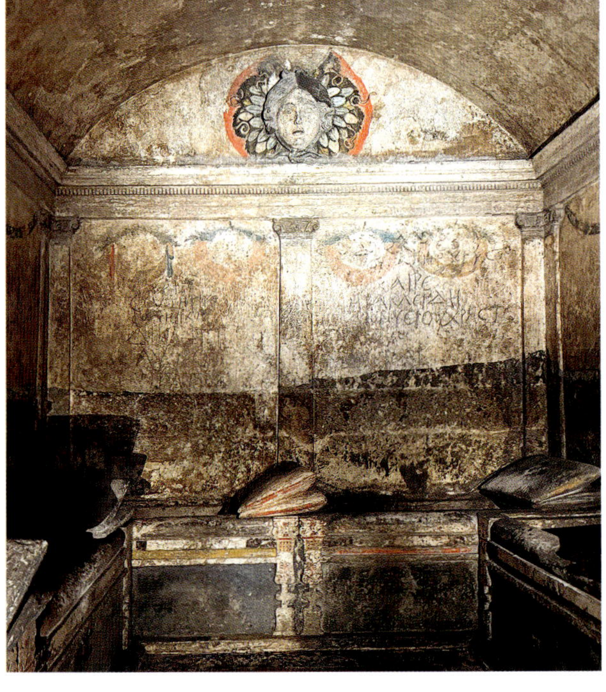

Medusa, Ipogeo dei Cristallini

wreathed in colored leaves and swirling brown snakes, and encircled in a band of red.

We had fear to thank, apparently, for these Greek remains of this Medusa, who presided over stone beds, topped with carved blue, red and ochre stone pillows, a painted rug, and what remained on the walls of a colorful painted landscape. When the catacombs were originally in use by the Greeks, we were told their ancient city, Neapolis, was increasingly falling under the influence of Roman expansion. Upon discovering these catacombs, the Romans were said to have stripped the tombs clean, preferring the purity of white to the Greek's more decorative flourishes — until the final chamber, where they were so terrified by the image of Medusa, they never dared enter, leaving the cursed Medusa alone, in all her ghoulish monstrosity.

On the steps leading back up toward evening, I remember pressing my palm against the cool jagged wall as much to steady myself as to prove that I was real. That this was all real. The effect of the catacombs was dizzying. Disorienting. Our trip through time had dislodged me from the present, such that I was suddenly floating, untethered in space.

After that visit, Alexis and I began to imagine the long string of contingencies that eventually came to shape Naples, the civilizations that had seized power, only to be decimated by erupting volcanoes, mudslides, disease, and — as often as not — insatiable human greed. But how did this landscape appear before it became a Greek colony? And what prehistoric contingencies had directed what was once an underwater landmass to the present day?

As if in answer to this question, we proceeded the next morning to the Stazione Zoologica Anton Dohrn with Mark, Dana, and Giulia. Opened in 1874, the world's first public aquarium also serves as an active center for scientific research. Designed by the German zoologist Anton Dohrn, it now occupies a main building featuring educational displays, labs, and specimens gathered from all over the world; an aquarium whose original tanks are still fed by sea water; an enchanting array of

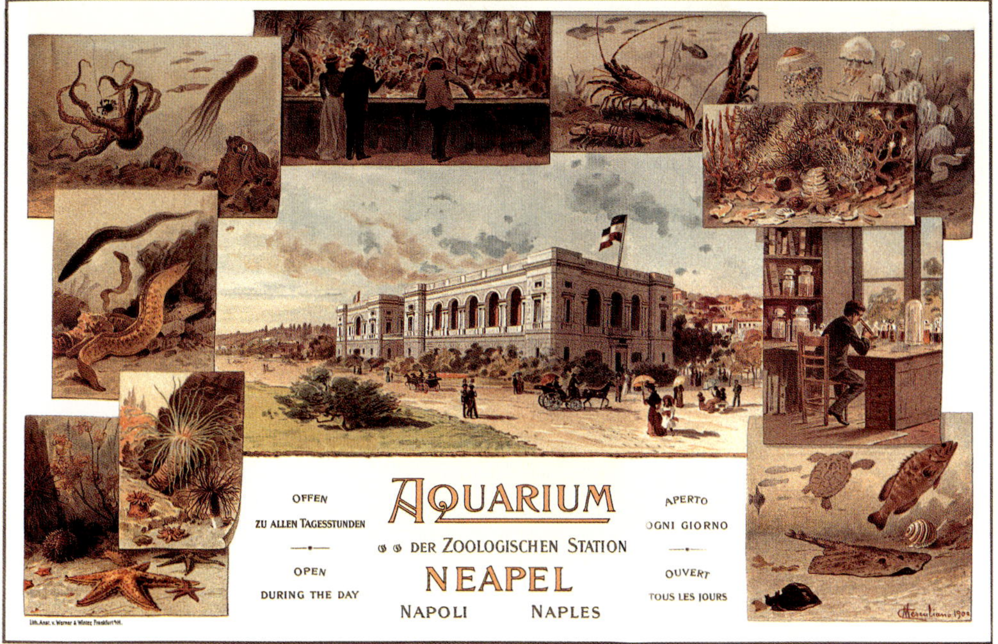

Vintage advertising poster by Comingio Merculiano for the Stazione Zoologica Anton Dohrn, which is recognized as the first public aquarium in the world. © Stazione Zoologica Anton Dohrn, Archivio Storico

living sea creatures; a library crammed with historic books; and the museum's extensive archives dating back to 1887.

Our tour guide, Ferdinando Boero, was a professor and researcher of marine biodiversity, evolution, and the impact of human activities on marine systems. We soon learned he also loved music, and in particular, the music of the late American rock legend, Frank Zappa. "Zappa wrote a song about a jellyfish for me," Boero informed us, "so I named a jellyfish after him." We were all duly impressed.

Continuing through the galleries, we passed wall diagrams charting ocean currents, glass shelves of undersea specimens, and a huge fossilized tooth of a megalodon, while Boero plied us with facts. "Oceans cover 70% of planet's surface," he said, "but in volume they occupy more than 90% of planet's space." It was a reminder of how small we were as humans, and how much damage we could cause.

Alexis, who has loved dioramas since he was a little boy in New York City, roaming the halls of the American Museum of Natural History, appeared mesmerized by a diorama known as "whale-fall," which presented a timeline of a whale after its carcass had sunk to the bottom of the ocean. In this particular diorama — which was free-standing — the carcass offered vital food for scavenging sharks, giant isopods and hagfish. Life after life, so to speak. It was this diorama, Alexis told me later, that planted the first seeds for his painting *The Fossil Record: Tethys Sea* (2024, p. 28), in which he applied the principle of "whale-fall" to an extinct marine reptile.

After a quick lunch, our group moved on to the aquarium, where we marveled over

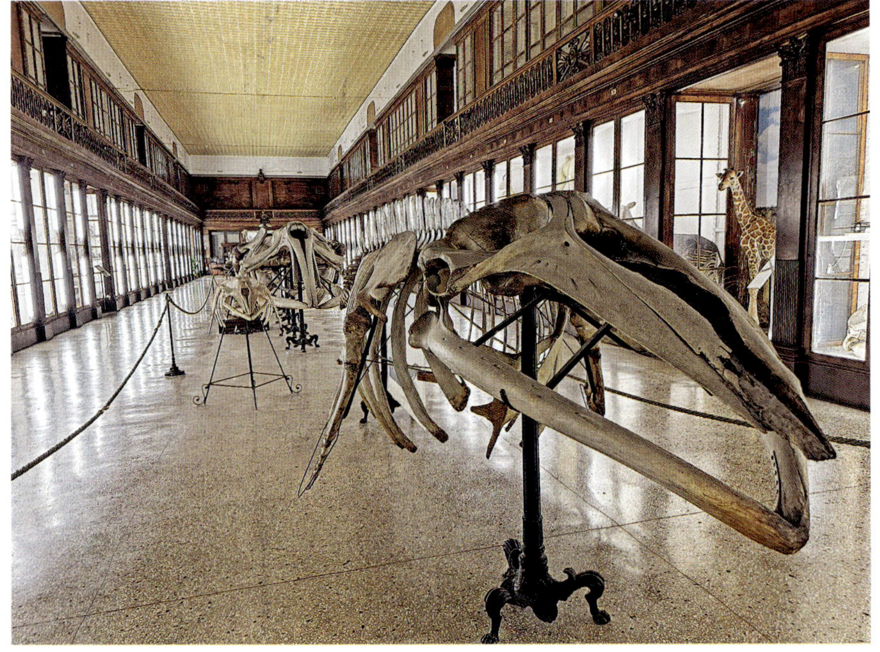

The Museum of Zoology, University of Naples Federico II

tanks of live fish, sharks and other dazzling sea creatures. In another part of the complex, we explored archives comprising the administrative and historical life of the museum. There, gray cardboard boxes were piled high with manuscripts, typed scientific documents, old photographs, and faded postcards. There was a suitcase full of letters written by Charles Darwin. But the biggest draw, at least for Alexis, were flat files filled with scientific drawings.

"I've never seen better drawings of specimens," he whispered, as we pored through illustration after extraordinary illustration of zooplankton, octopus, crabs, and whelk by Neapolitan artists from the late-19th and early-20th century. The drawings came out of a tradition that preceded photography — and how beautifully they revealed the vivid colors of individual sea creatures before they slipped into gray as they died!

Alexis would remember these specimen drawings when he painted the invasive orange and white lionfish, the purplish dusky spinefoot, and the backlit blue reticulated leatherjacket in *Acquario di Napoli - Stazione Zoologica Anton Dohrn* (2024, p. 58). "I took the lionfish out of the aquarium," he told me afterward, "and put it outside in front, as part of the rising sea." In the painting, the historic museum/research center/aquarium appears submerged underwater, due to the inevitable sea rise caused by human-generated climate change.

The specimen drawings in the Stazione archives would also inform Alexis' field drawings of flora and fauna native to Vesuvius, and his painting, *The Departed* (2024, p. 52). Except instead of celebrating the abundant biodiversity of the Mediterranean, *The Departed* reads like a funeral. Its succession of historical boats — from primitive canoes to more recent commercial fishing boats — loom above the water while, below, a colorful parade of marine life — from tiny prehistoric diatoms, to brine shrimp, bottlenose skate, smalltooth sawfish, and assorted sharks — represents species now either extinct or under threat due to human pollution and activities such as over-fishing.

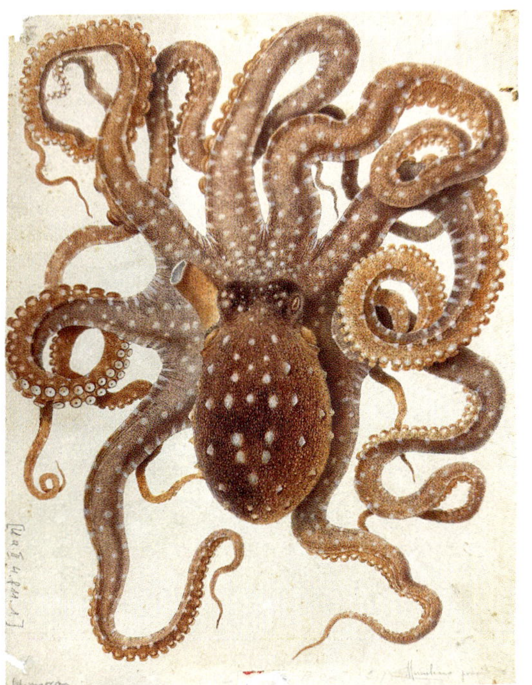

Comingio Merculiano (1845–1915), *Atlantic White Spotted Octopus (Callistoctopus macropus)*, 1897. Watercolor and gouache on paper, 17 × 14½ inches (43.1 × 36.1 cm). Collection Stazione Zoologica's Historical Archives, Stazione Zoologica Anton Dohrn

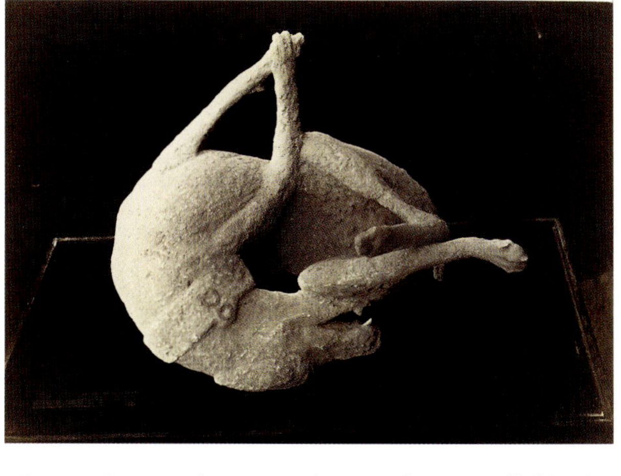

Giorgio Sommer (1834–1914), *Cast of a Dog Killed by the Eruption of Mount Vesuvius, Pompeii - Catalogue nr. 1287*, 1863. Albumen silver print, 7⅝ × 9⅞ inches (16.9 × 25.1 cm)

At the Anatomical Museum the next morning, we passed many congenital anomalies, mummified bodies, shrunken heads from South America, skeletons of conjoined twins. Collections of skulls were used for studying the human brain. Collections of eyes — the largest in the world, we were told — were used for teaching about pathologies. Large jars filled with formaldehyde contained a variety of human body parts. Displays of hands appeared to reach through time, as if to touch us.

But for Alexis, even the skulls unearthed from Pompeii after the eruption of Mount Vesuvius felt peripheral to his work. Of his painting, *Plague in the Kingdom of Naples, 1656–1658* (2024, p. 46), he said, "I'd been dying to make a plague painting since I first saw Pieter Bruegel the Elder's *The Triumph of Death* (1862), and Arnold Böcklin's *Die Pest* (1898) in the early 1980s." The subject

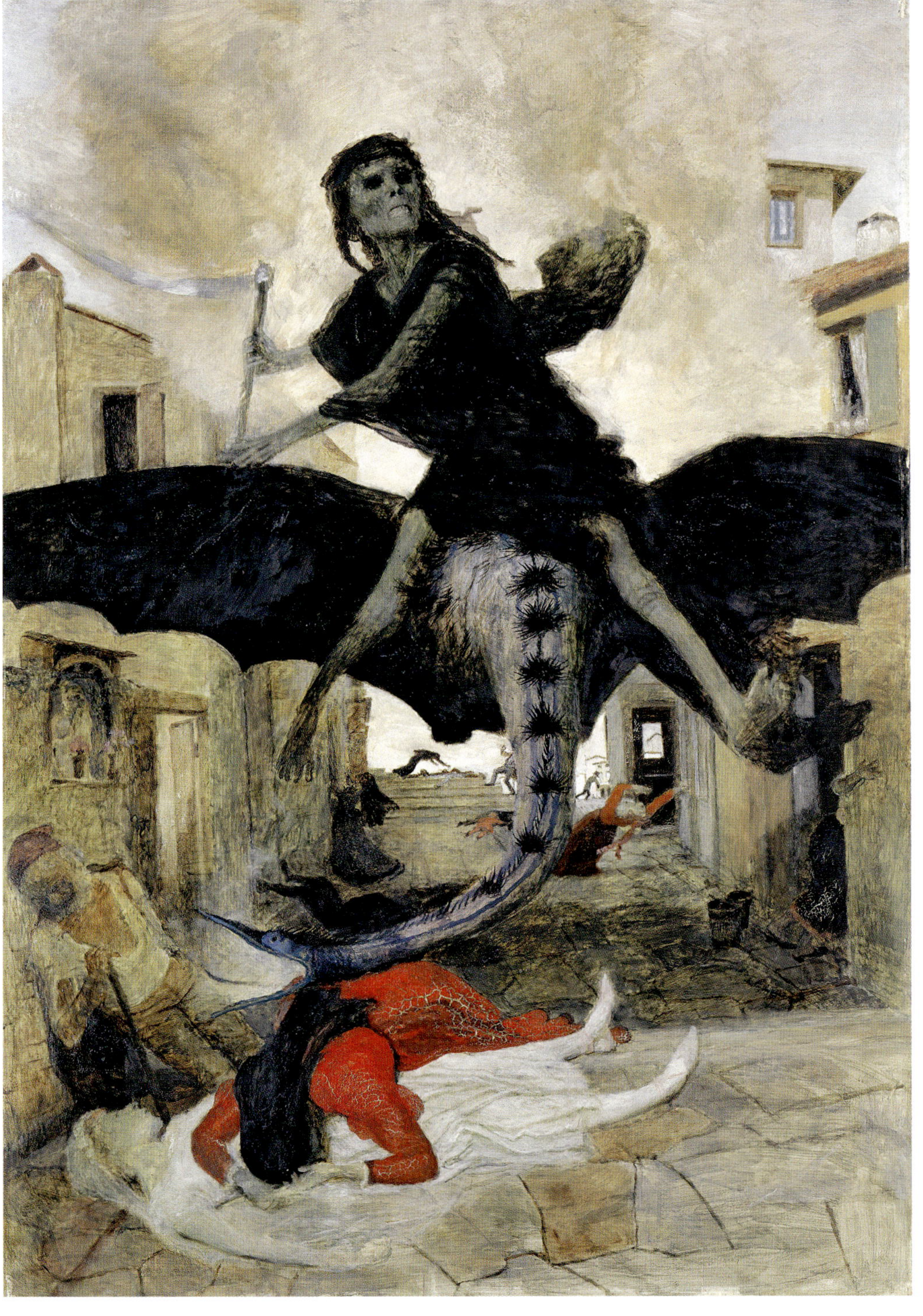

Arnold Böcklin (1827–1901), *The Plague (Die Pest)*, 1898. Tempera on wood, 59 × 41⅜ inches (149.8 × 105.1 cm). Kunstmuseum Basel

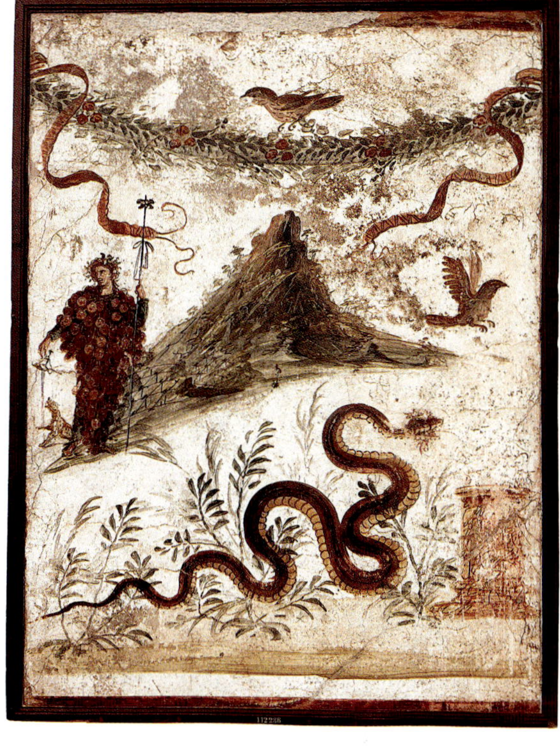

Roman Fresco of the God Bacchus and Mount Vesuvius, National Archeological Museum, 1st century AD

of plagues also figured importantly in film history, an obsession of Alexis which, like his fascination with natural history, goes all the way back to his childhood.

"It's where body-horror, science, and history all collide," he said. That the bubonic plague, one of the most destructive plagues in Western history, was a direct result of trade between different bio-geographies only made him more determined finally to make a painting about this subject. As for the Anatomical Museum's copious collections, he remained indifferent, "I've seen it all before," he said. "I'm just grateful I have five fingers."

The Archaeology Museum, by contrast, Alexis and I will always remember as a highlight of our trip. Opened to the public in the early 19th century, the museum's unrivaled collections can be credited to a long line of Neapolitan kings and nobles, for whom acquiring beautiful rare objects was tantamount to power and status. Many of the objects on view date back to antiquity, including much of what was rescued from the ruins of Pompeii, when the site was first excavated in 1738.

Among the astounding trove of ancient paintings and mosaics, one from Pompeii depicting a roundup of marine life in the Bay of Naples caught Alexis' eye. Another, featuring a mountain with snakes and birds hurtling away from it, would influence the structure of his painting, *Mt. Vesuvius, Autumn, 79 AD* (2024, p. 40), in which a wild rabbit, a red fox, a European toad, and various birds attempt to flee the catastrophe as the erupting volcano shoots red-hot embers into the air. Instead of lamenting the human loss, Alexis' version of the disaster memorializes the myriad animals that once made their home in this unstable ecosystem, only to be obliterated in a rushing surge of lava.

Saturday was our group's day off, so in the morning, Alexis and I enjoyed a leisurely few hours sketching and writing, before catching a taxi to Capodimonte, a sprawling palace on a hill overlooking the Bay of Naples.

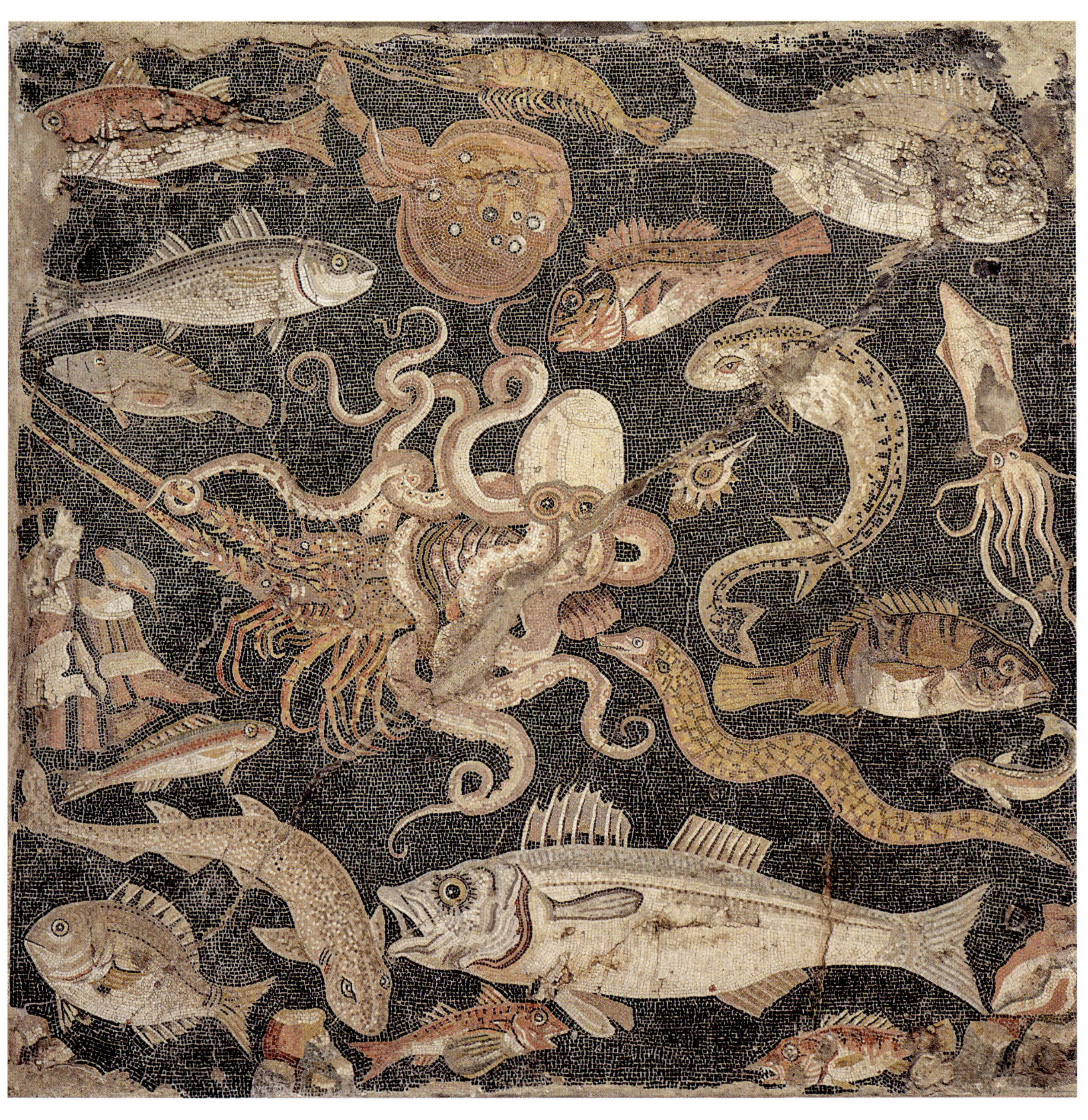

The *Catalog of fish* mosaic, 34⅝ × 34⅝ inches (88 × 88 cm), found in Pompeii (triclinium of house viii, 2, 16), today in Naples in the National Archaeological Museum

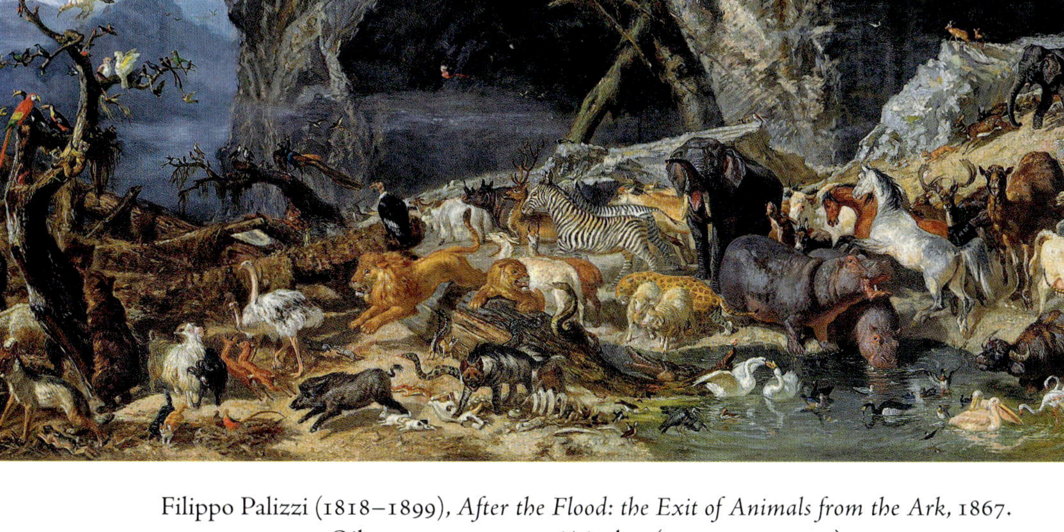

Filippo Palizzi (1818–1899), *After the Flood: the Exit of Animals from the Ark*, 1867.
Oil on canvas, 41 × 59½ inches (104.5 × 150.5 cm)

Excited to take in its vast holdings, which included paintings by Pieter Bruegel the Elder, Titian, Caravaggio, and a lesser-known artist, Filippo Palizzi, we were greeted by the shaking of heads, as several guards informed us the galleries were closing in a half-hour for a two-hour lunch break.

It was a hot, sultry afternoon. Alexis bought me a ricotta and prosciutto panino at an outdoor café, and we wandered the grounds, admiring a huge cinnamon tree from China, and staking a place in the crowded shade to sit and read until the museum re-opened at 3pm. Once inside, we discovered a wide range of art, and period rooms that had witnessed the comings and goings of nobles, from the Italian Farnese, to the Bourbon kings of Naples and Spain, to the family of Napoleon Bonaparte. Alexis was thrilled to find *After the Flood: The Exit of Animals from the Ark* (1867), an epic painting by Filippo Palizzi, which, as opposed to Alexis' *The Departed,* revels in the world's biodiversity spilling out of a ship.

Afterward, paying homage to Caravaggio's *Madonna della Misericordia* which, remarkably, still hangs in its original spot above an altar at the 17th-century Pio Monte della Misericordia, Alexis felt so inspired by Caravaggio's handling of light. He would keep it in mind, he said, when he painted the light streaming down from the upper left in *Acquario,* and plunging into the dark sea in *The Departed.*

Alexis was excited to go to the flea market with Mark that Sunday, something he had not yet done in all their decades of friendship. Mark and Dana were flea market regulars. The one they wanted to check out one was a twenty-minute drive, behind a racetrack in Agnano. Maurizio and Giulia joined us, as did Mark and Dana's son, Fairfield.

When we arrived, just before midday, the heat was like a wall, closing in on us from all sides. Umbrellas shaded a few stands, at least partially, but the further we wandered into the market the sparser they became. Maurizio and Giulia didn't seem to mind. Dana's wide-brim hat kept her face shaded. Fairfield and I had both applied huge dollops of sunscreen. But Alexis never used sunscreen, and without a hat, I could tell he was miserable.

Mark proceeded unfazed. Protected by a small cloth hat, he bargained for tools and assorted implements, such as string, for a piece he was considering about human cruelty to animals. Haggling like a pro with dealer after dealer, he attempted to reach his ideal price which, he confessed, was about a third of what was originally offered.

The sun bore down, merciless.

Seeing a beautiful cameo hanging from a cord around Dana's neck, I asked where she'd gotten it. "Mark gave it to me," she said. She'd been collecting cameos ever since. "But my first is still my best," she said, smiling, as she scoured

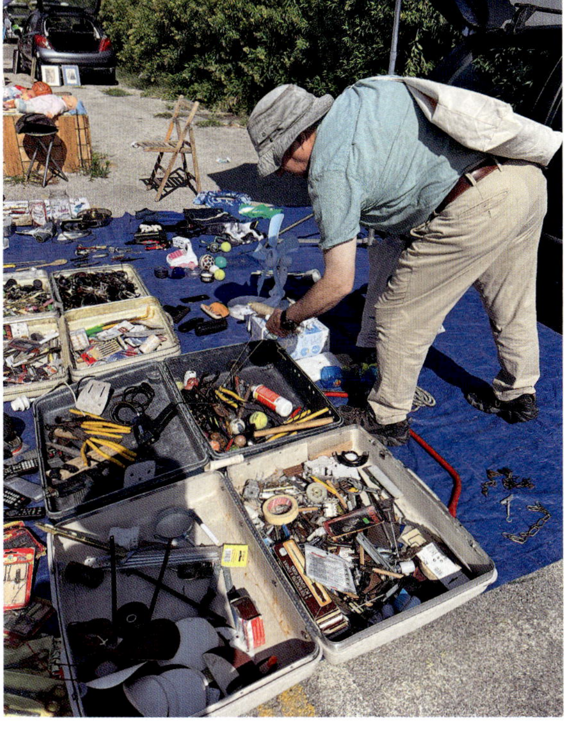

Mark Dion, flea market, Agnano

display cases crammed with cast-off jewelry. The tradition of carving cameos originated in Naples, Mark said. You could tell when a certain cameo was made, Dana added, by the type of profile that was in fashion at the time.

I was enjoying our discussion, a welcome distraction from the heat. But Alexis and Fairfield were sweaty and irritable. It was time for us to leave.

Driving along the coast, the hot wind blowing in through our open windows, we stopped for coffee, before continuing past a well-to-do neighborhood, and the Palazzo Donn'Anna, which would appear in Alexis' painting *Post Human: Palazzo Donn'Anna,* (2024, p. 64). Once back in Naples, we enjoyed a wonderful lunch at Baccalaria, a restaurant serving only cod.

"How many cods have been killed, thanks to this one restaurant?" Alexis half-joked, glaring at no one in particular, as he devoured his own delicious cod to the tune of 50s American big band music, which played absurdly in the background. (He would later cite Baccalaria as a source for *The Departed,* cod being yet another overfished species in the Mediterranean.)

The Museo di Fisica, a collection of institutions, encompasses a Minerology Museum, a Zoological Museum, an Anthropology Museum, and a Paleontology Museum. Visiting all four on our last day felt like the grand finale of a fireworks display. It was while examining the 6,000-odd specimens in the Minerology Museum, Alexis said, that he came up with the idea for his painting, *Grotte di Pertosa* (2024, p. 34). A popular tourist destination in modern-day Naples, the eponymous *grotte,* are a cave system located about an hour away by car from the city center. Since recent studies of the human genome have revealed that Neanderthals and humans interbred when humans arrived in the area around 45,000 years ago, Alexis chose to depict a romance between a Neanderthal and a modern human — modeled by me — in his painting.

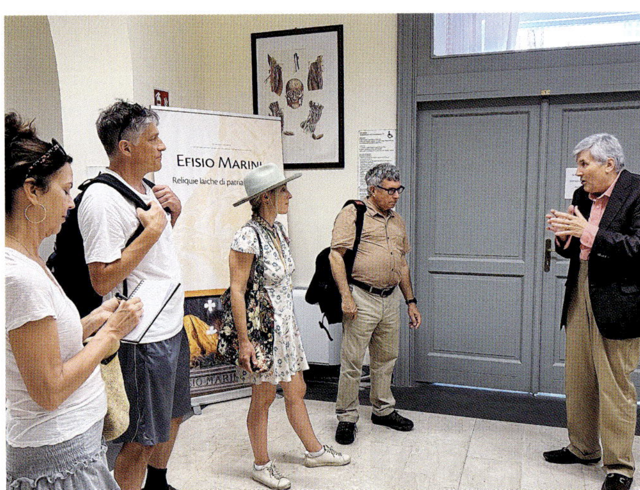

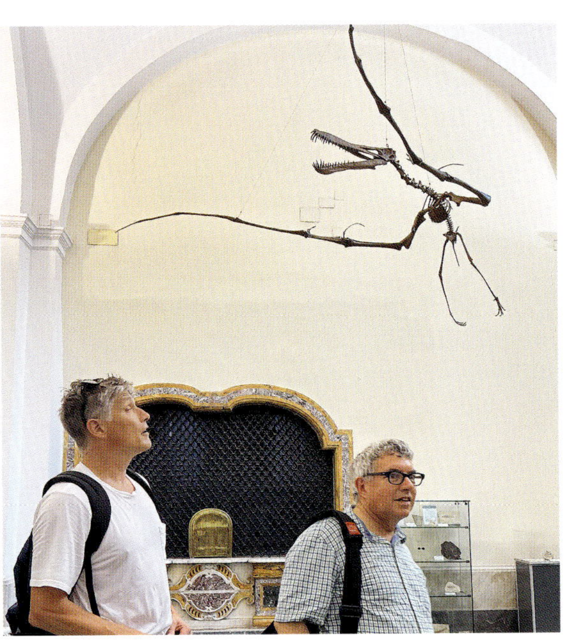

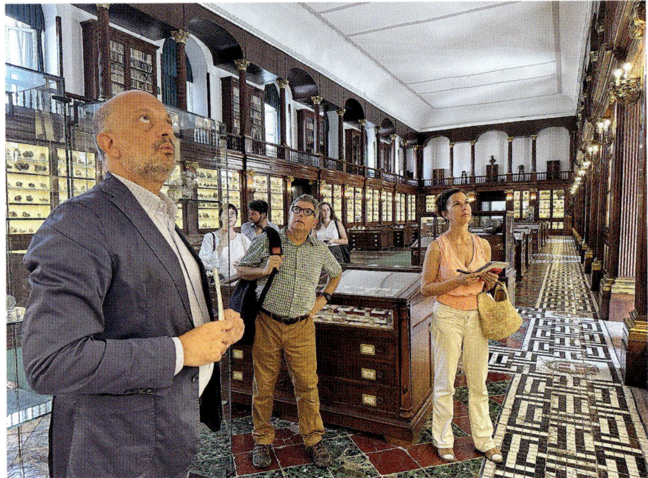

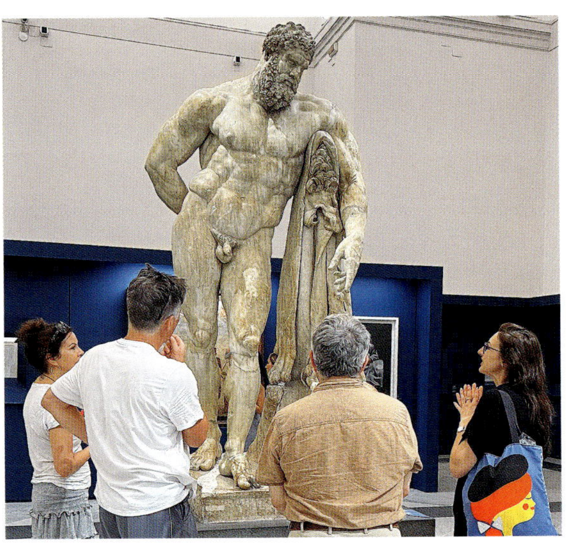

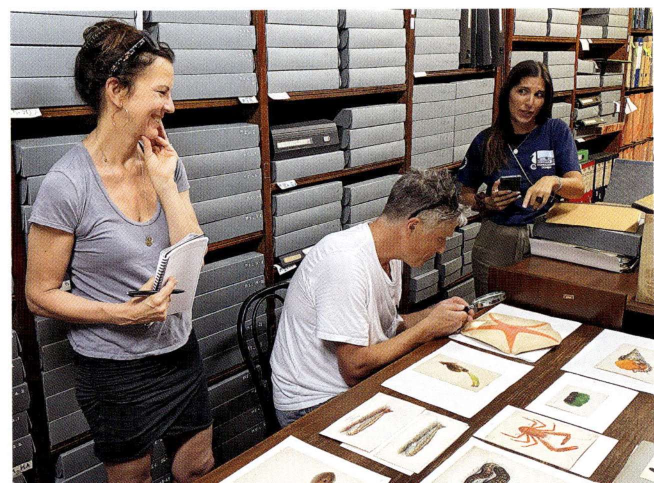

Clockwise from top left: Dorothy Spears, Alexis, Dana Sherwood, Mark Dion, and Professor Michele Papa, Chief Curator, The Anatomy Museum of the University of Naples Federico II; Paleontology Museum of the University of Naples Federico II; with Professor Laura Massetti, Naples National Archaeological Museum; looking at watercolors, Anton Dohrn Archive; with Professor Piergiulio Cappelletti, Royal Mineralogy Museum Center of Natural Sciences, July, 2023

Part of the lore surrounding Alexis' long friendship with Mark stems from their seven-week expedition in Guyana thirty-two years ago, which inspired Alexis' first field drawings, of native plants and wildlife, using material collected from the Essequibo River. Eying the Vesuvius collection with its impressive specimens of copper, iron, gold nuggets, lava, molten rock and ash, all of which were originally retrieved from slopes of the exploded volcano, Alexis told Mark, "I've got to make field drawings from this shit."

During a follow-up trip to Naples, Mark, loyal friend that he is, generously stopped a cab on the side of the volcano, to collect lava and other debris in ziplock bags for Alexis, who then used it to make thirty-three field drawings of mammals, birds, plants and insects living on Vesuvius for *Course of Empire*.

When artists are inspired ideas cross-fertilize. Having seen a whale skeleton outside the aquarium on our first day, we saw a second one on our last, at the Zoological Museum. As a counterpoint to the ichthyosaur in *The Fossil Record*, which appears washed up on a beach, Alexis began to envision a living whale for his final painting, *Post Human*.

The cast fossil of an extinct flying reptile suspended from the ceiling in the Paleontology Museum, would also inspire the flying pterosaur in *The Fossil Record*. Both appear in the same pose. In the Paleontology Museum, Alexis told me later, "it really hit home that part of Europe was underwater off and on from 270 to 66 million years ago," a realization that would serve as *The Fossil Record's* organizing principal.

In the months following our visit to Naples, the dates for Alexis, Mark, and Dana's exhibition at the Fondazione would get pushed back once, twice, three times, and there would be no accompanying book, we were told, due to cuts in government funding. In other words, in

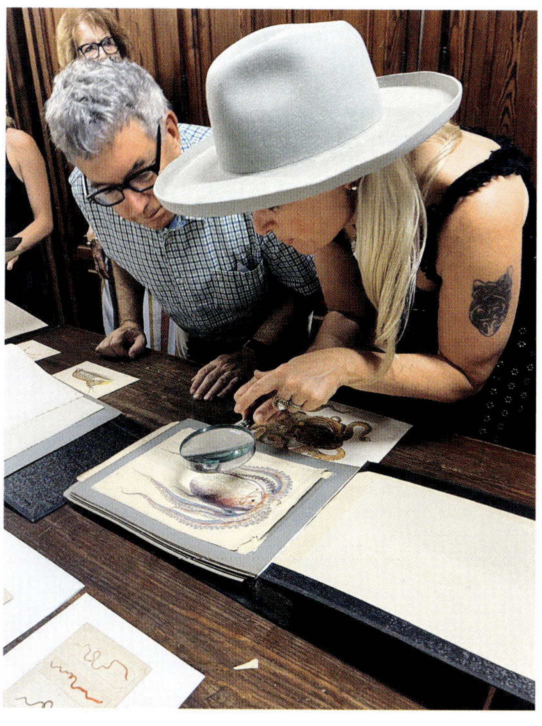

Mark and Dana at Stazione Zoologica's Historical Archives, Stazione Zoologica Anton Dohrn

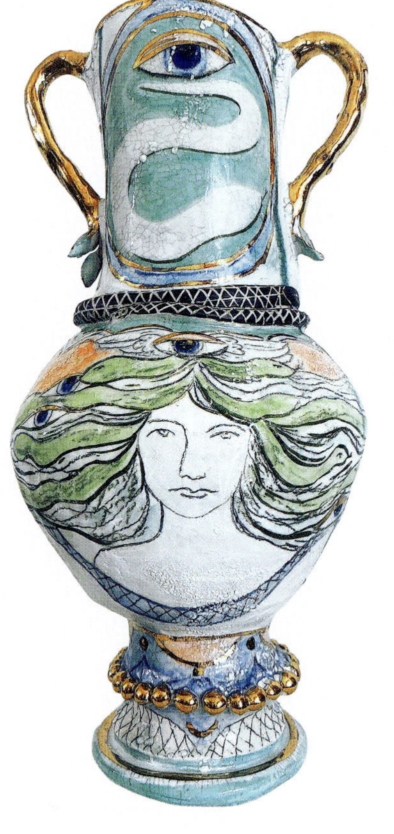

Dana Sherwood, *Golden Medusa*, 2024. Glazed porcelain with gold lustre, 11 × 6 inches (27.9 × 15.2 cm)

keeping with the long succession of empires that have come and gone over the course of our world's three-hundred-million-year history, the course of our humble project would take an unexpected turn. After nearly three years, the future of the exhibition at the Fondazione Morra Greco in Naples remains uncertain.

In the meantime, Magenta Plains gallery in New York hosted *Alexis Rockman: Course of Empire*, featuring the paintings, watercolors, and field drawings Alexis originally made for the Fondazione, in early 2025. The exhibition has since traveled to the Herbert F. Johnson Museum of Art, where it is currently on view. Thanks to Elisabeth Rochau-Shalem, Hirmer Publishers have published this book, with its gorgeous reproductions of Alexis' work, and my essay, based on copious notes scribbled long-hand in a black wire notebook.

Things have turned out differently than any of us expected, but the art and writing inspired by our magical time in Naples lives on, which feels like further proof of something that became stunningly clear when we were there: the best-laid plans, like the most powerful empires, are subject to events beyond anyone's control. Everything is contingent on everything else. Nothing is permanent. But maybe — hopefully — if we're lucky enough, at least a small part of what we've achieved during our brief flicker of time here will resonate for future generations, independent of us.

At our final dinner in Naples, a convivial affair hosted by Maurizio, I found myself contemplating the shallow sea that used to be Italy and feeling a connection to geological time for the first time in my life. Would climate change one day return what had begun as an underwater landmass to its watery origins? Would the restaurant where we were sitting become a ruin, like the *Acquario di Napoli* in Alexis' painting. Was the entire empirical

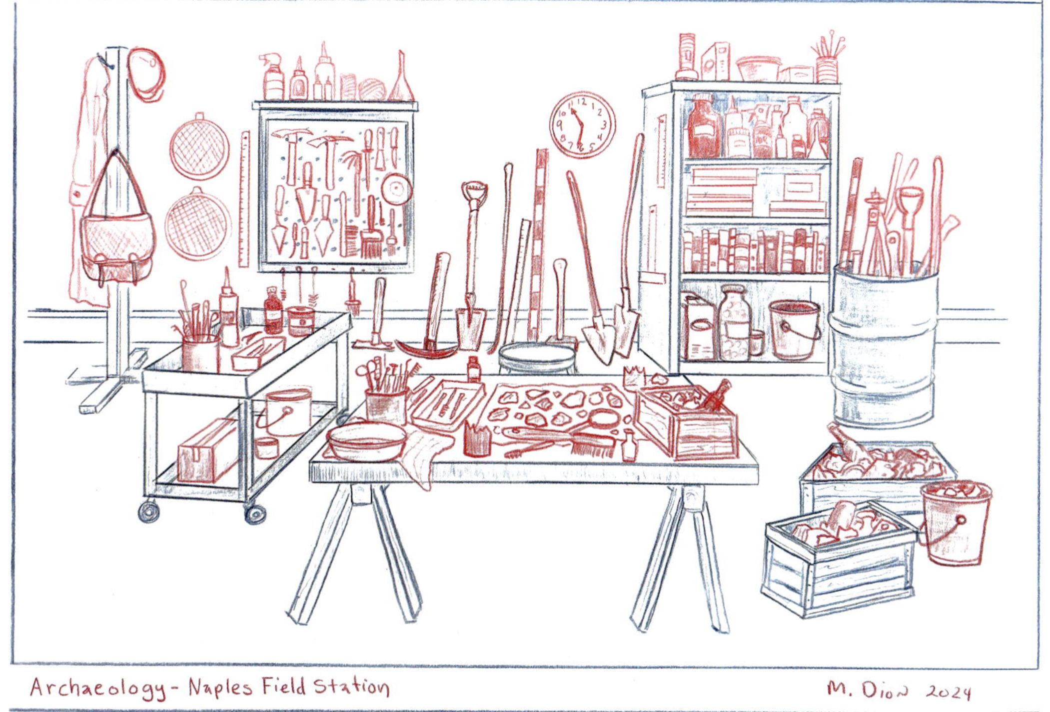

Mark Dion, *Archaeology – Naples Field Station*, 2024. Pencil on paper, 9 × 12 inches (22.8 × 30.5 cm)

course of humans on our beloved planet doomed to drown in its over-abundant waters?

"We think of Naples as a place for human endeavors," Alexis would later tell me. "But there were hundreds of millions of years of animal life before that, that are often overlooked."

His painting, *Post Human: Palazzo Donn'Anna*, would be the last in his series. And in it, the work inspired by Naples would appear to come full circle. *Post Human* foresees a future without humans. Off to the right, in the distance, the Palazzo Donn'Anna, mentioned earlier, appears on its familiar Rocks of Siren, but as a ruin, sprouting palm trees. Meanwhile, in the foreground, a humpback whale breaches with joyful abandon. As if resurrected — miraculously — from its recent near-extinction, the beautiful animal arches through the air, exposing its vulnerable gray belly to bright sun as a spray of seawater forms a rainbow in its wake.

Alexis has credited the fossilized whale skeletons outside the Stazione, and in the Zoological Museum, with inspiring *Post Human*. But did he intend for his painting to be seen as a revenge scenario for animals? Was the final chapter of life's three-plus billion-year empire on our planet, for him, a utopian world without humans? Without *us?*

I decided to ask him.

"Well, I don't really believe that," he answered, slowly, his gray-green eyes glittering with mischief. "But do I love the idea."

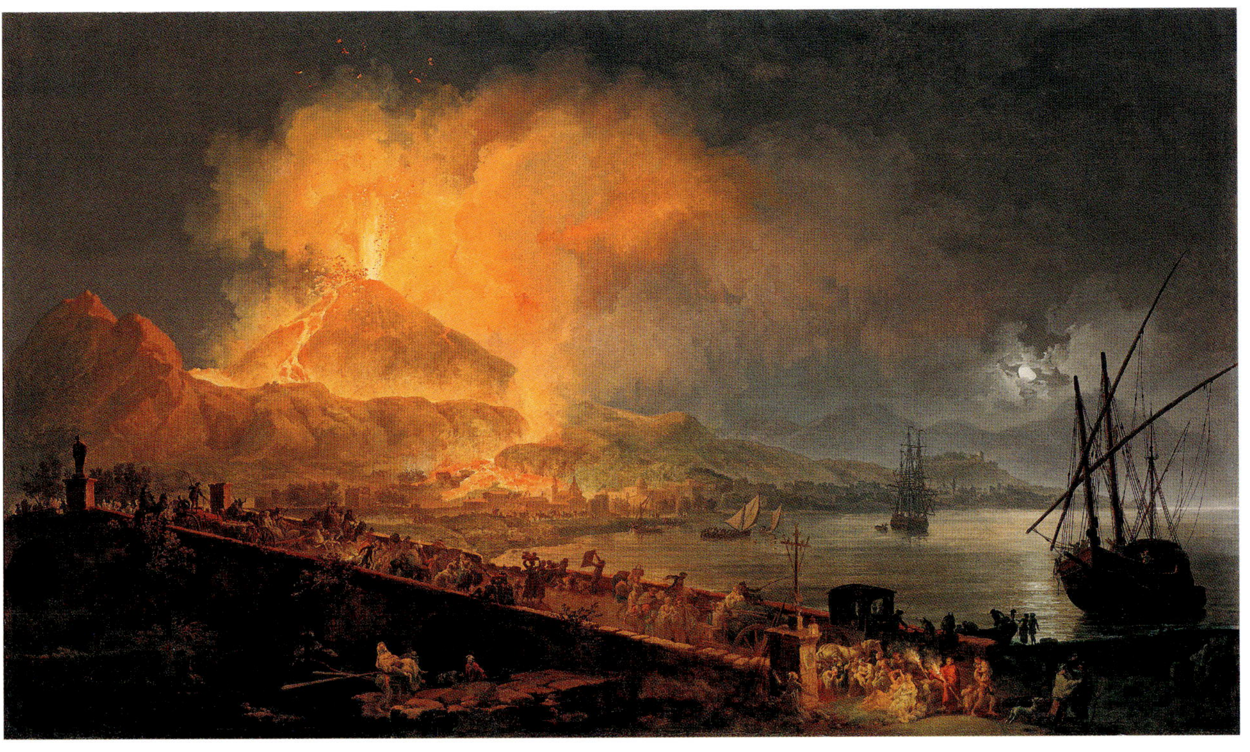

Pierre-Jacques Volaire (1729–1799), *The Eruption of Mt. Vesuvius*, 1777. Oil on canvas, 53⅛ × 89 inches (134.9 × 226.1 cm). North Carolina Museum of Art, Raleigh, NC. Purchased with funds from the Alcy C. Kendrick Bequest and the State of North Carolina, by exchange

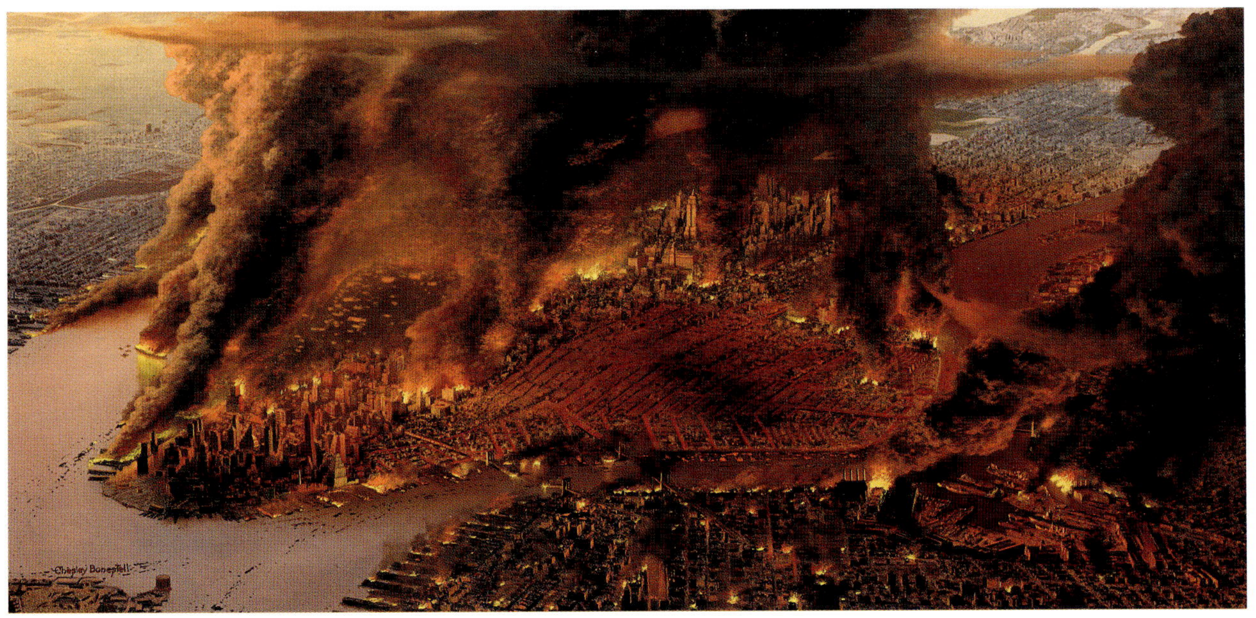

Chesley Bonestell (1888–1986), *Atom Bombing of New York City*, 1950. Oil on paper laid on masonite, 17⅜ × 32¾ inches (44.1 × 83.2 cm). The New York Historical, New York. Gift of Chesley Bonestell

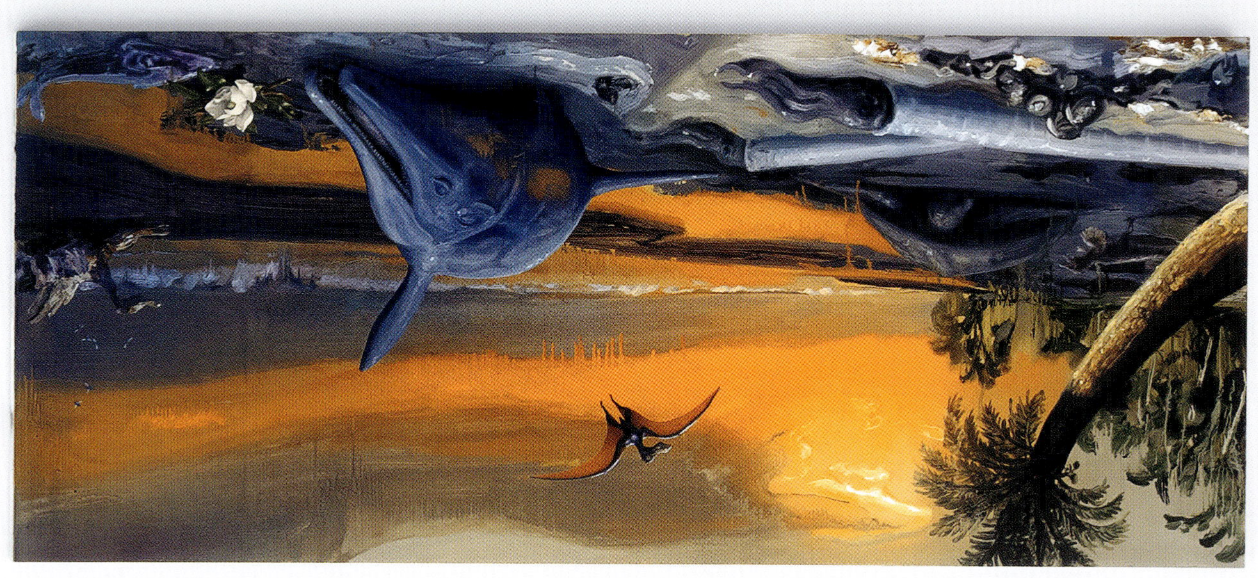

ALEXIS ROCKMAN

Naples: Course of Empire

Magenta Plains, New York, NY

January 16 – March 1, 2025

Herbert F. Johnson Museum of Art, Cornell University, Ithaca, NY

January 20 – June 7, 2026

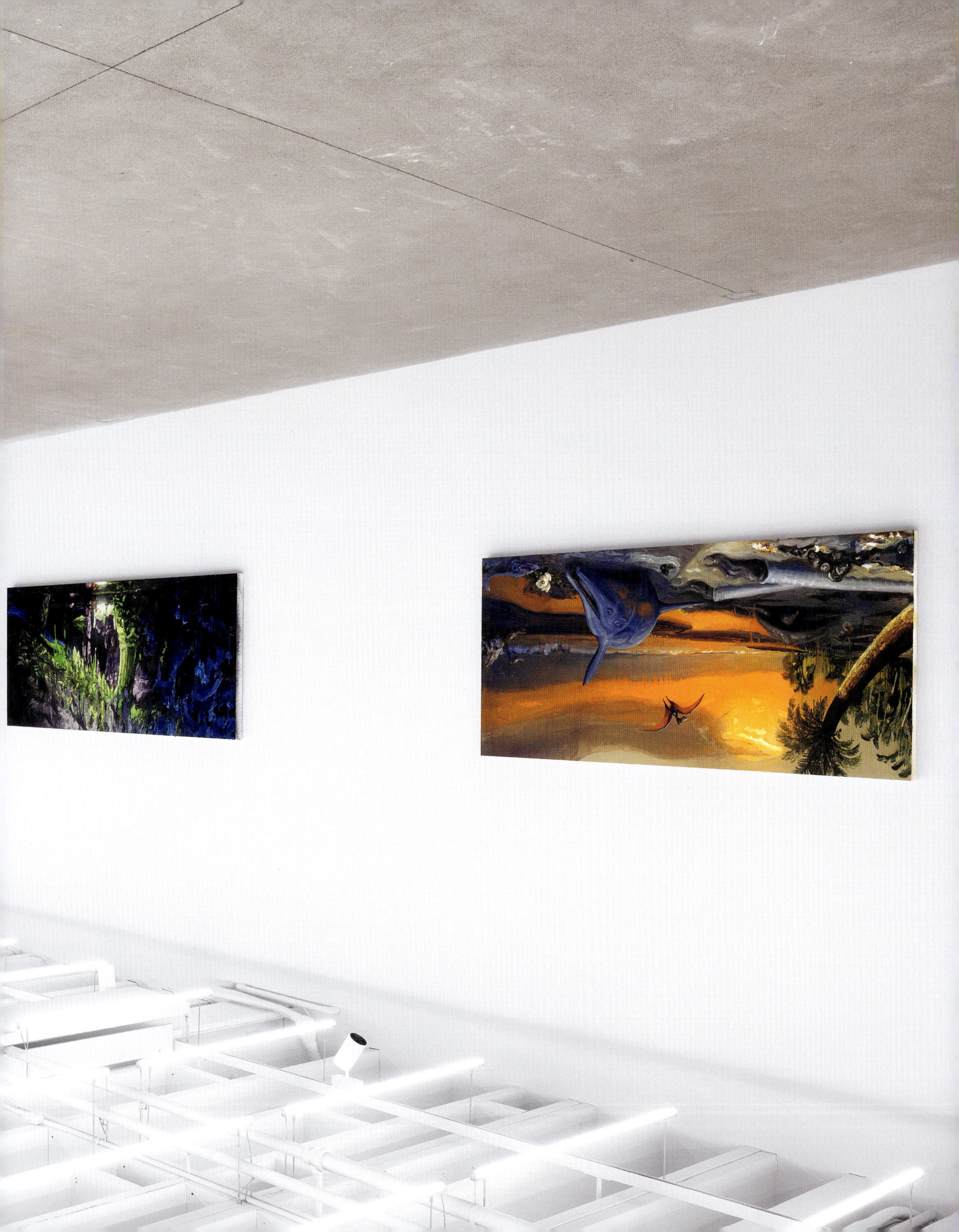

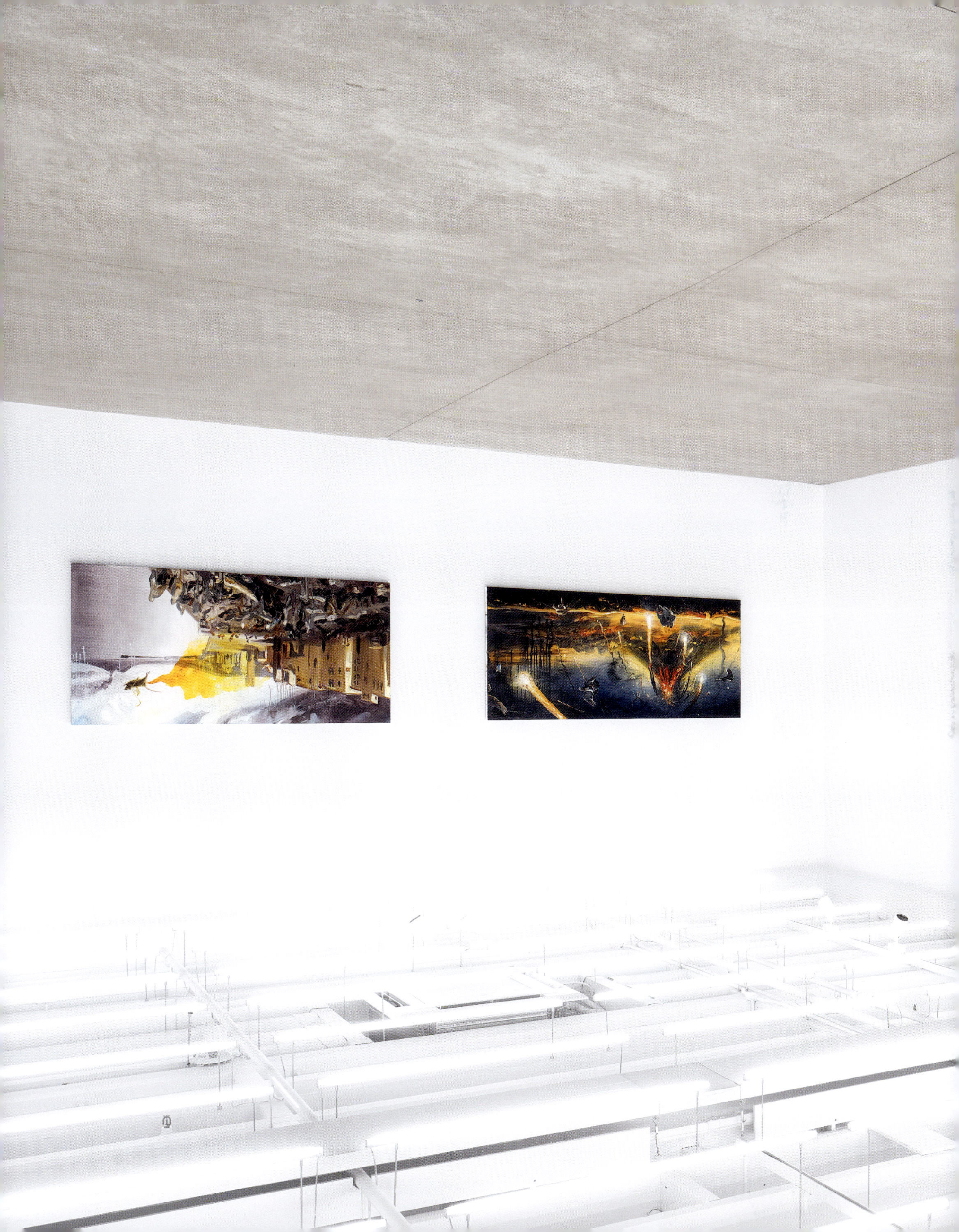

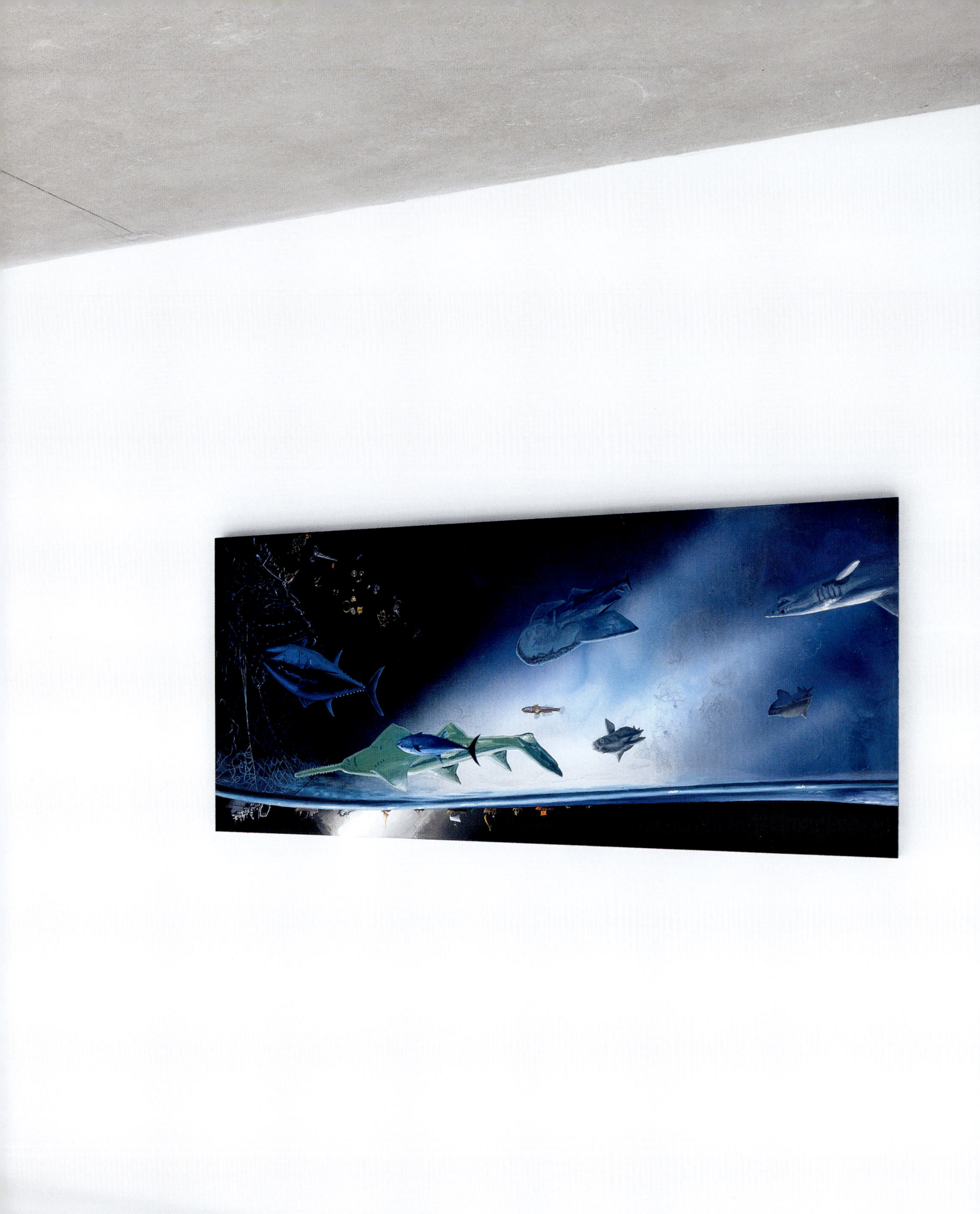

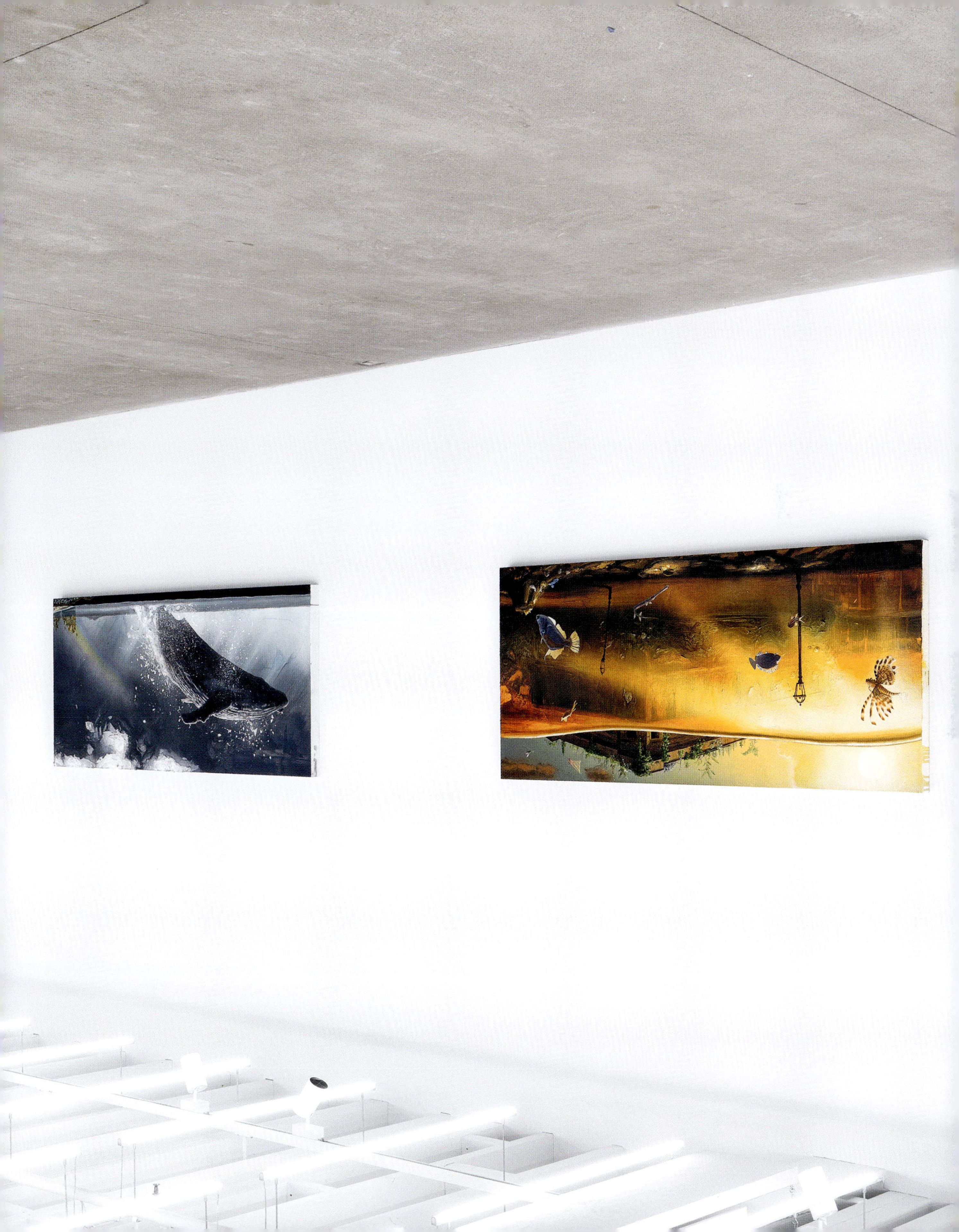

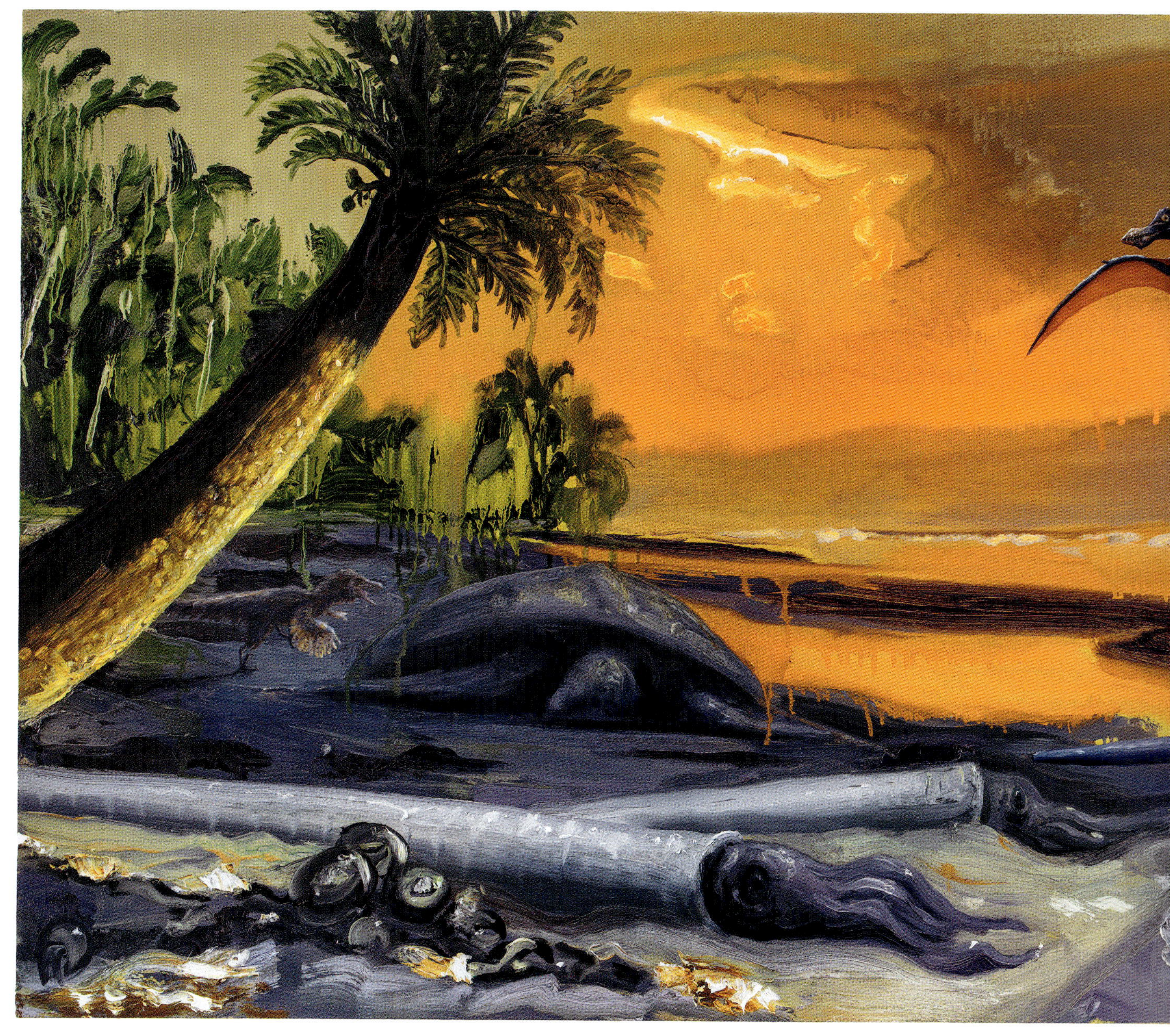

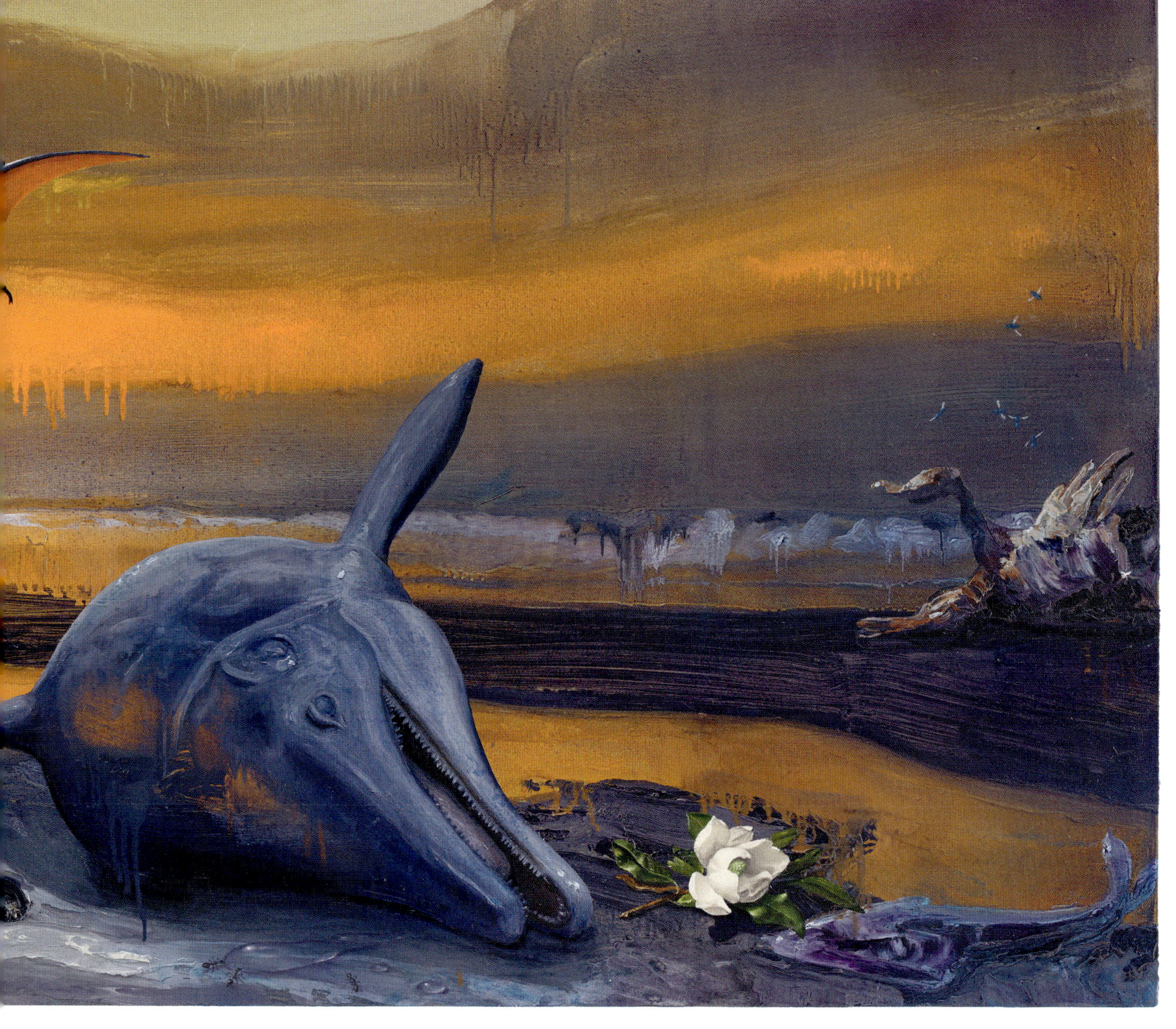

The Fossil Record: Tethys Sea, 2024
Oil and cold wax on wood, 36 × 84 inches (91.4 × 213.4 cm)

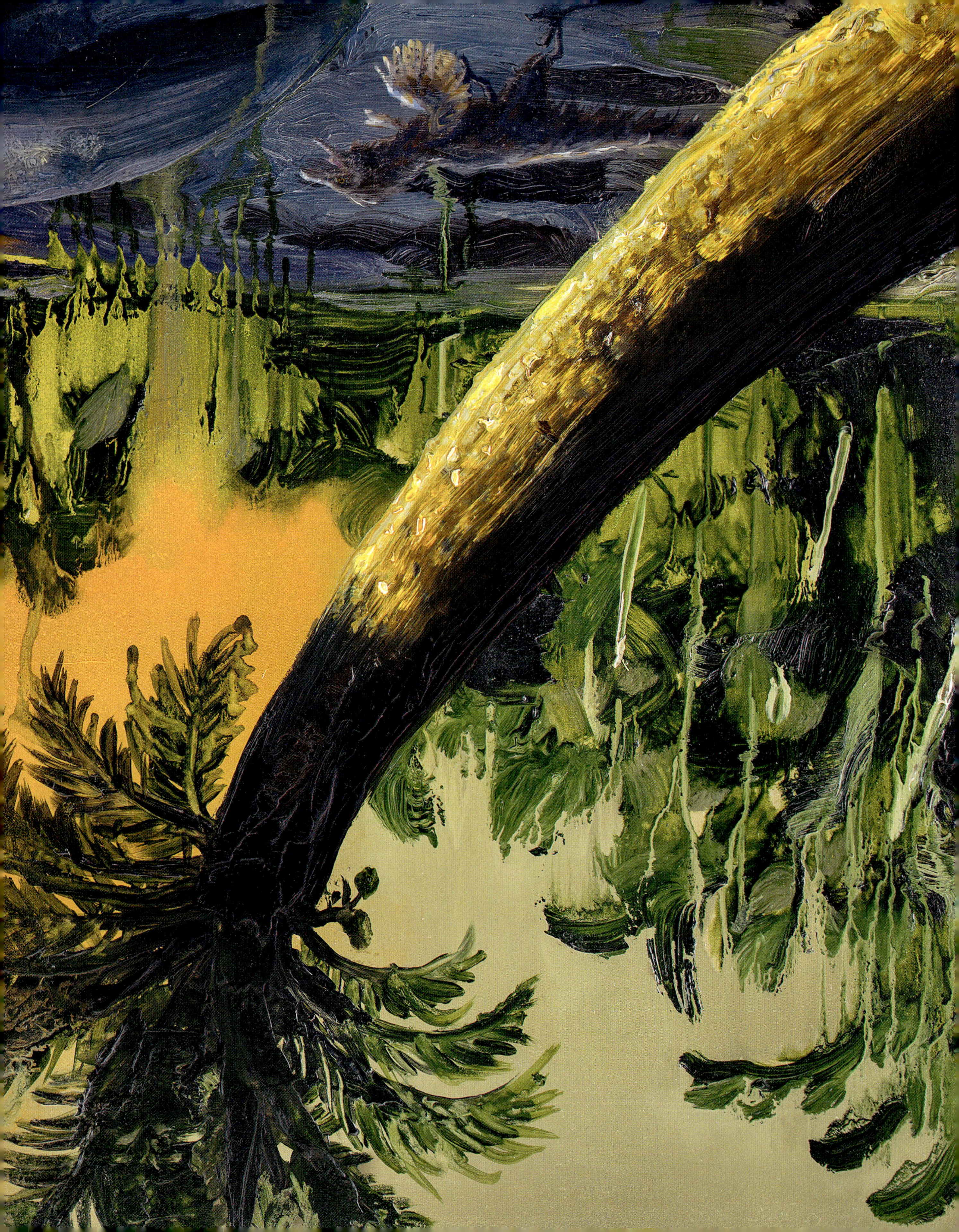

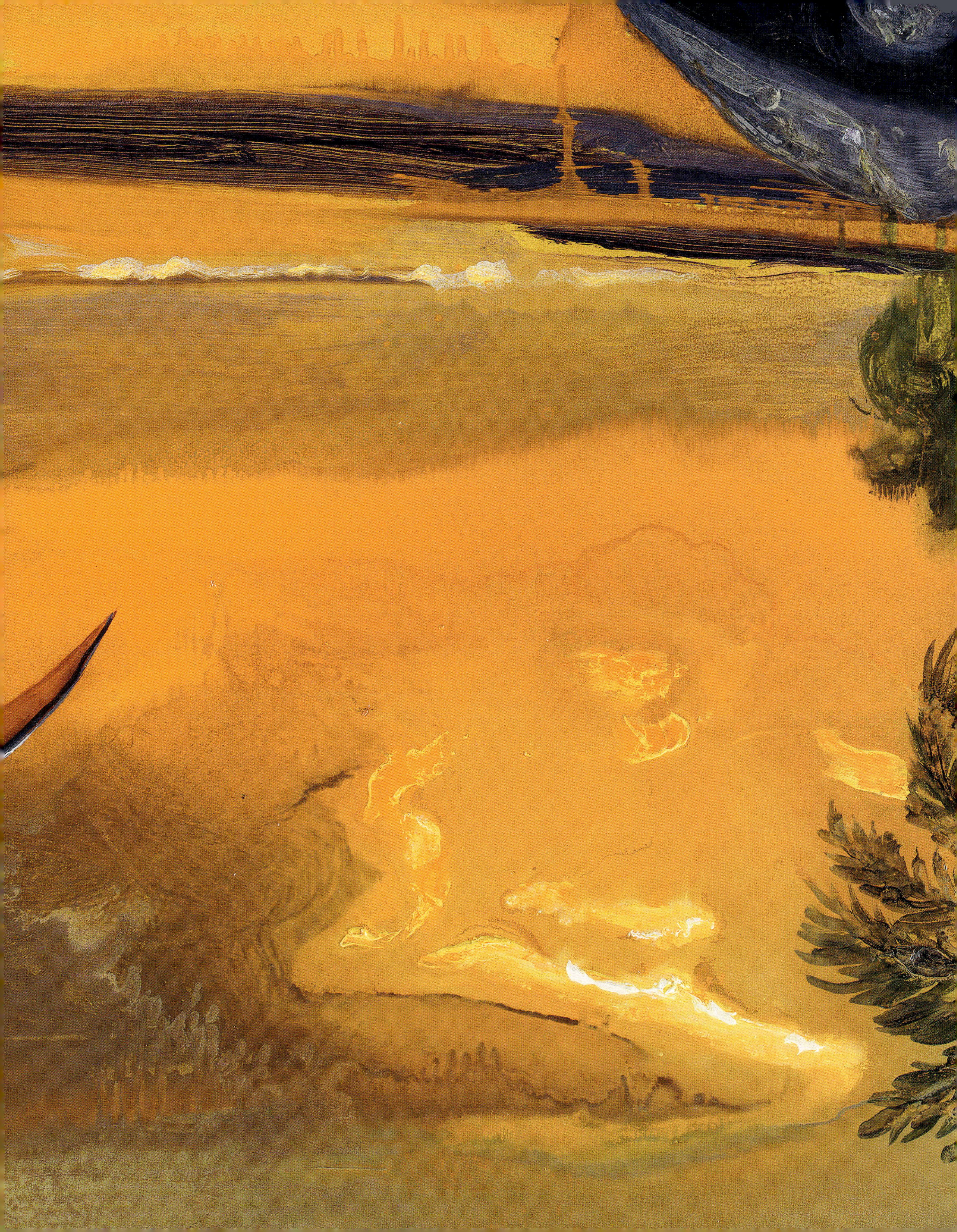

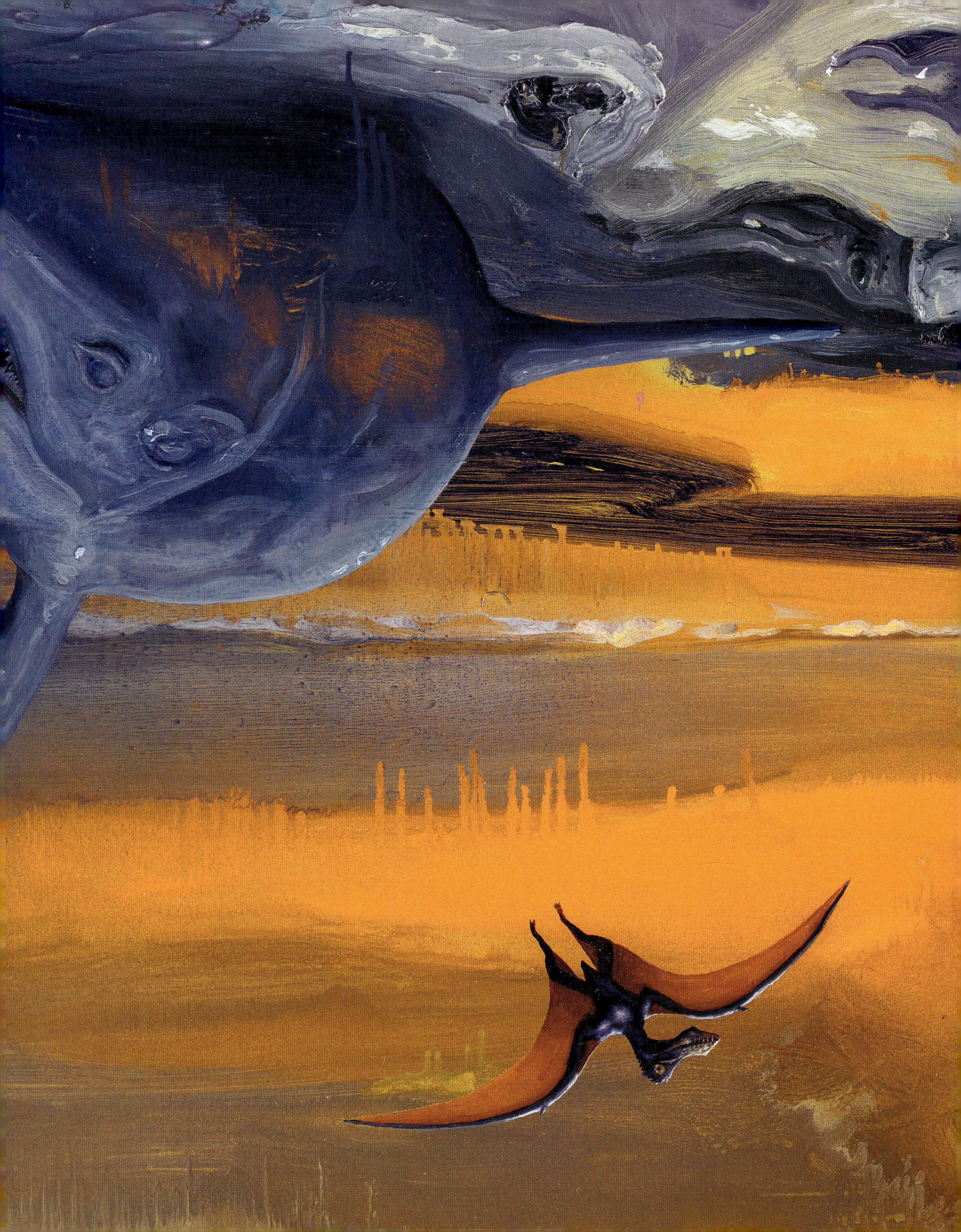

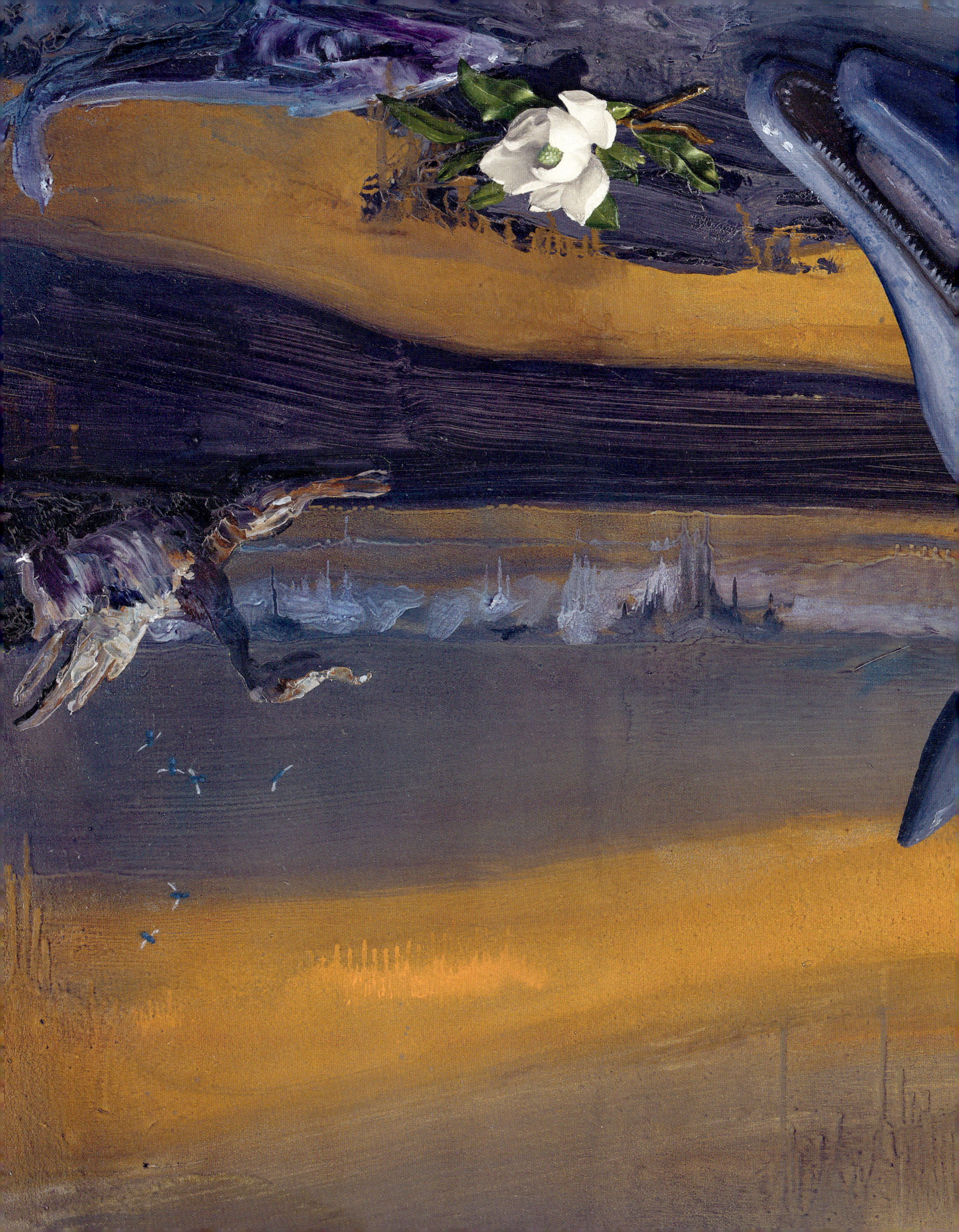

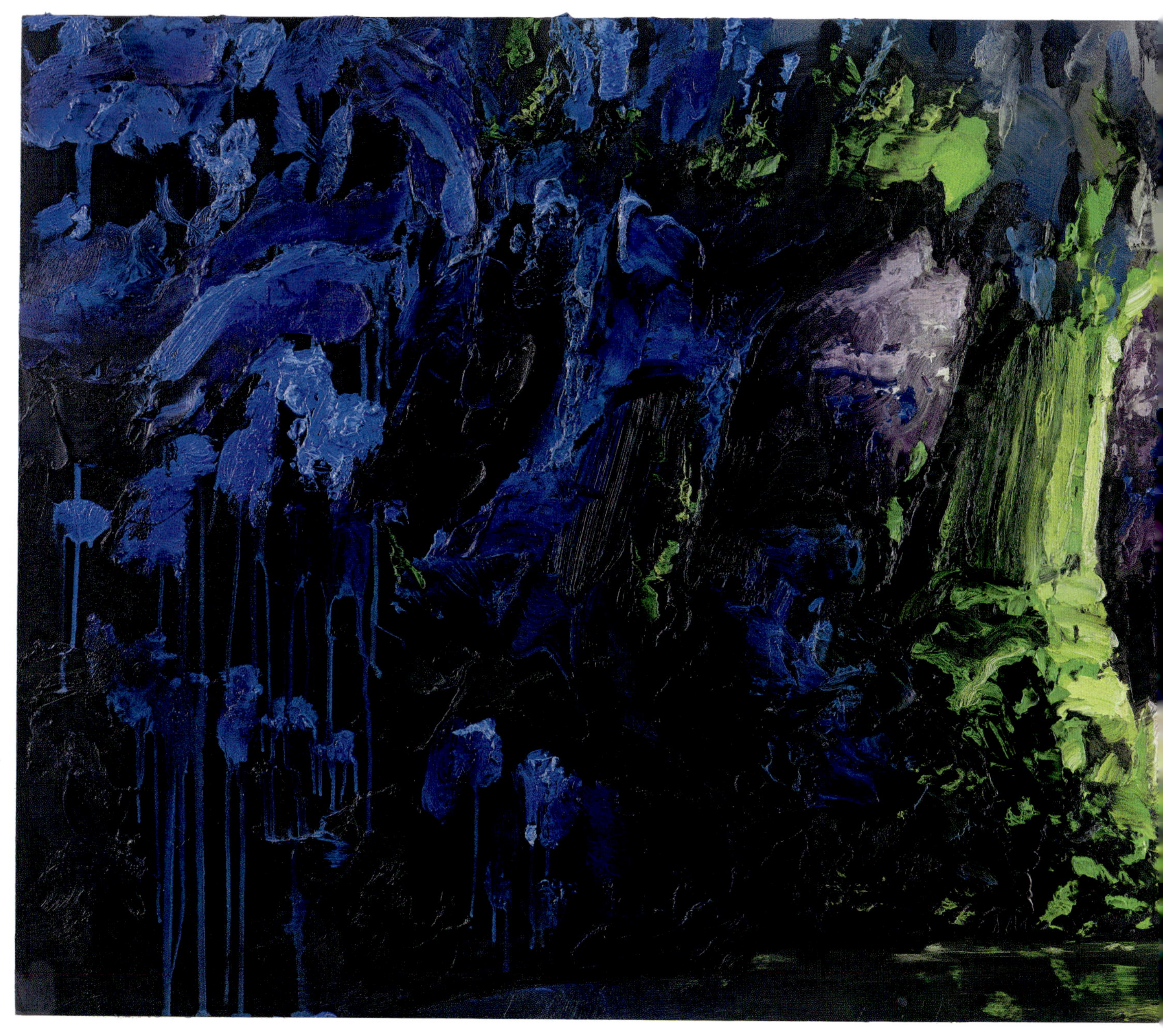

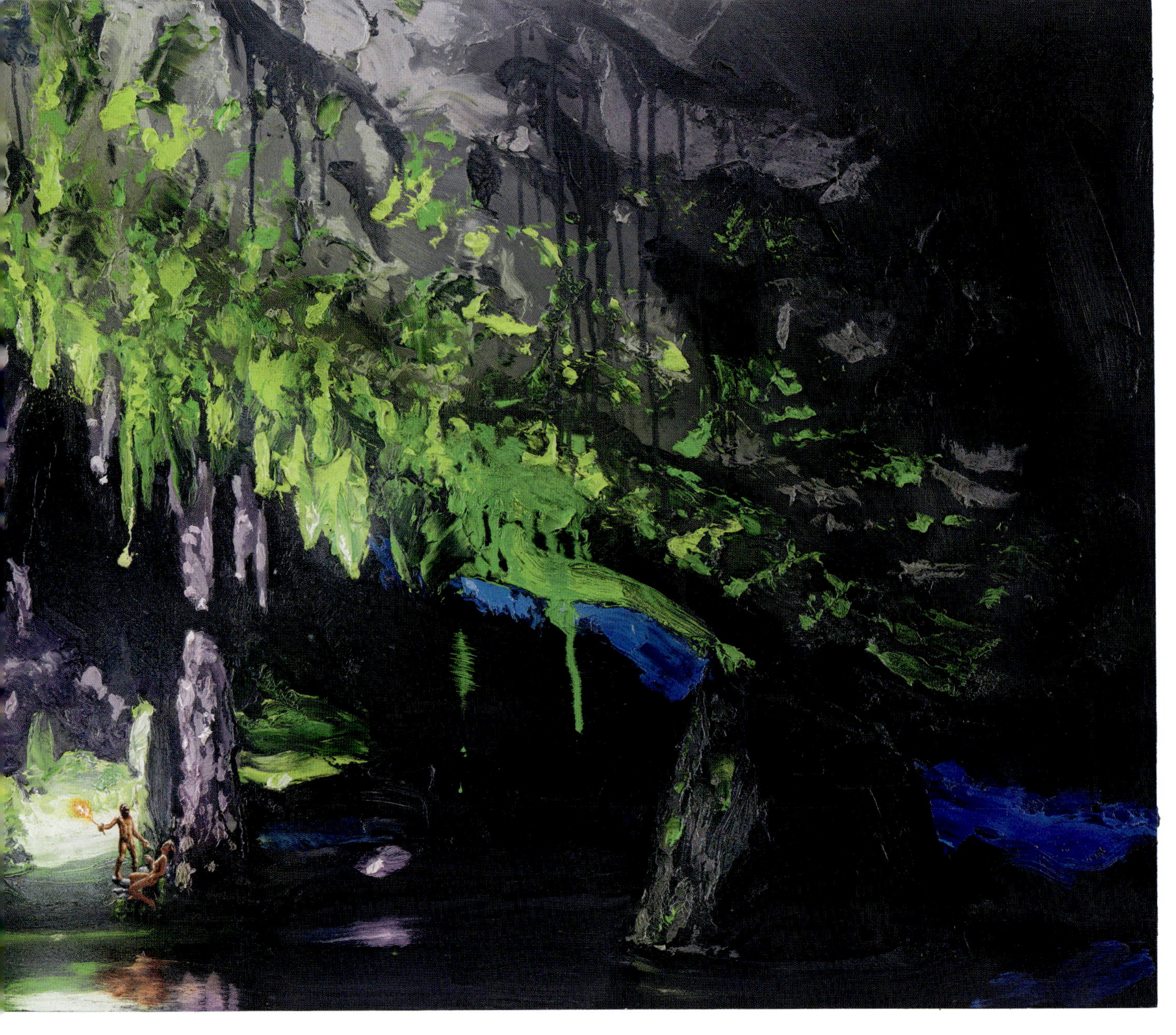

Grotte di Pertosa, 2024
Oil and cold wax on wood, 36 × 84 inches (91.4 × 213.4 cm)
Collection of Bram and Lara Hechtkopf

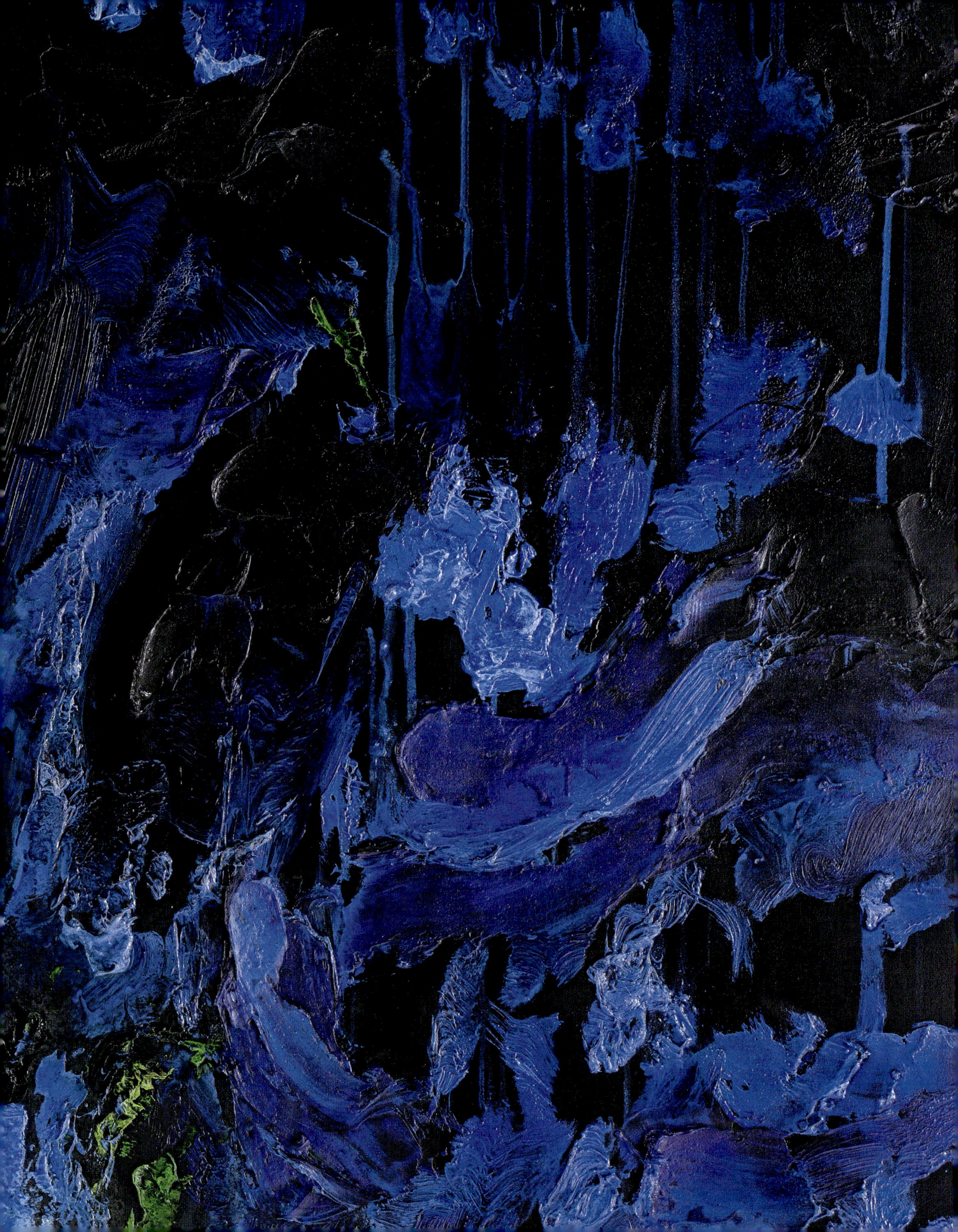

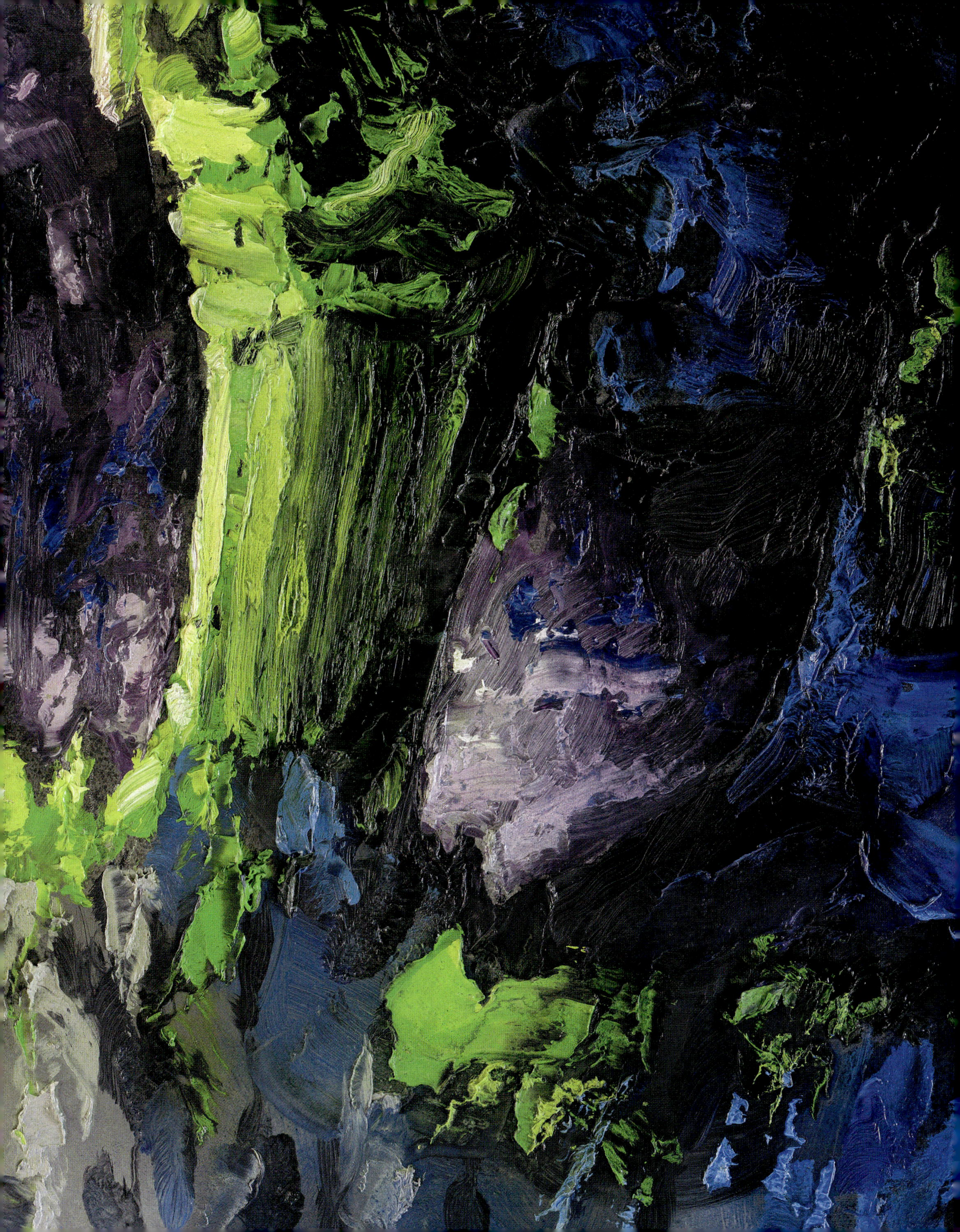

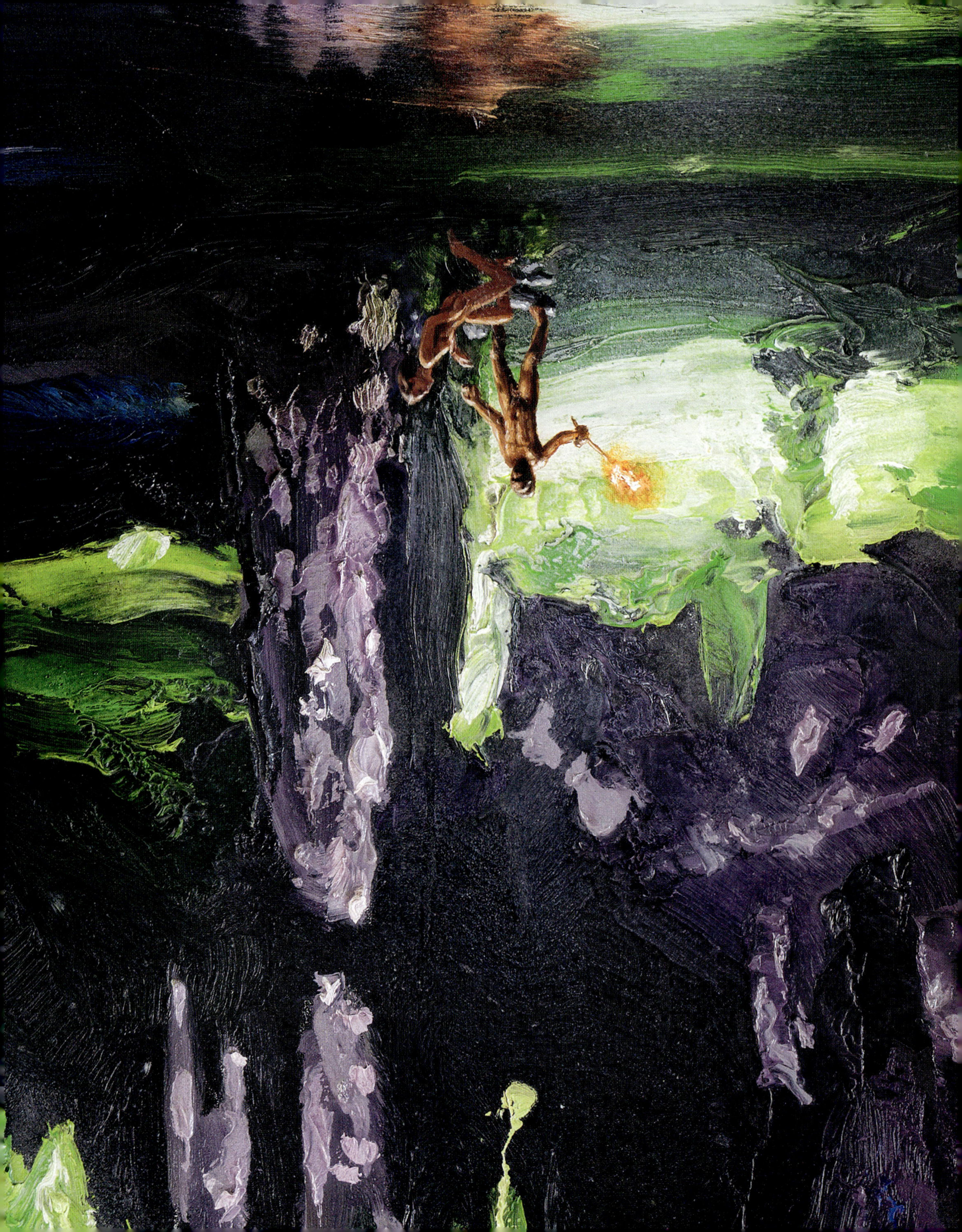

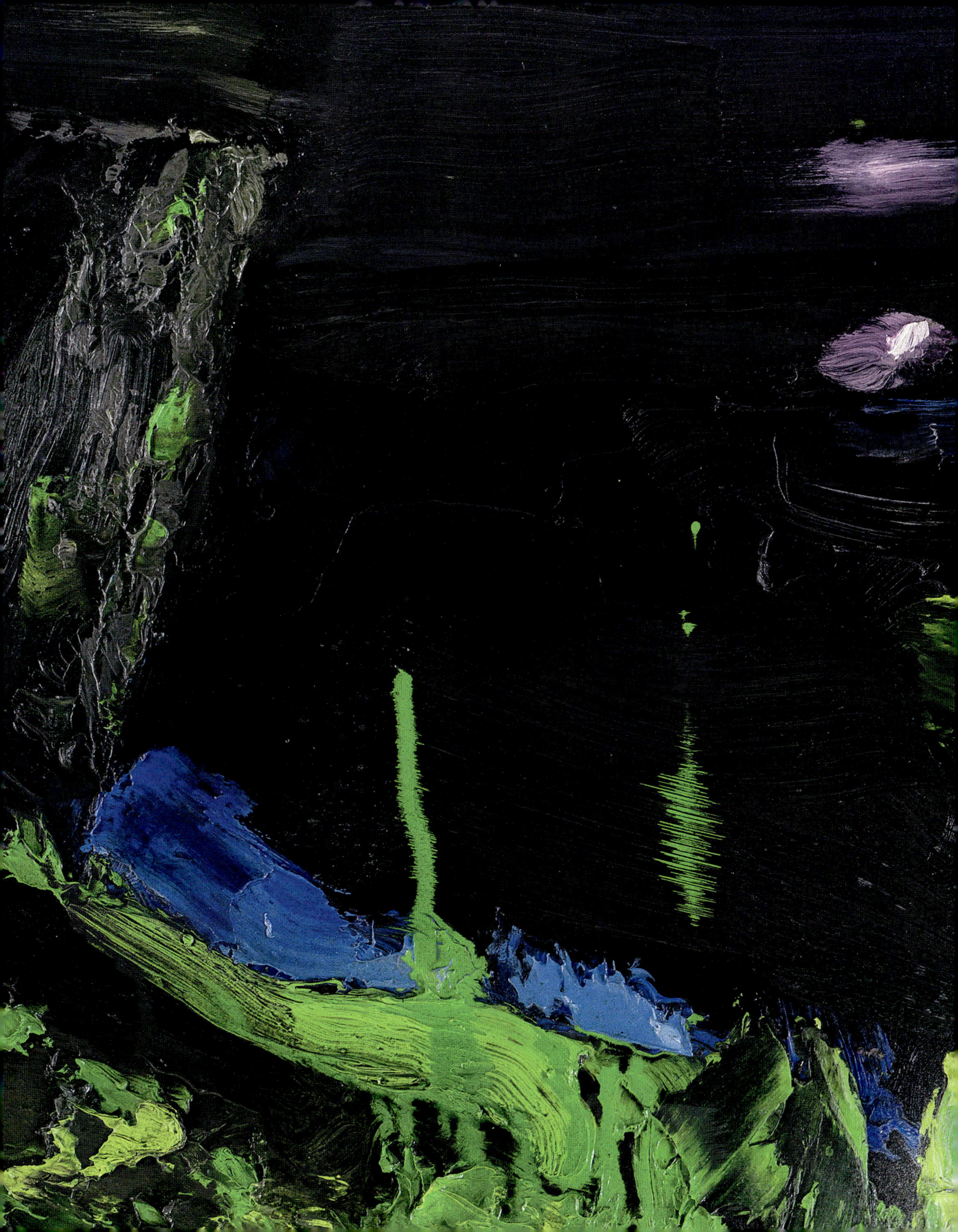

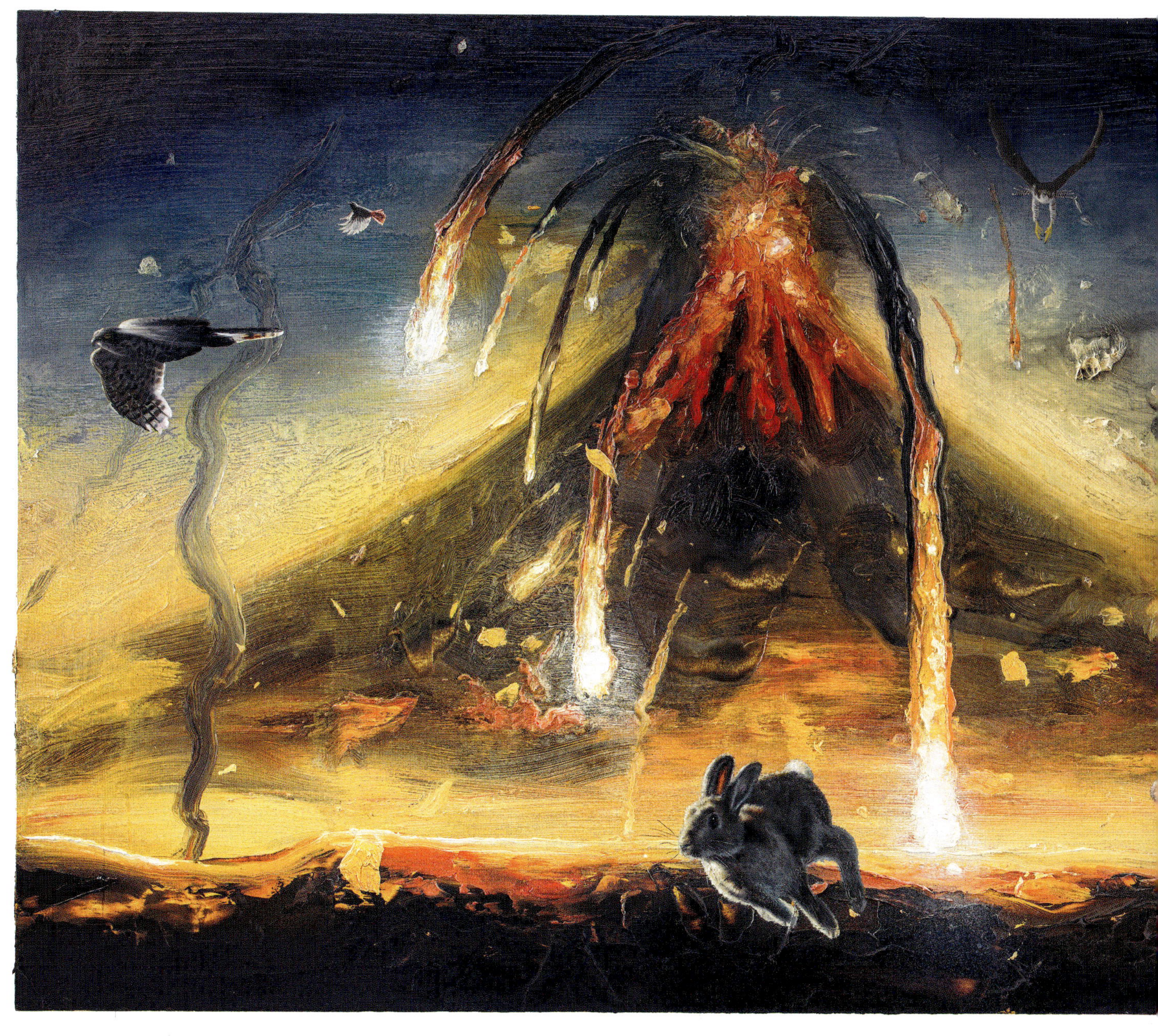

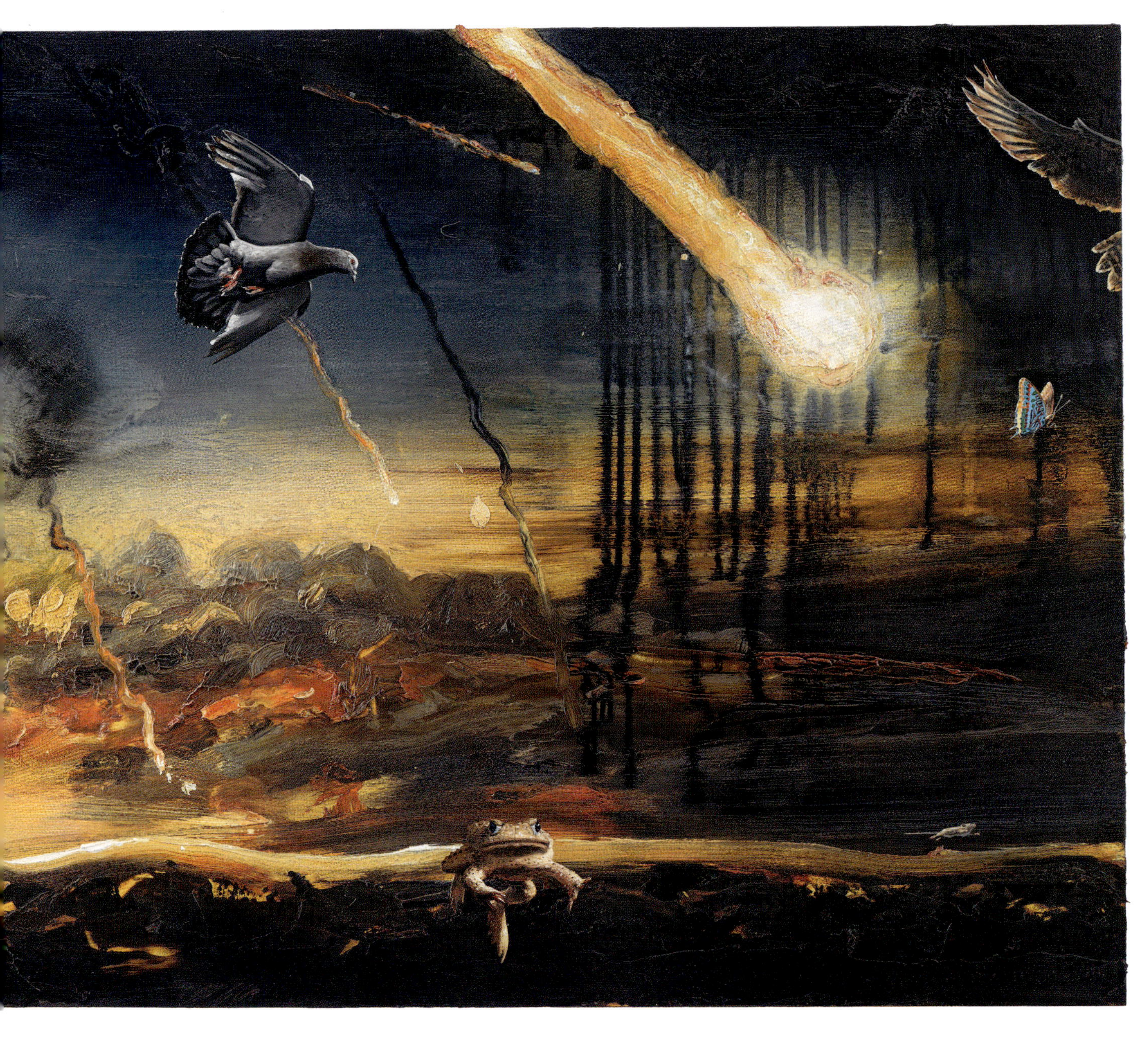

Mt. Vesuvius, Autumn, 79 AD, 2024
Oil and cold wax on wood, 36 × 84 inches (91.4 × 213.4 cm)
Collection of Bram and Lara Hechtkopf

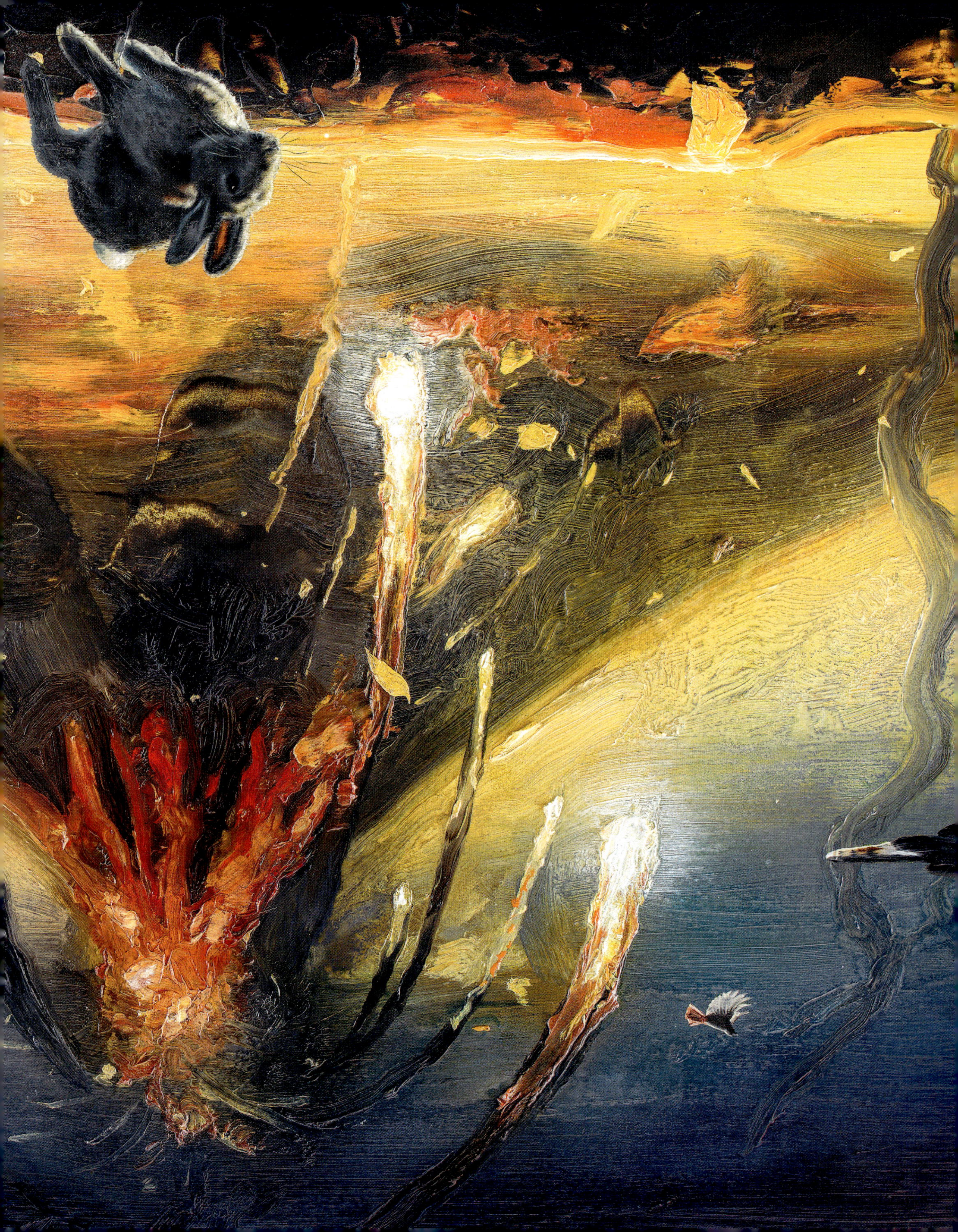

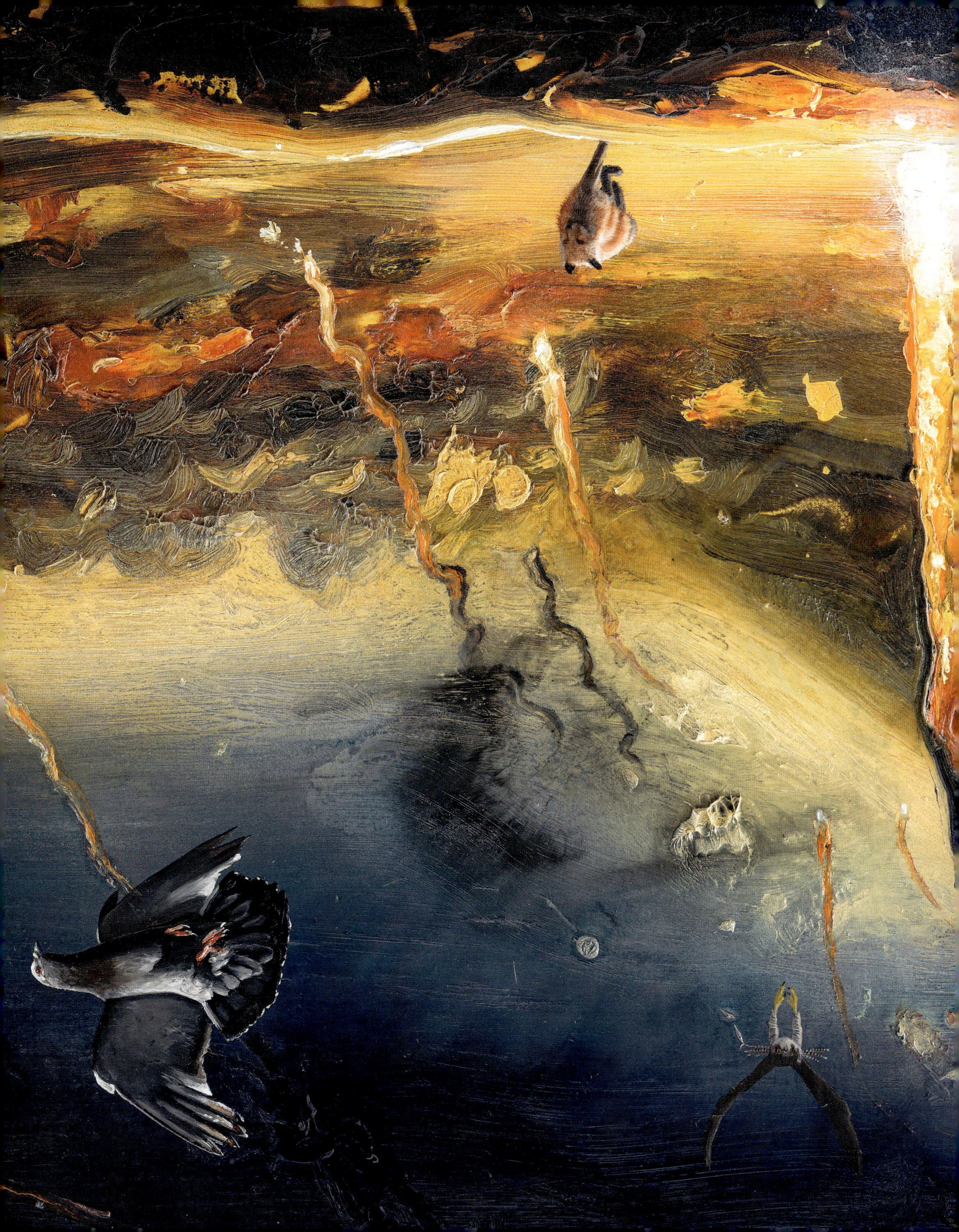

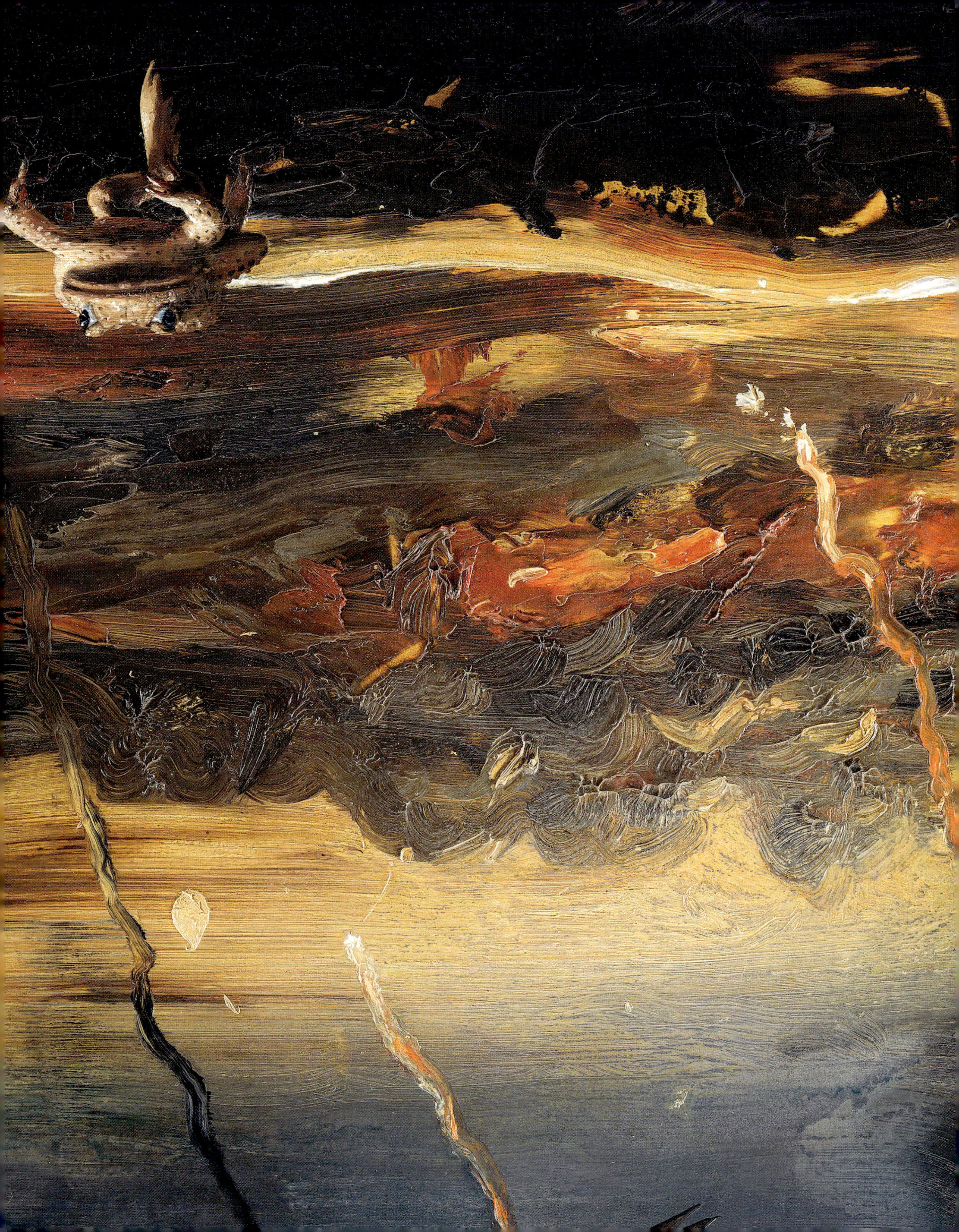

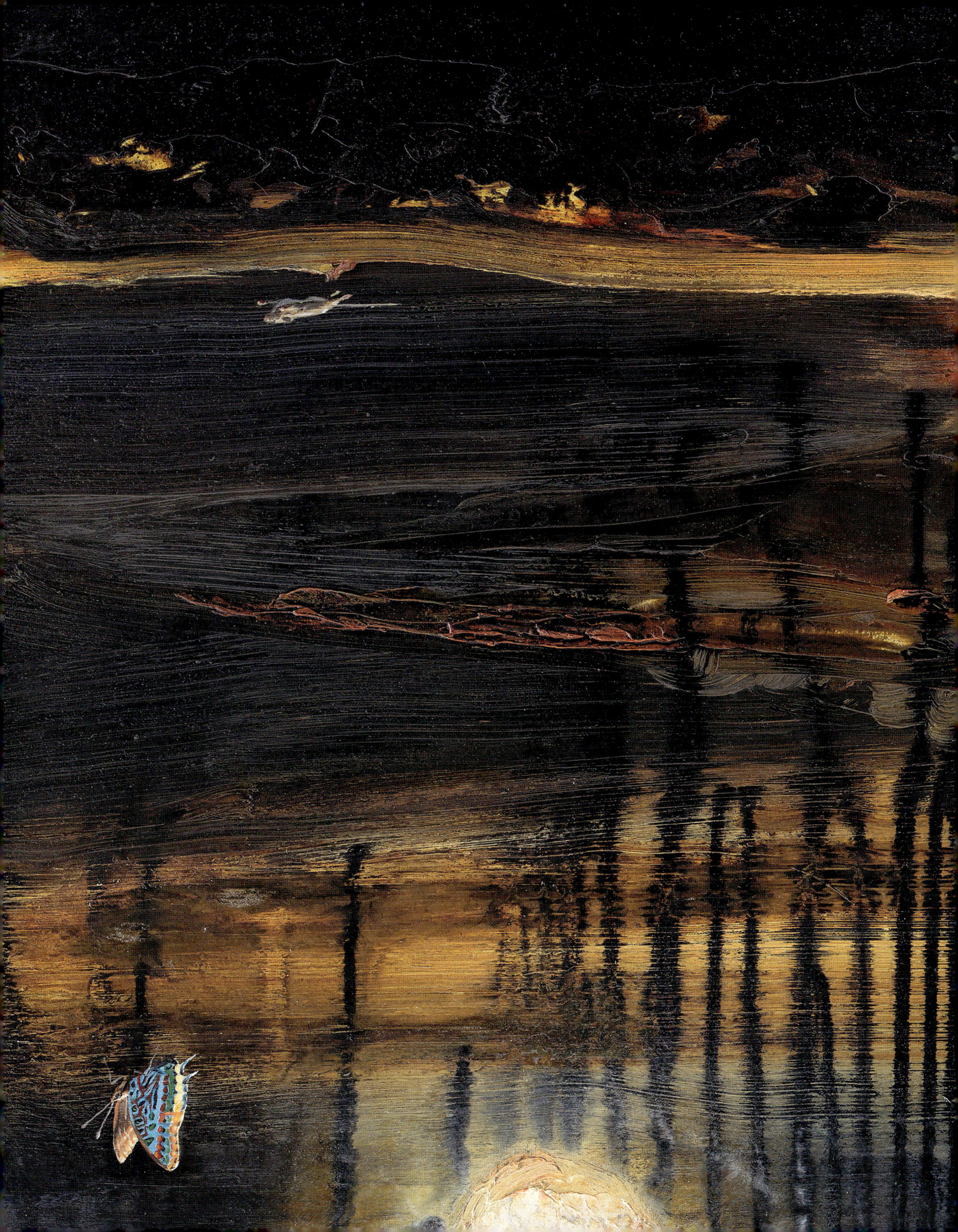

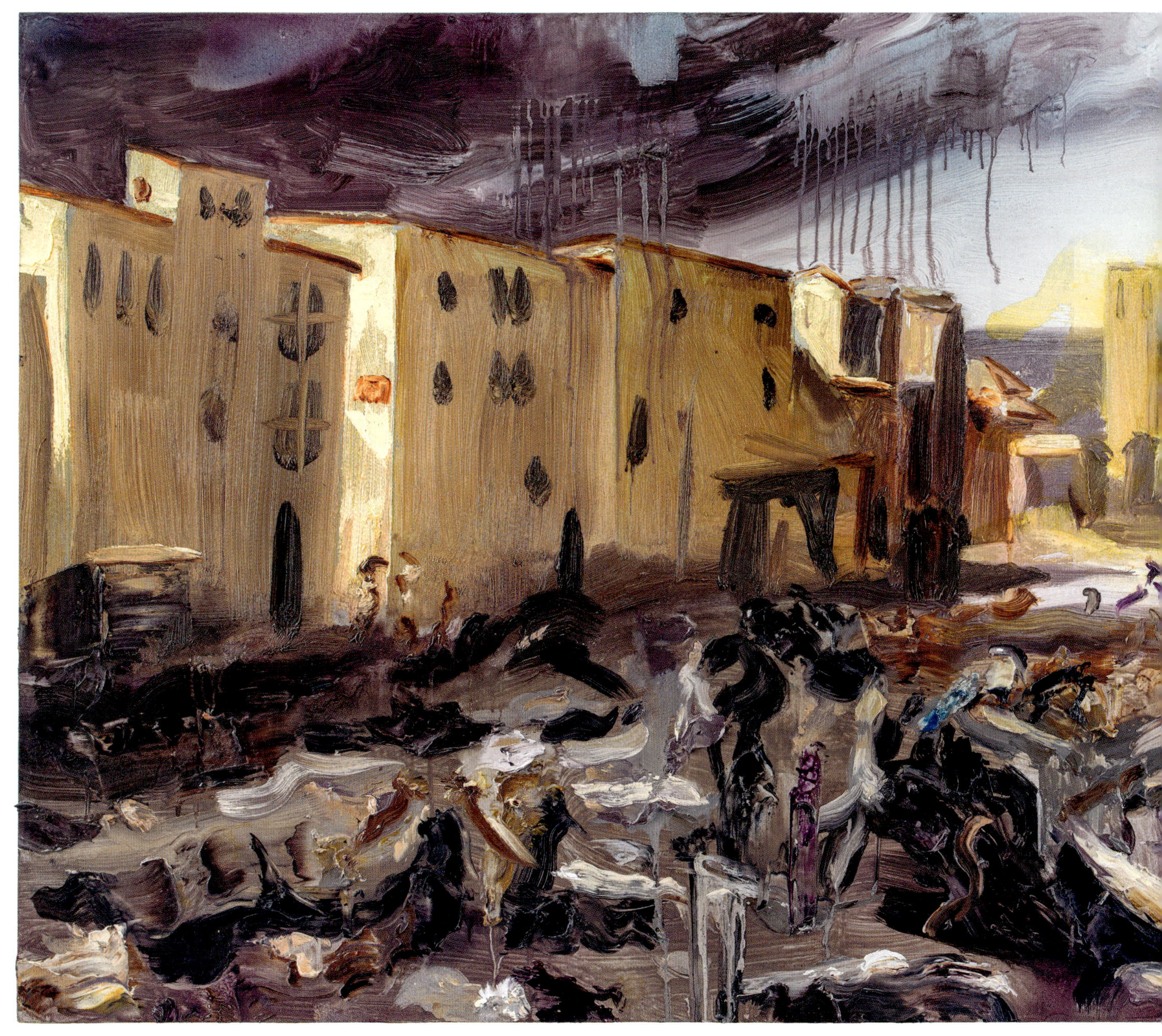

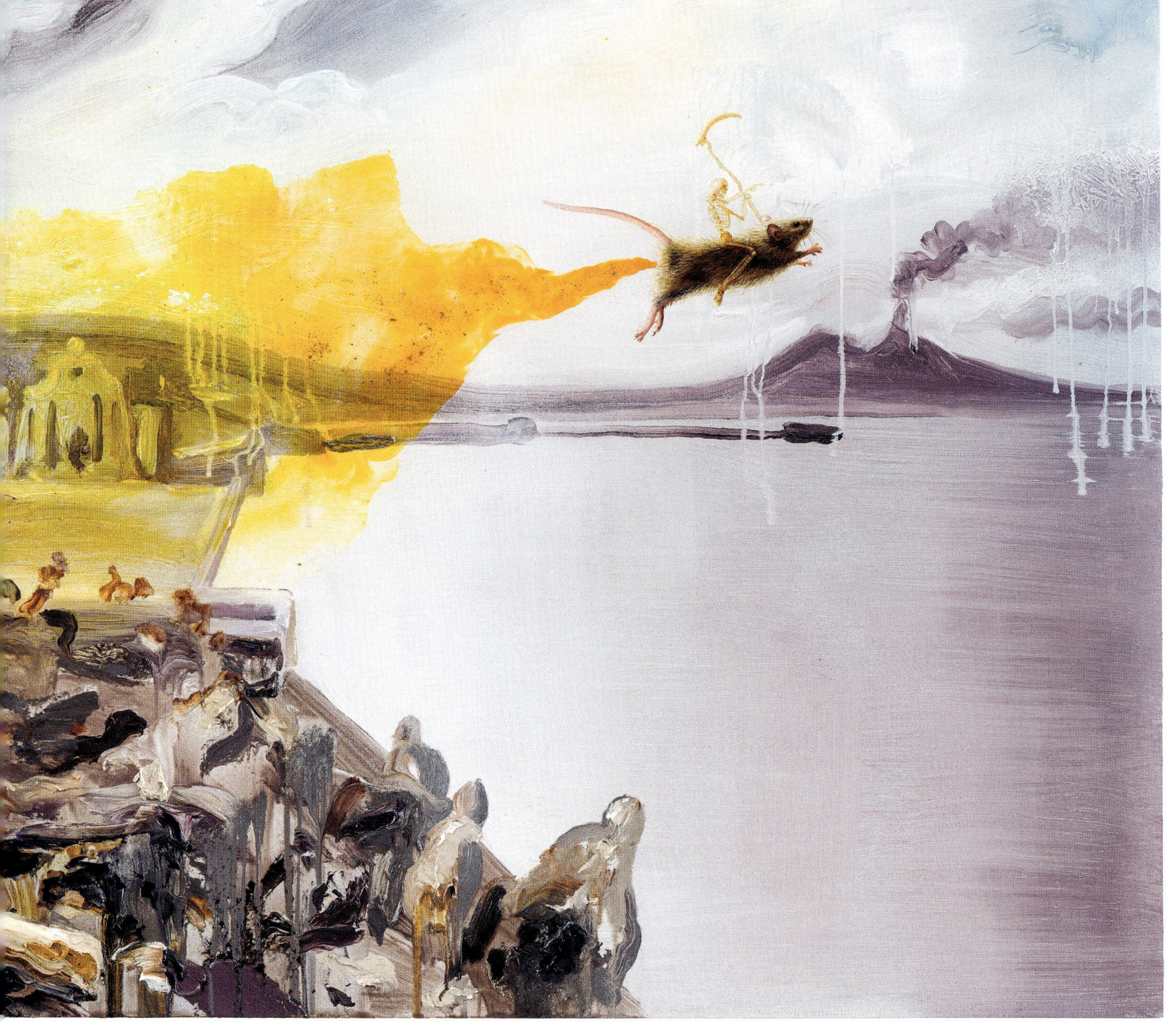

Plague in the Kingdom of Naples, 1656–1658, 2024
Oil and cold wax on wood, 36 × 84 inches (91.4 × 213.4 cm)

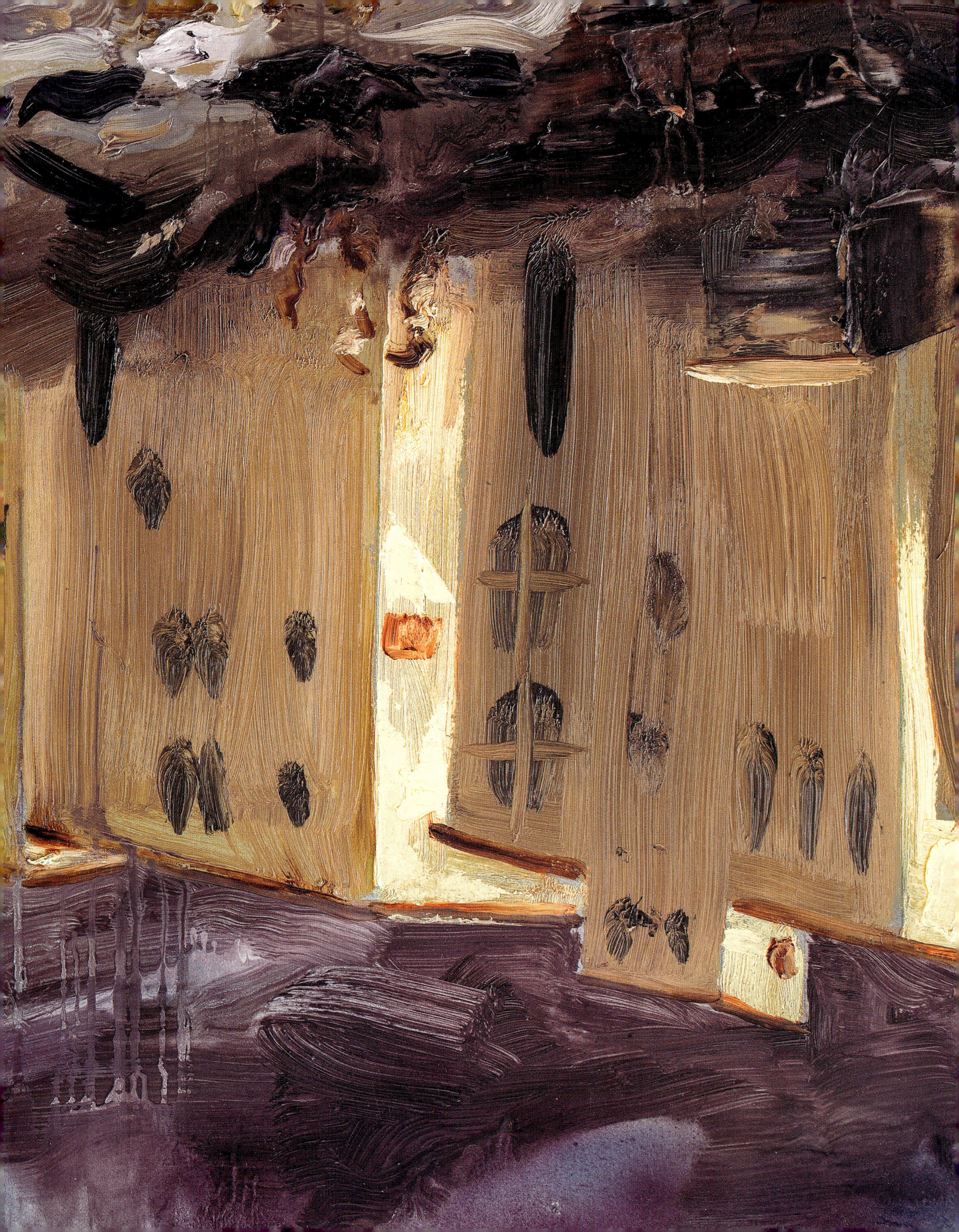

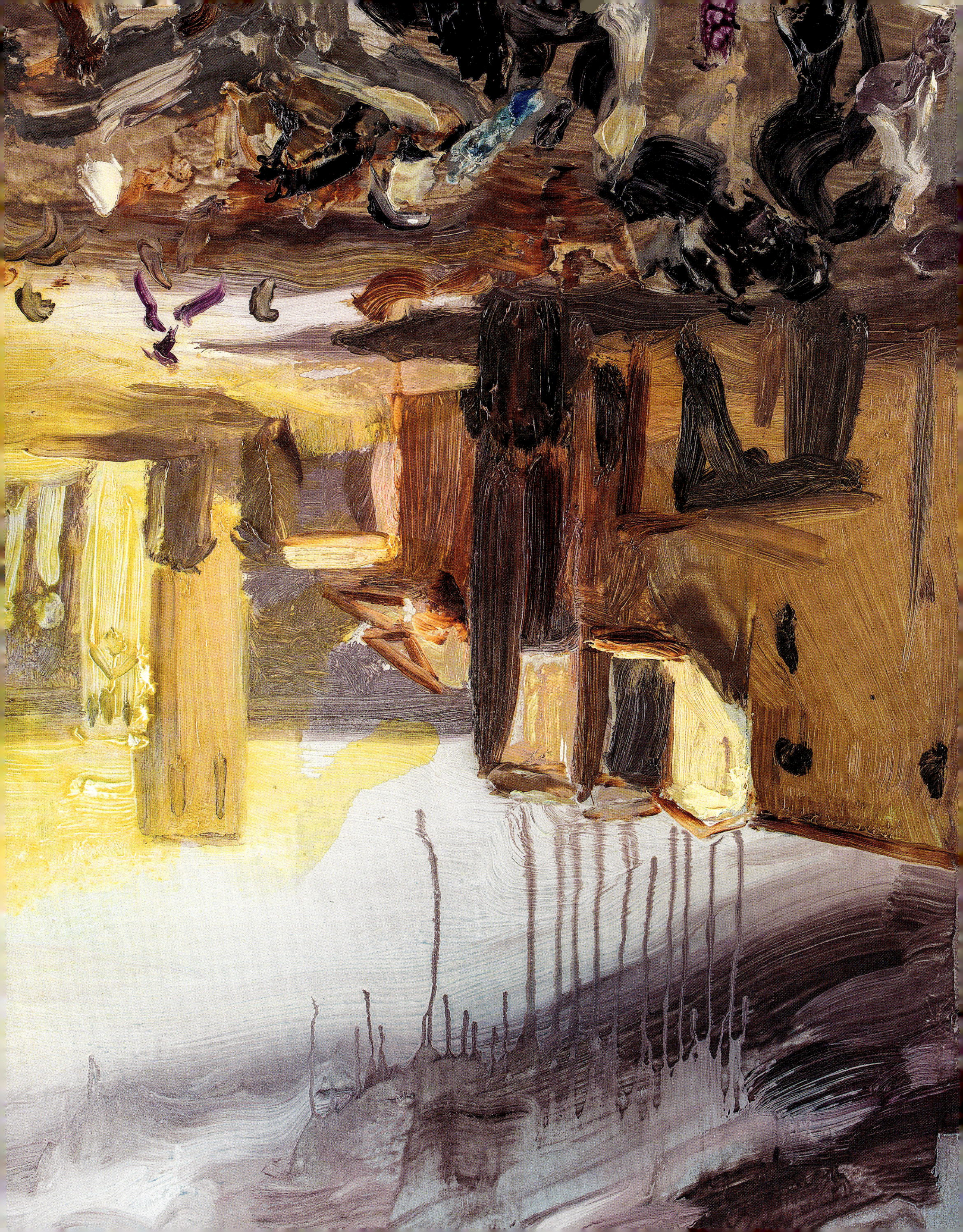

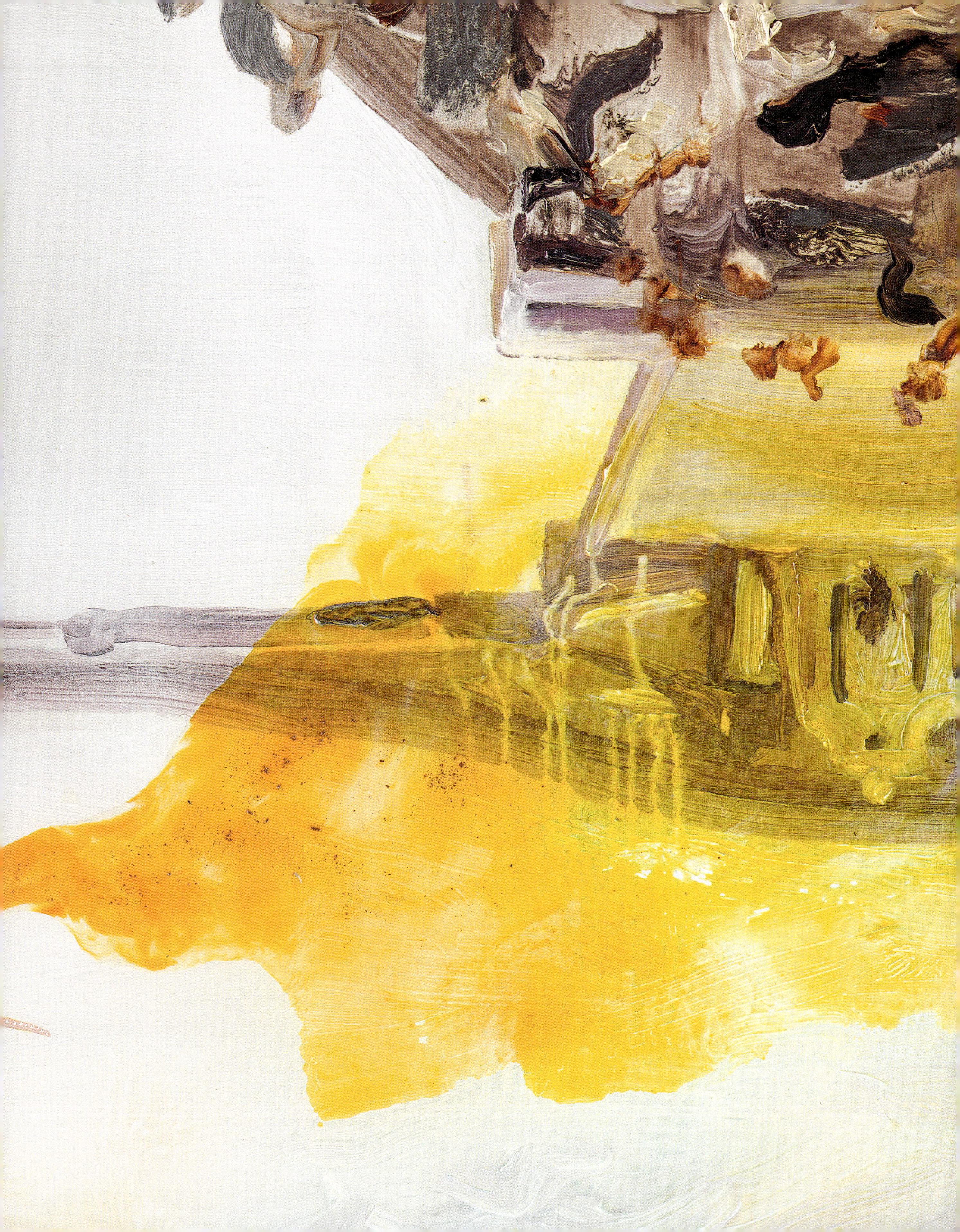

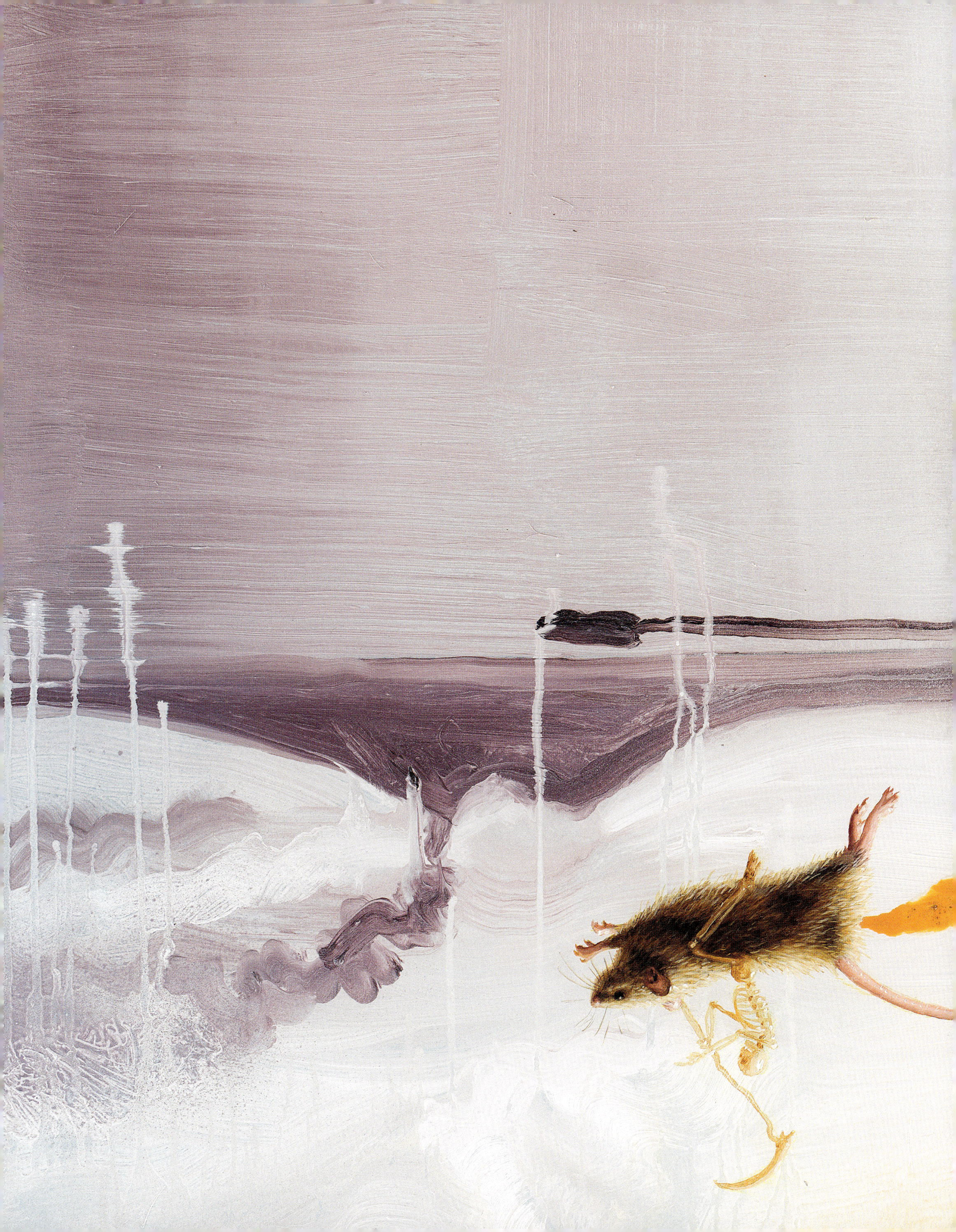

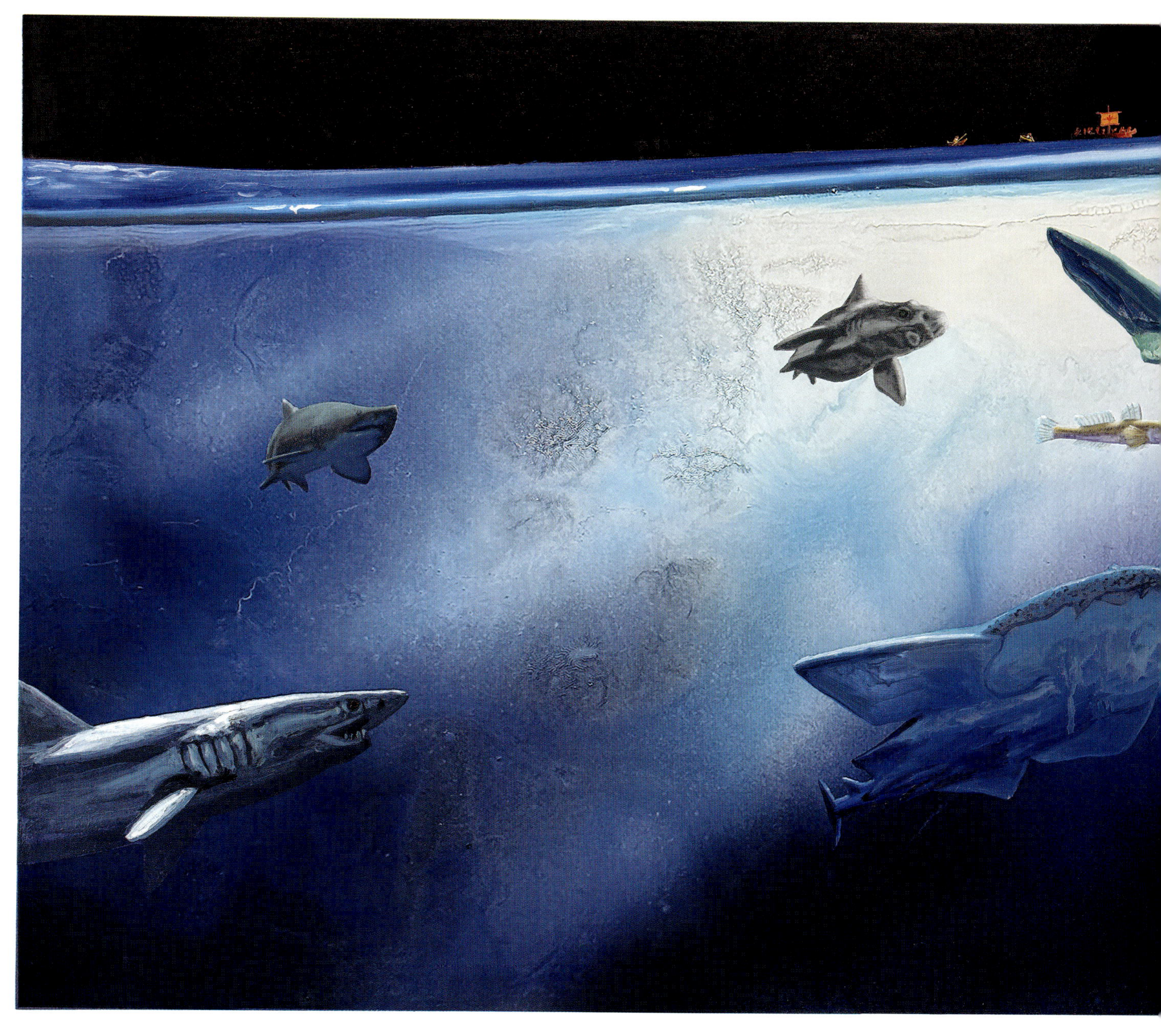

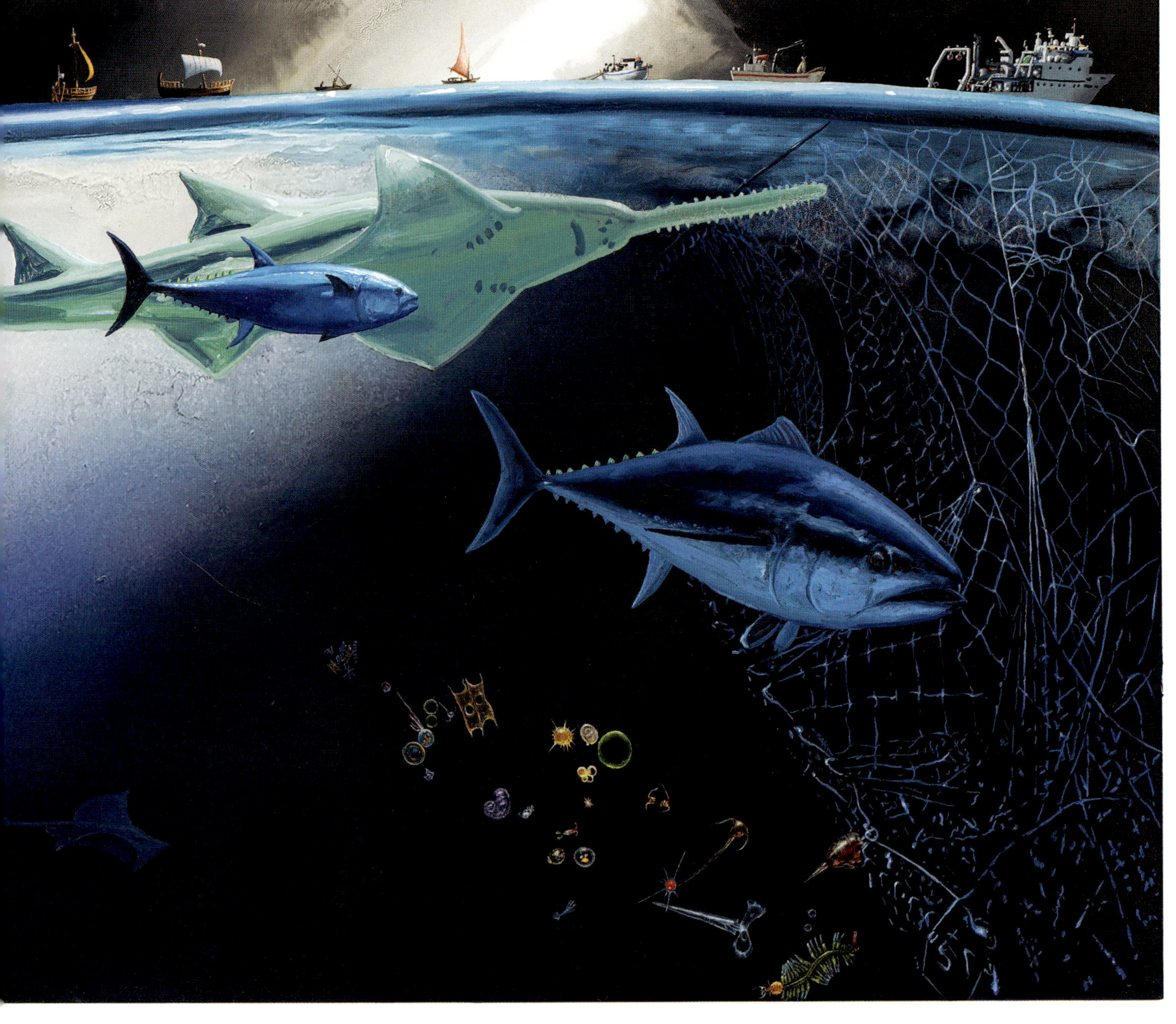

The Departed, 2024
Oil and cold wax on wood, 36 × 84 inches (91.4 × 213.4 cm)

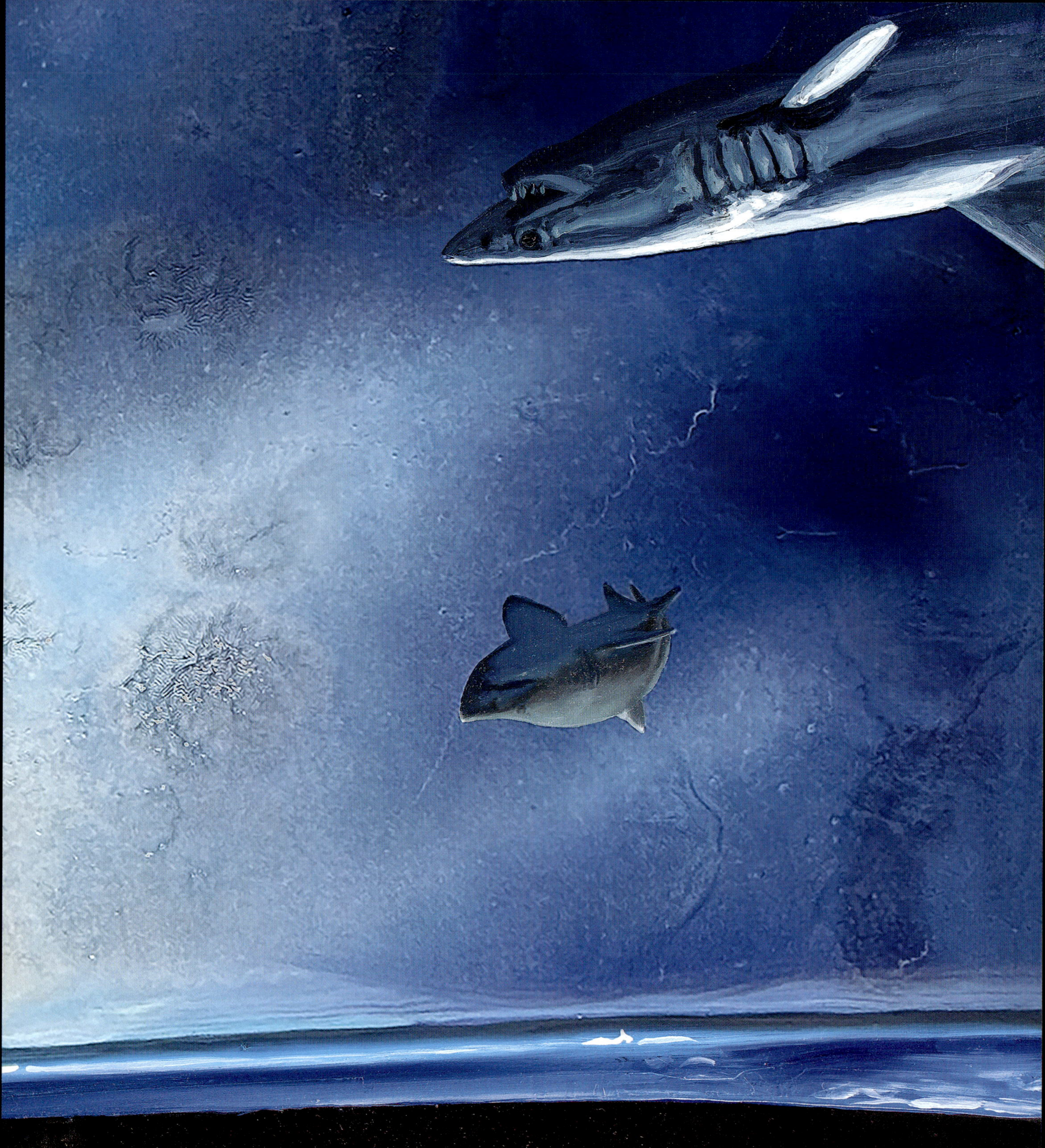

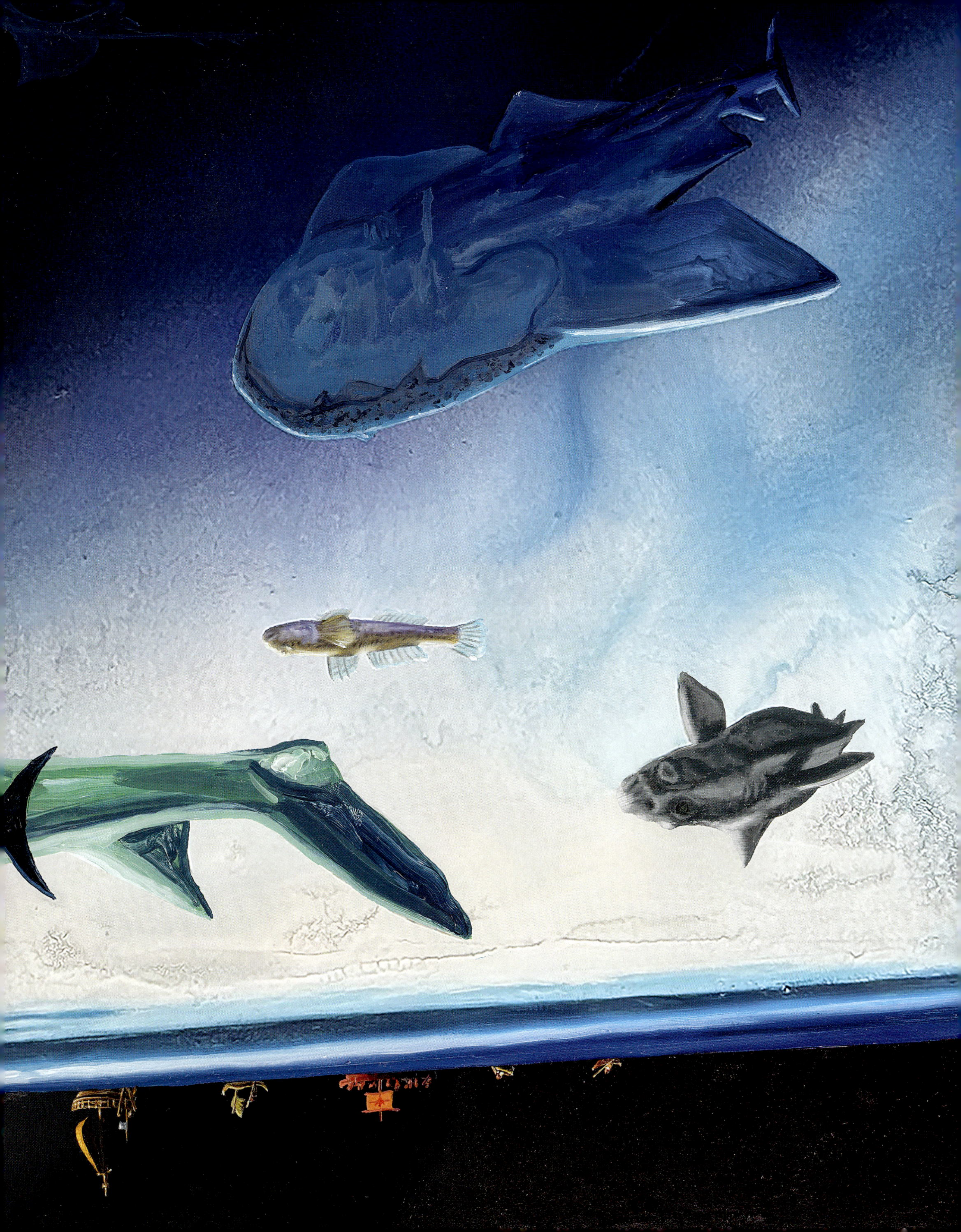

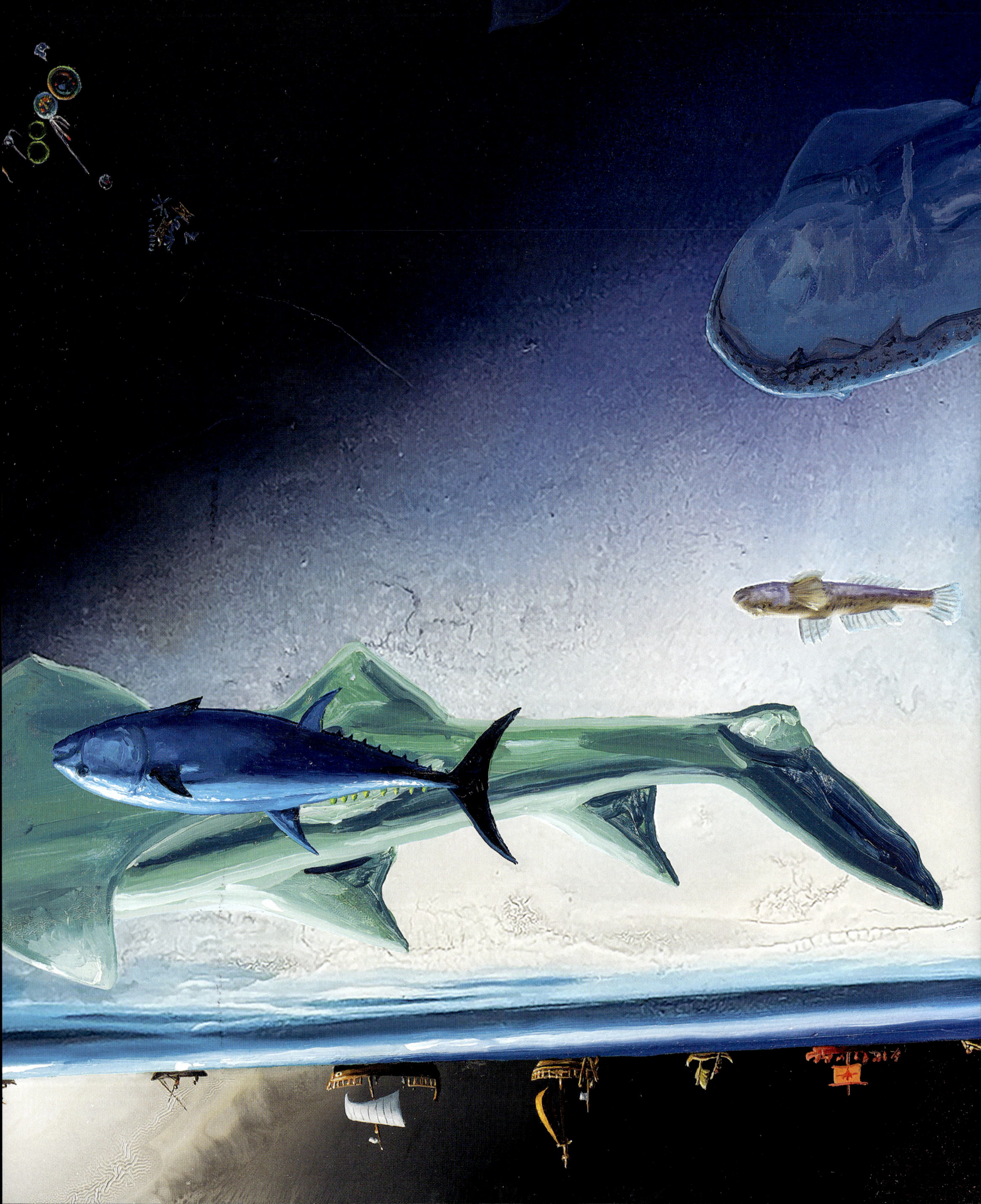

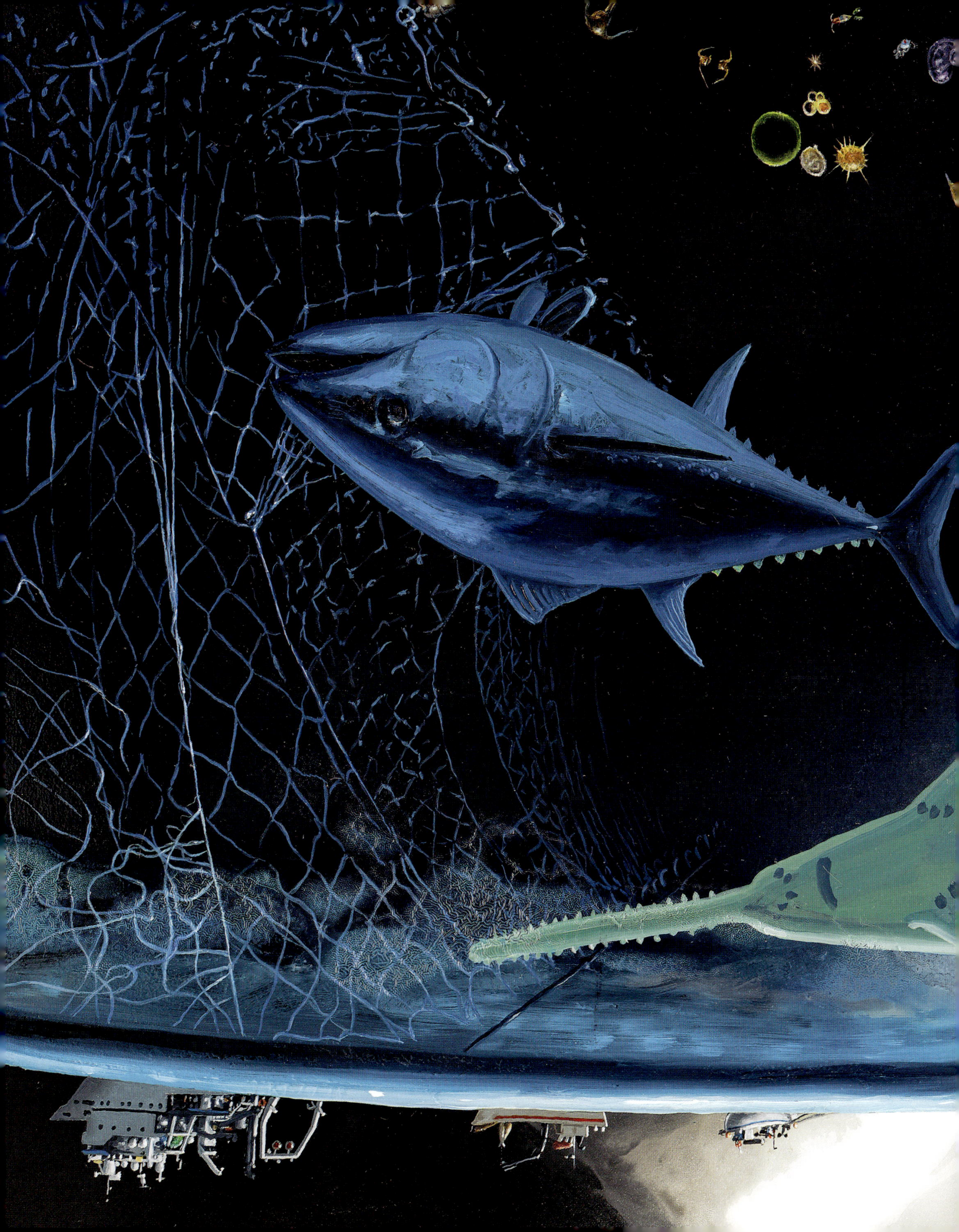

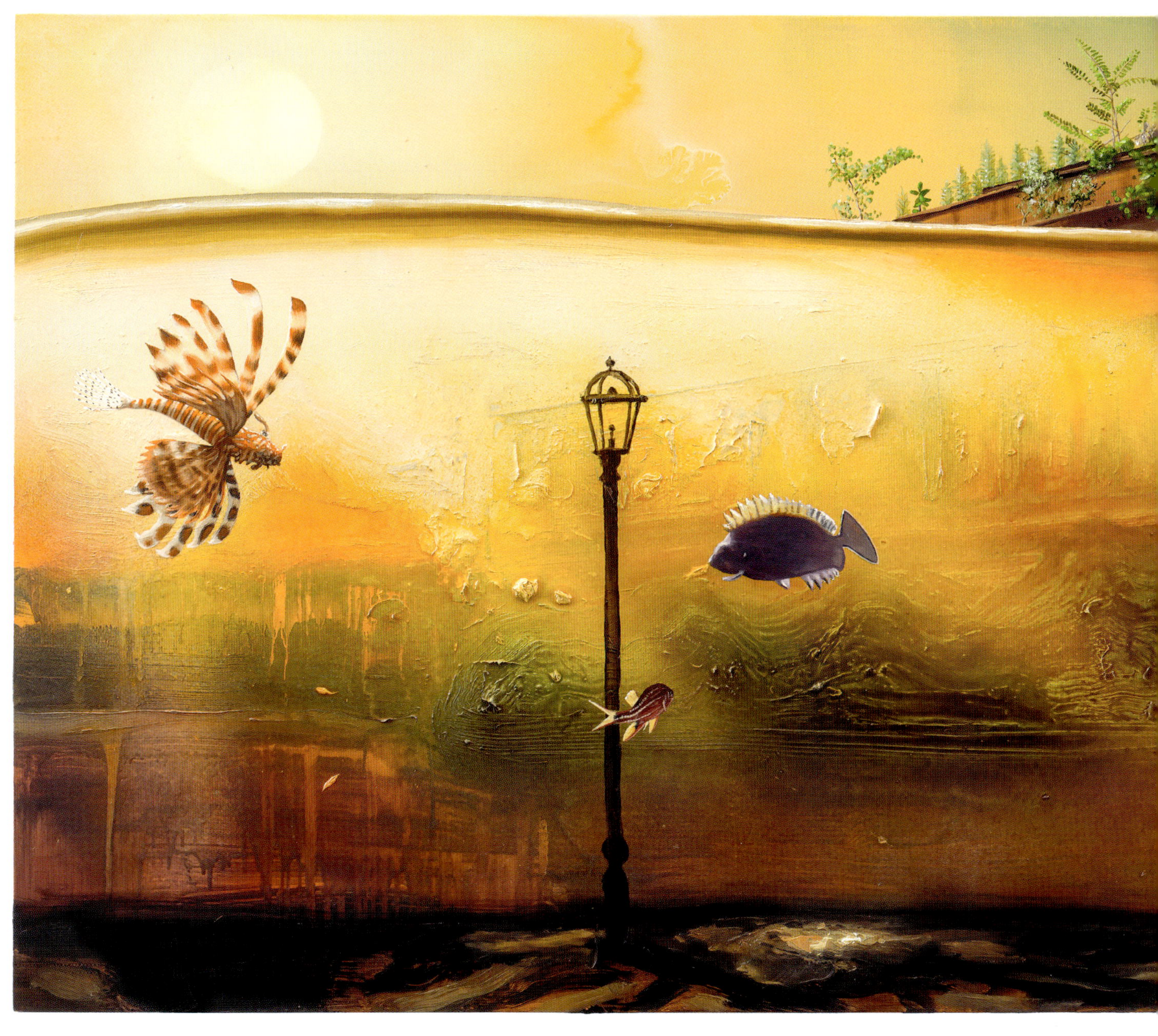

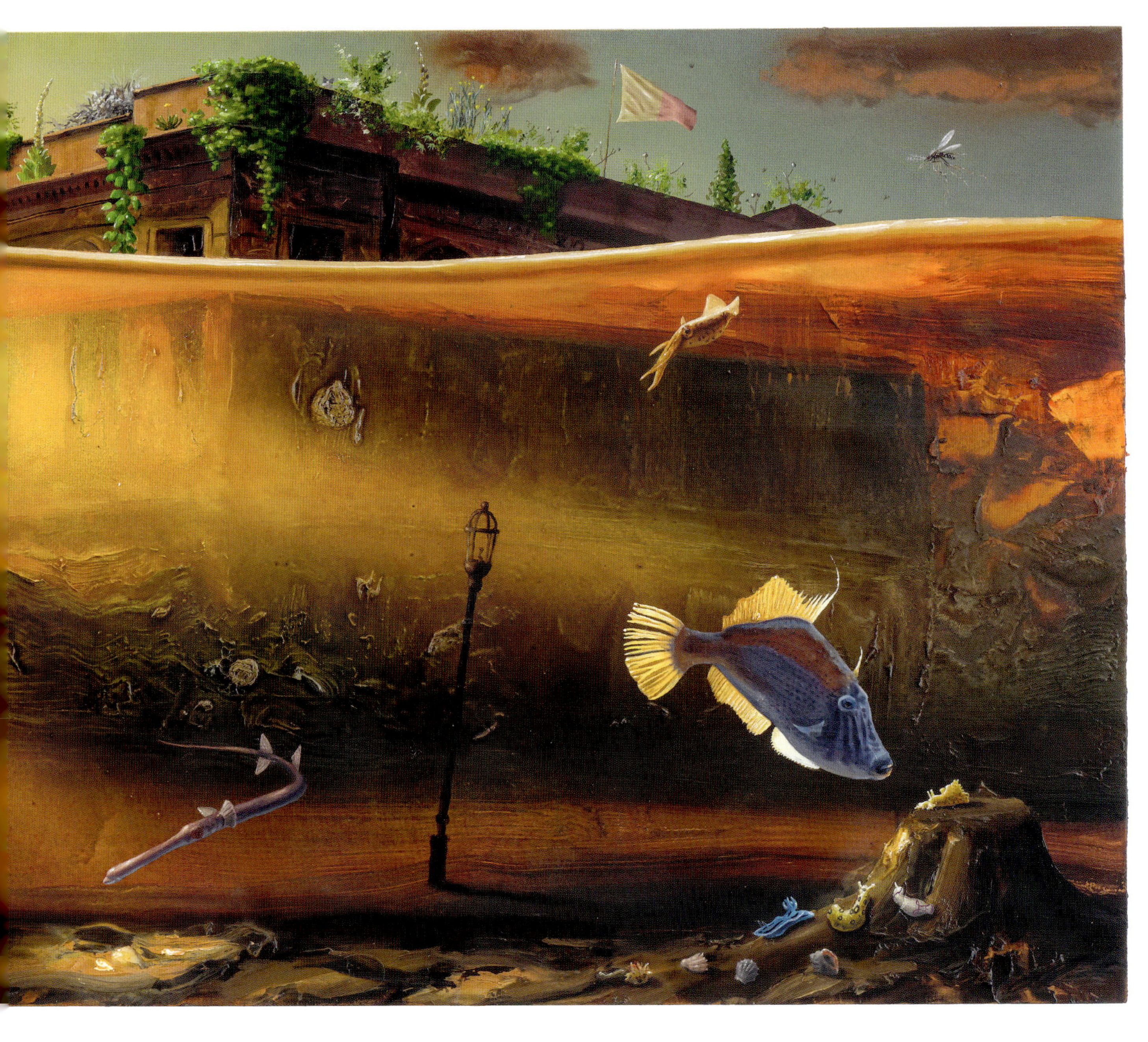

Acquario di Napoli - Stazione Zoologica Anton Dohrn, 2024
Oil and cold wax on wood, 36 × 84 inches (91.4 × 213.4 cm)
Collection of Gerard and Ilaria Viganò-Francis

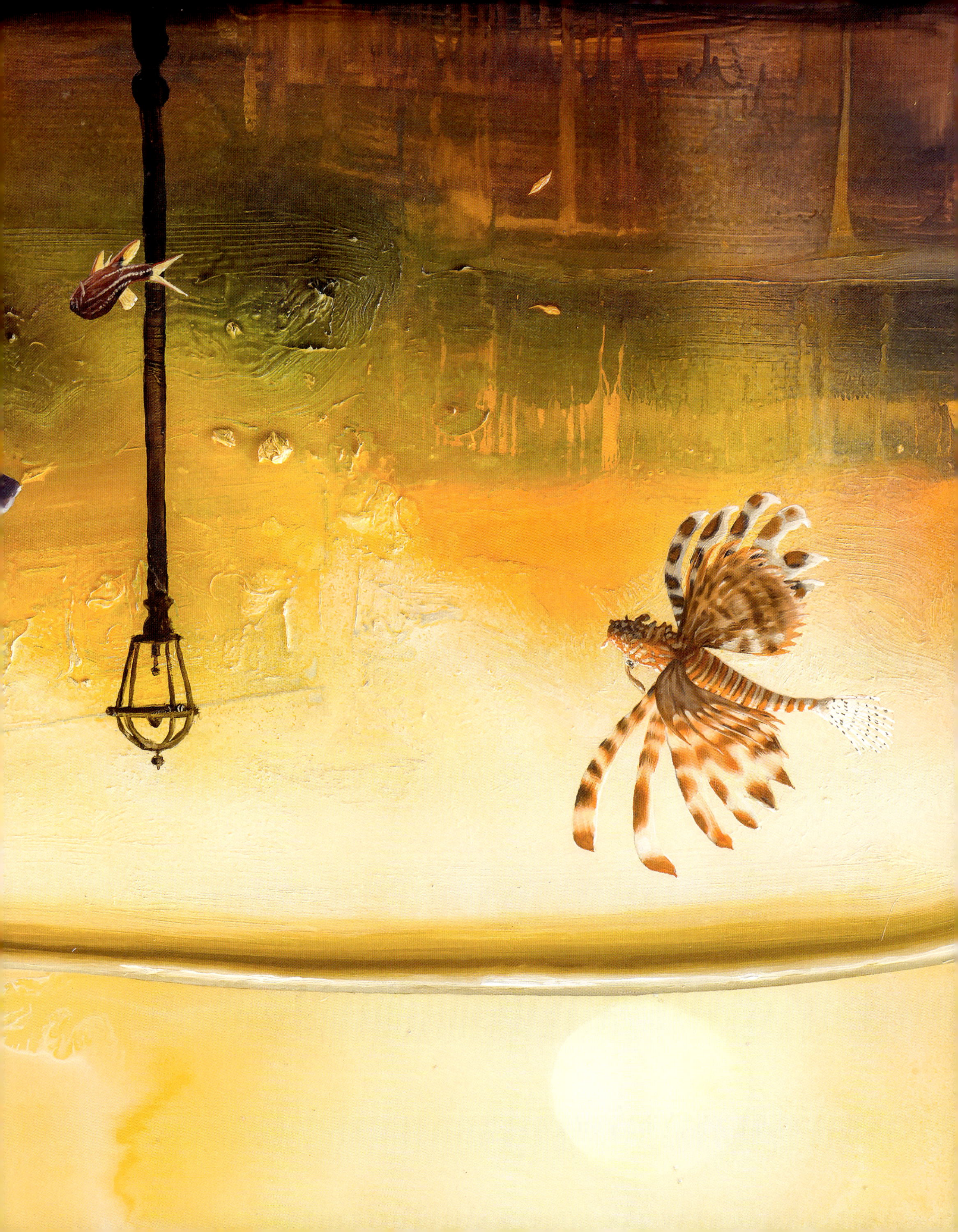

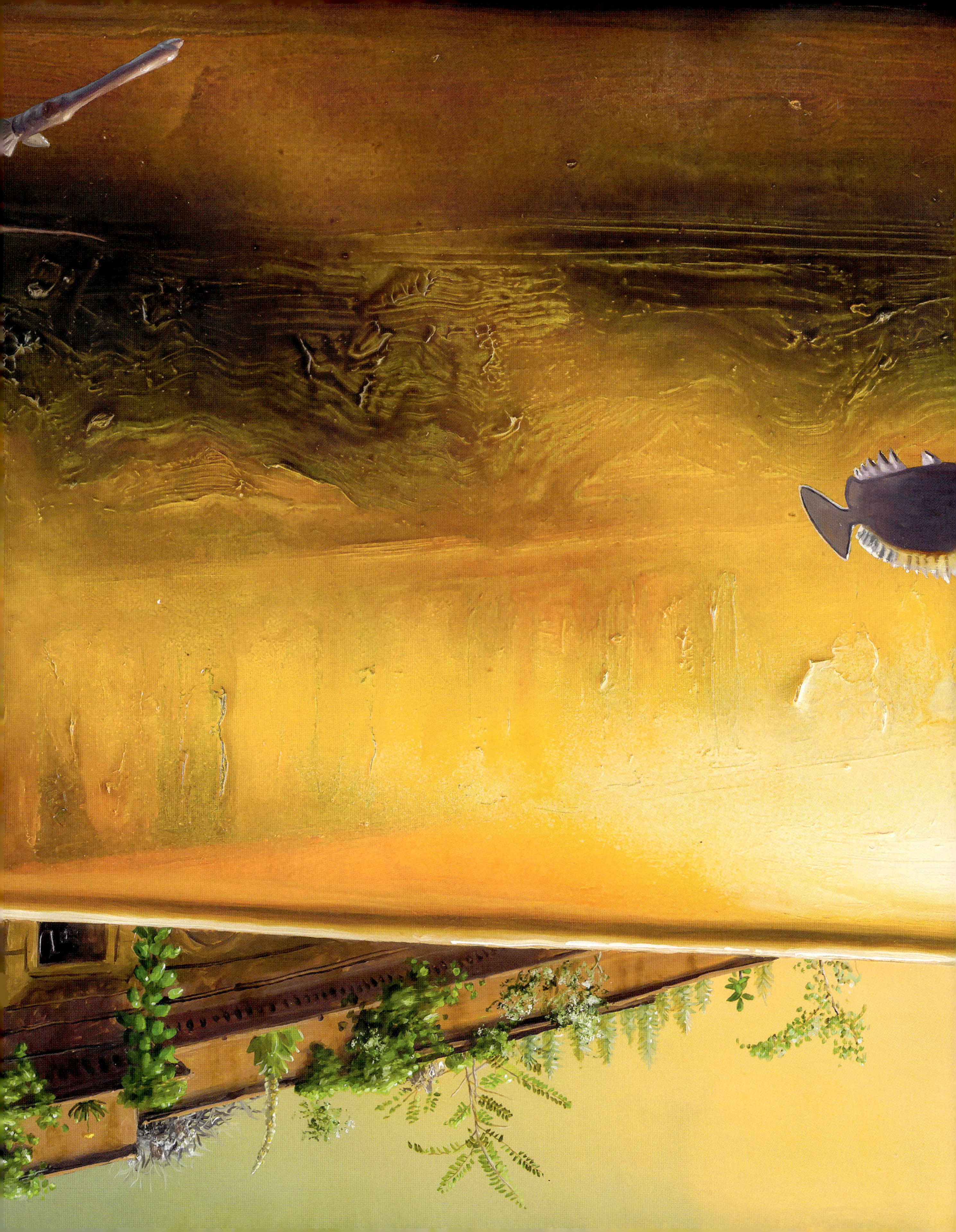

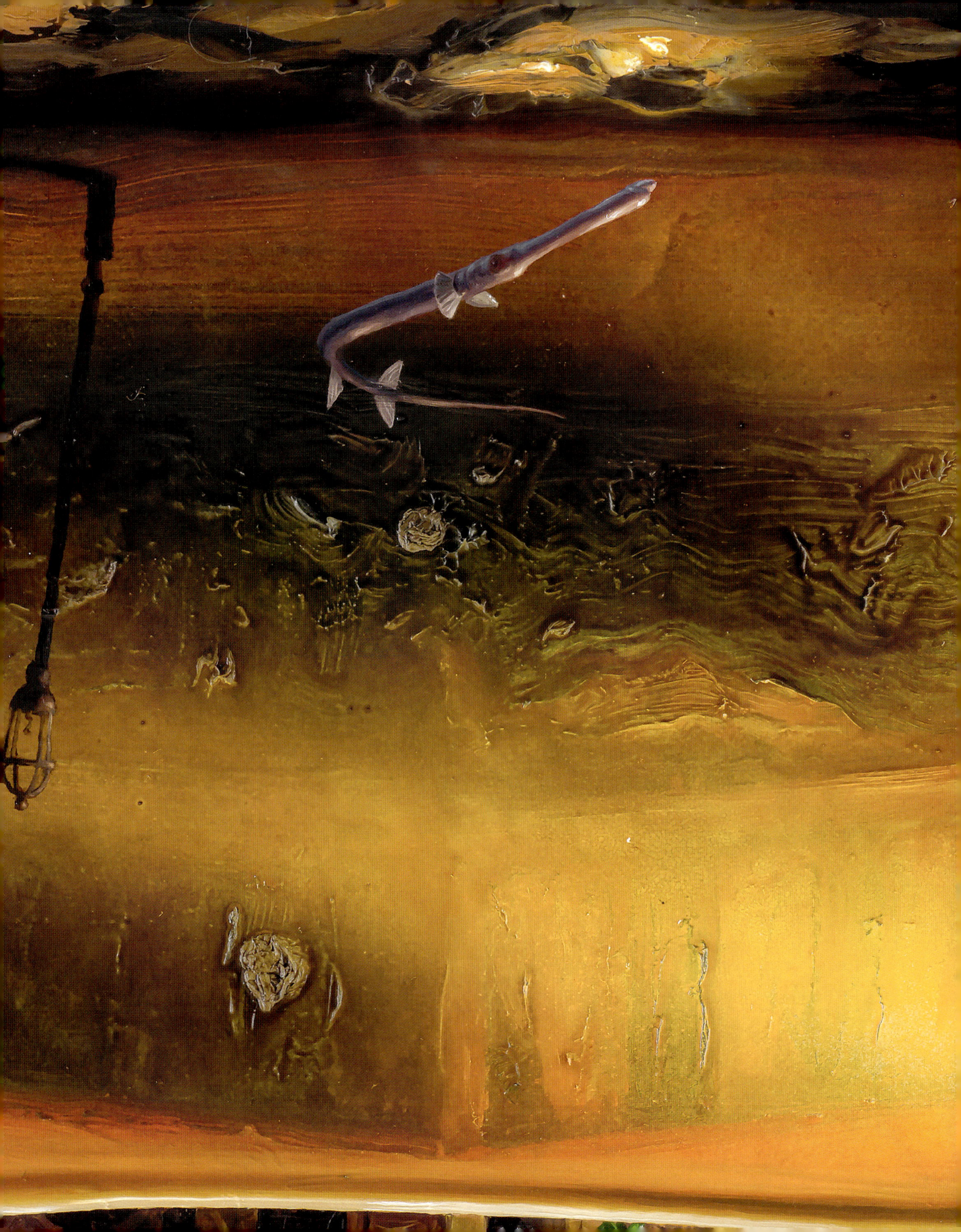

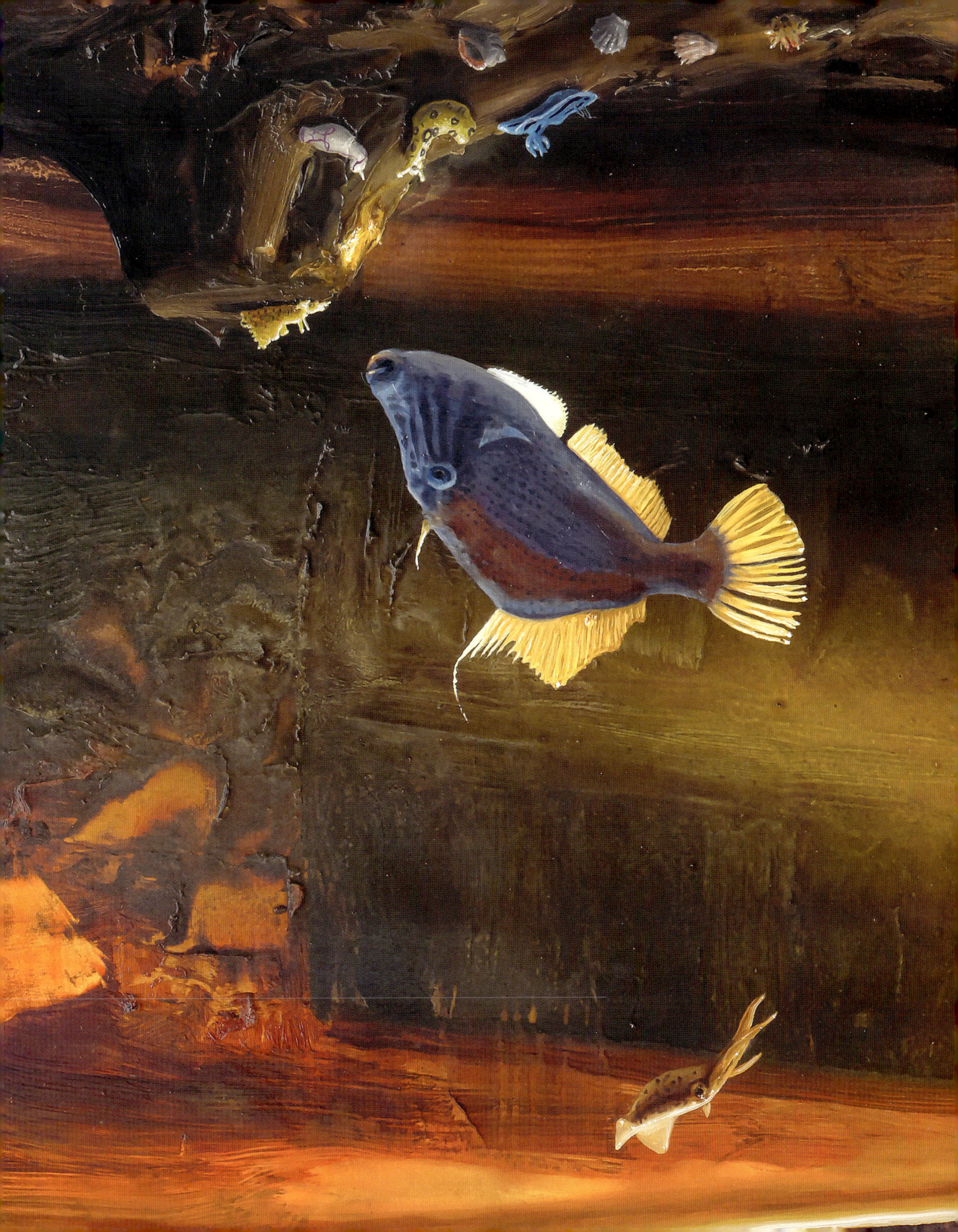

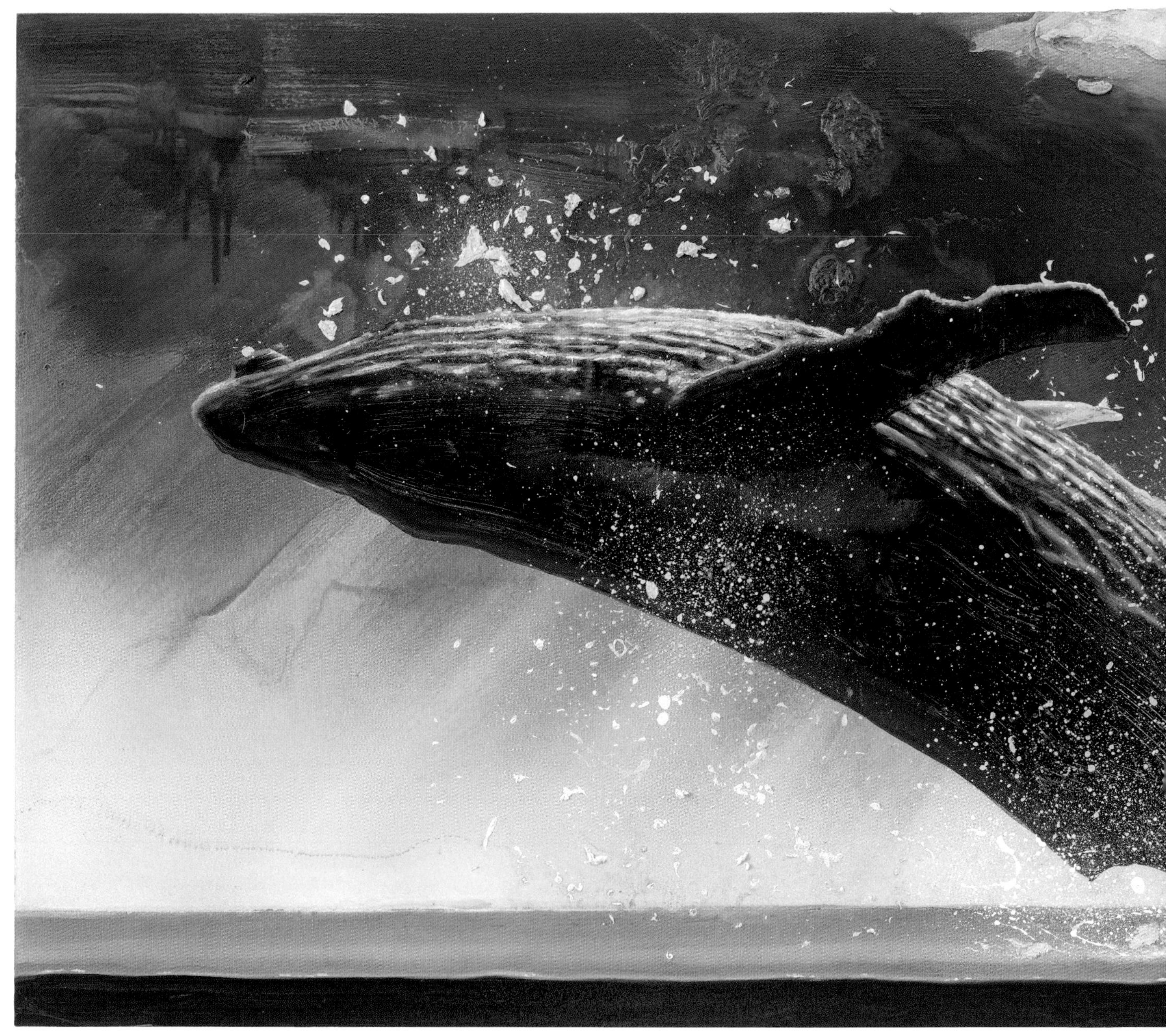

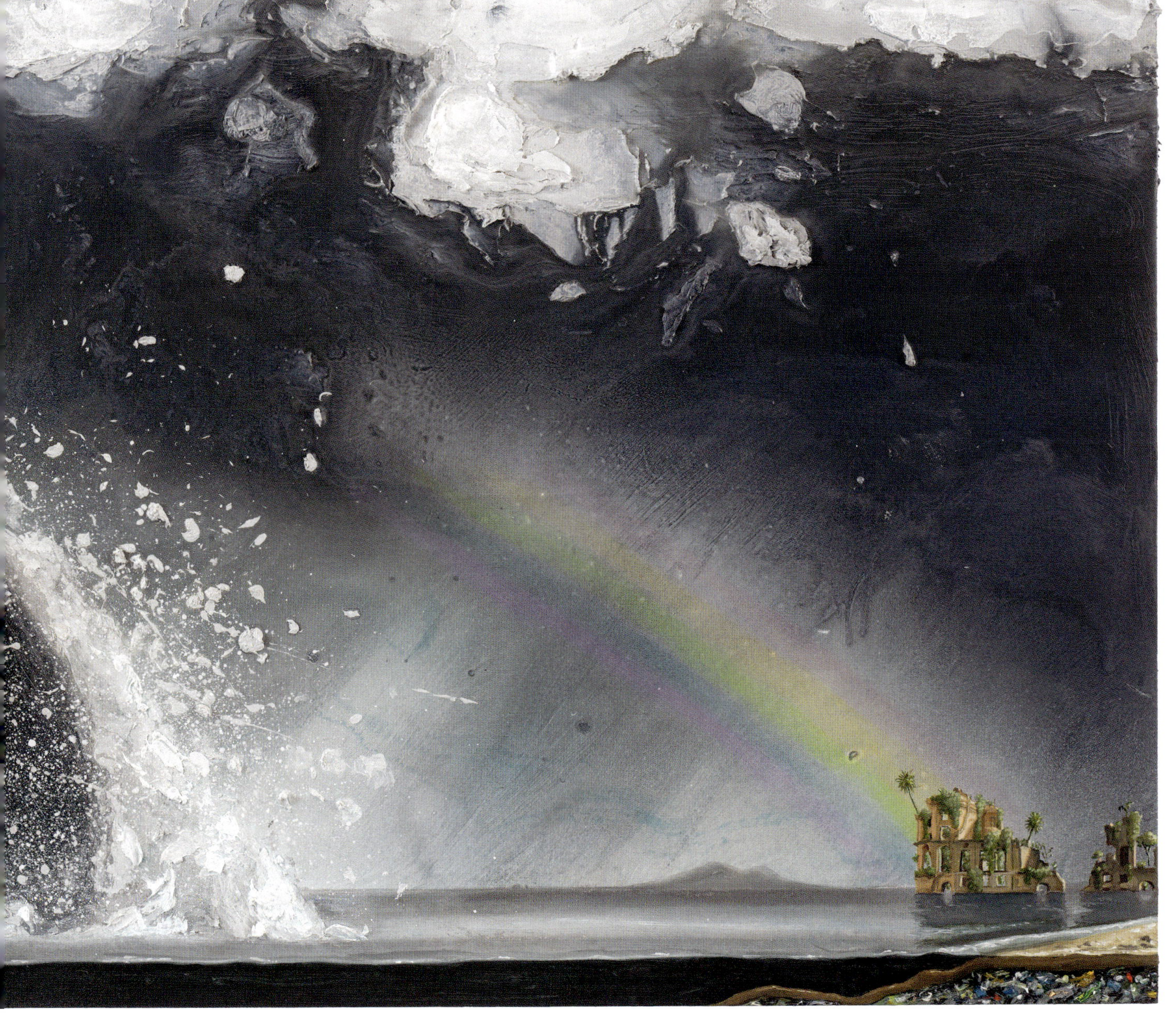

Post Human: Palazzo Donn'Anna, 2024
Oil and cold wax on Dibond, 36 × 84 inches (91.4 × 213.4 cm)

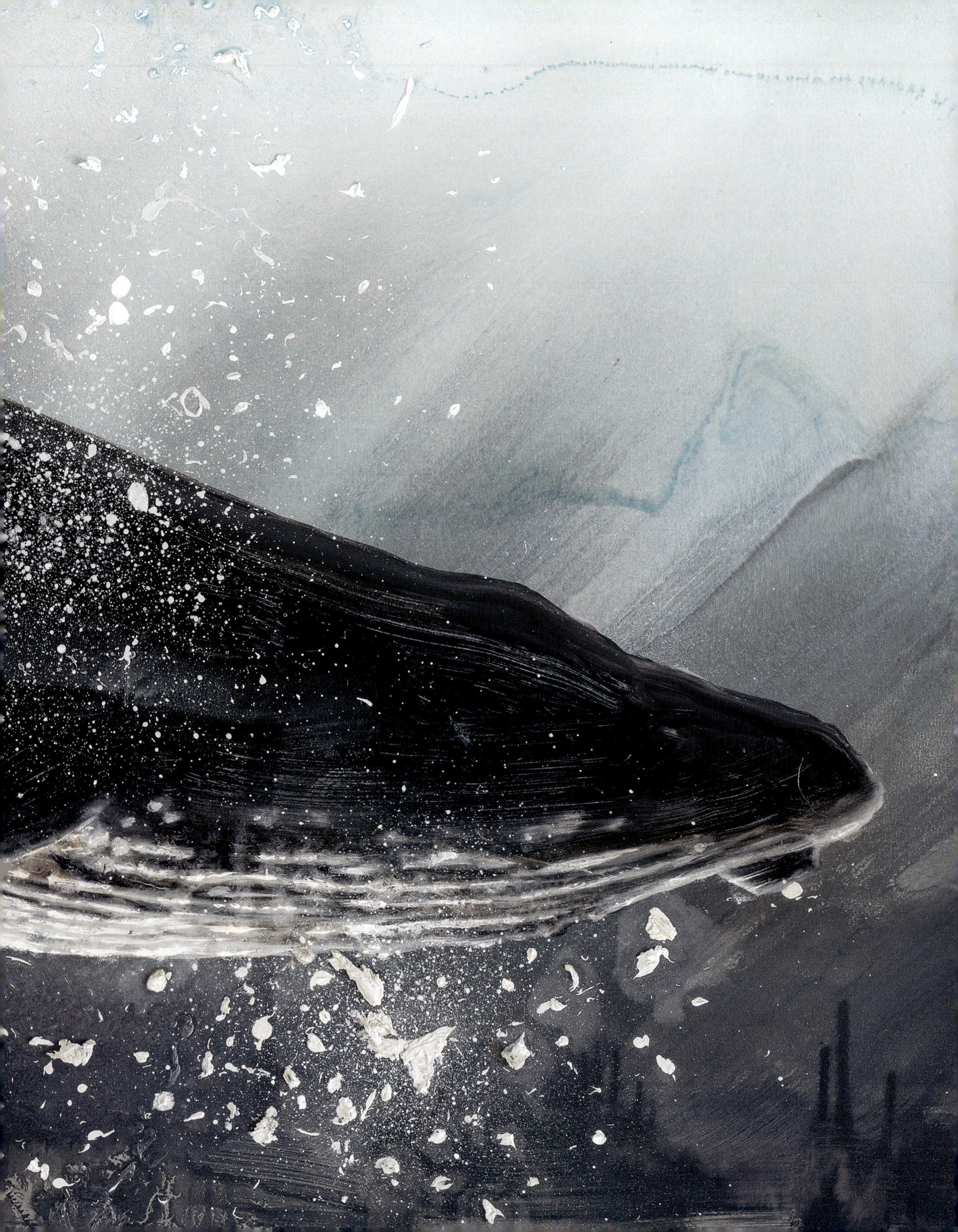

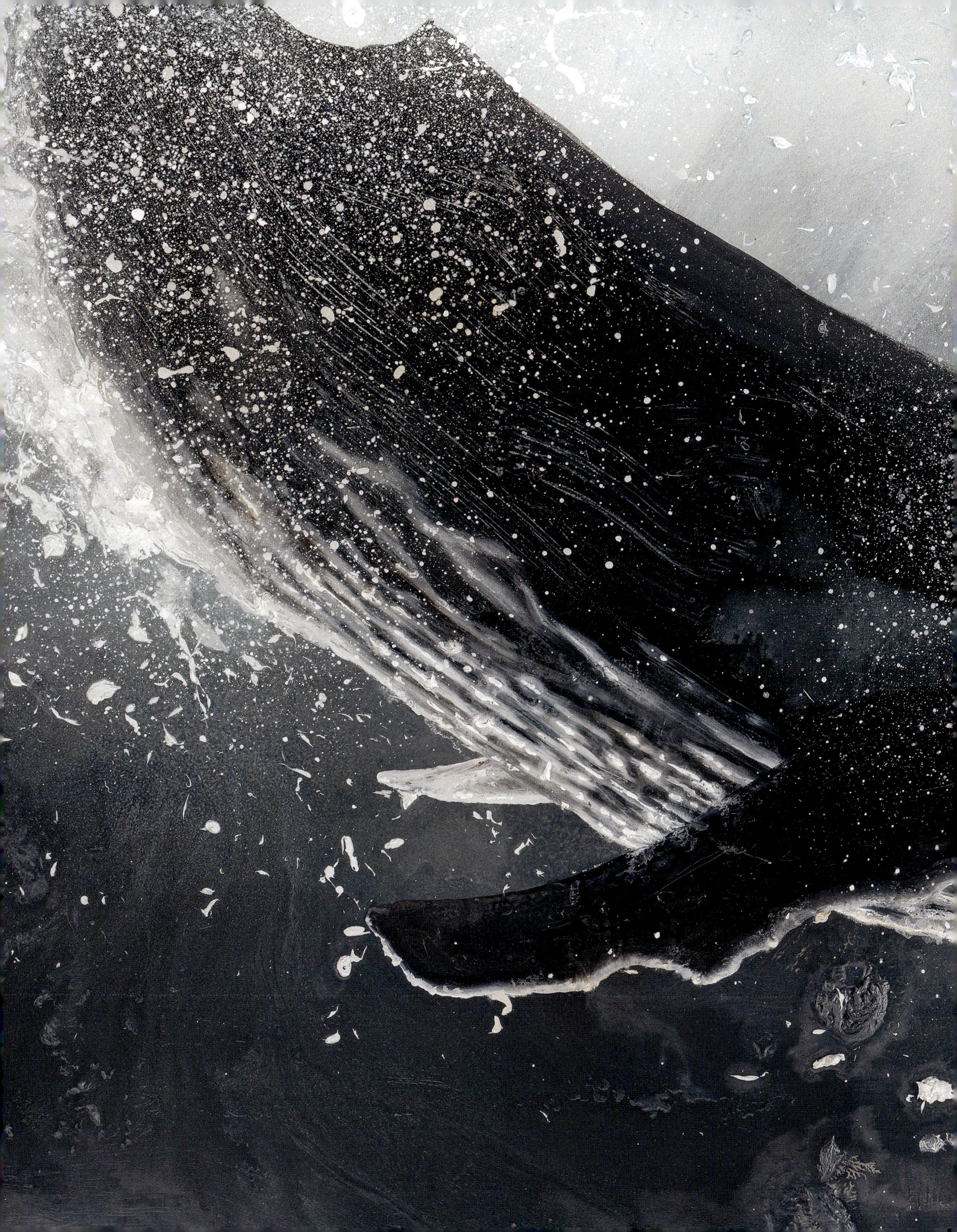

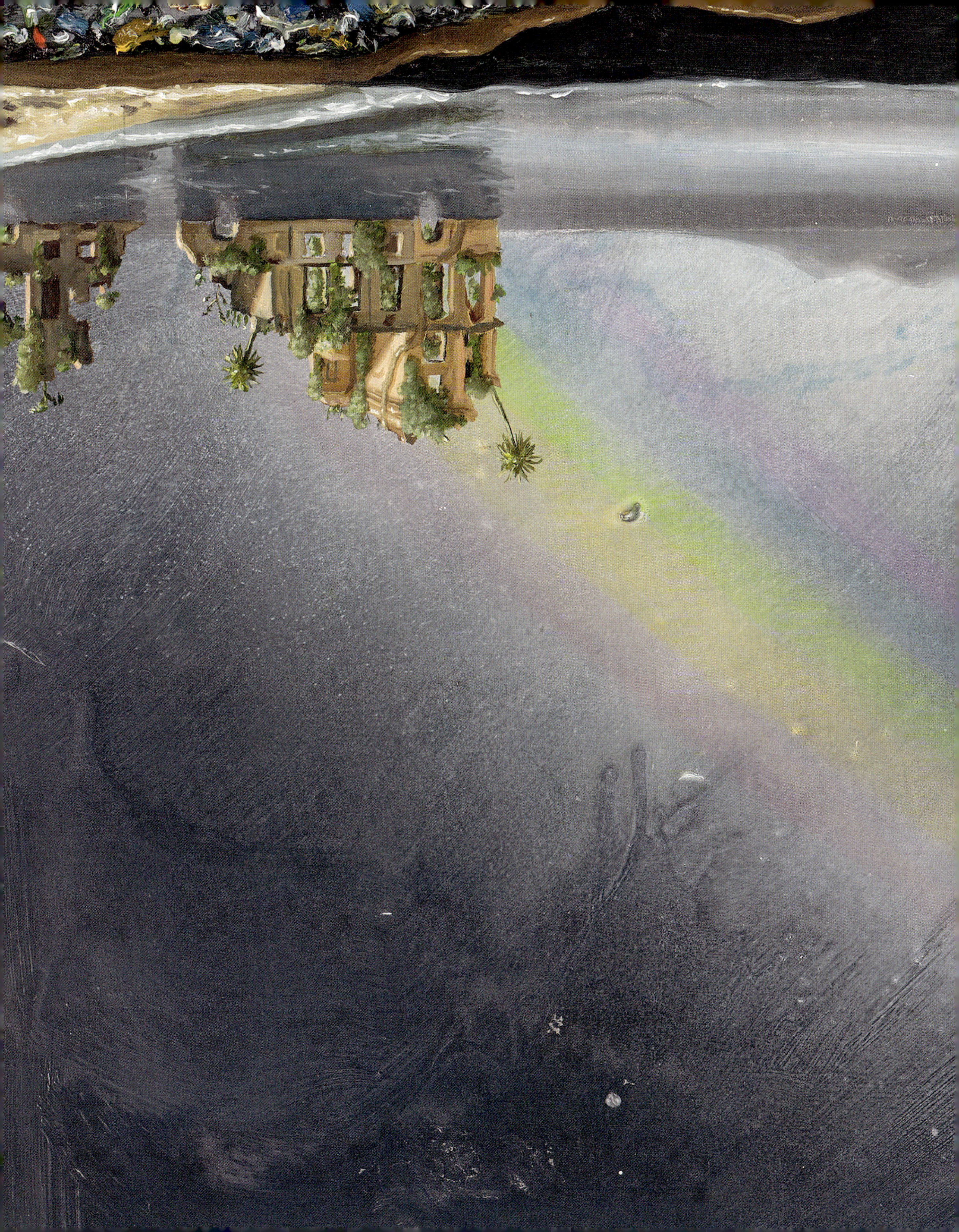

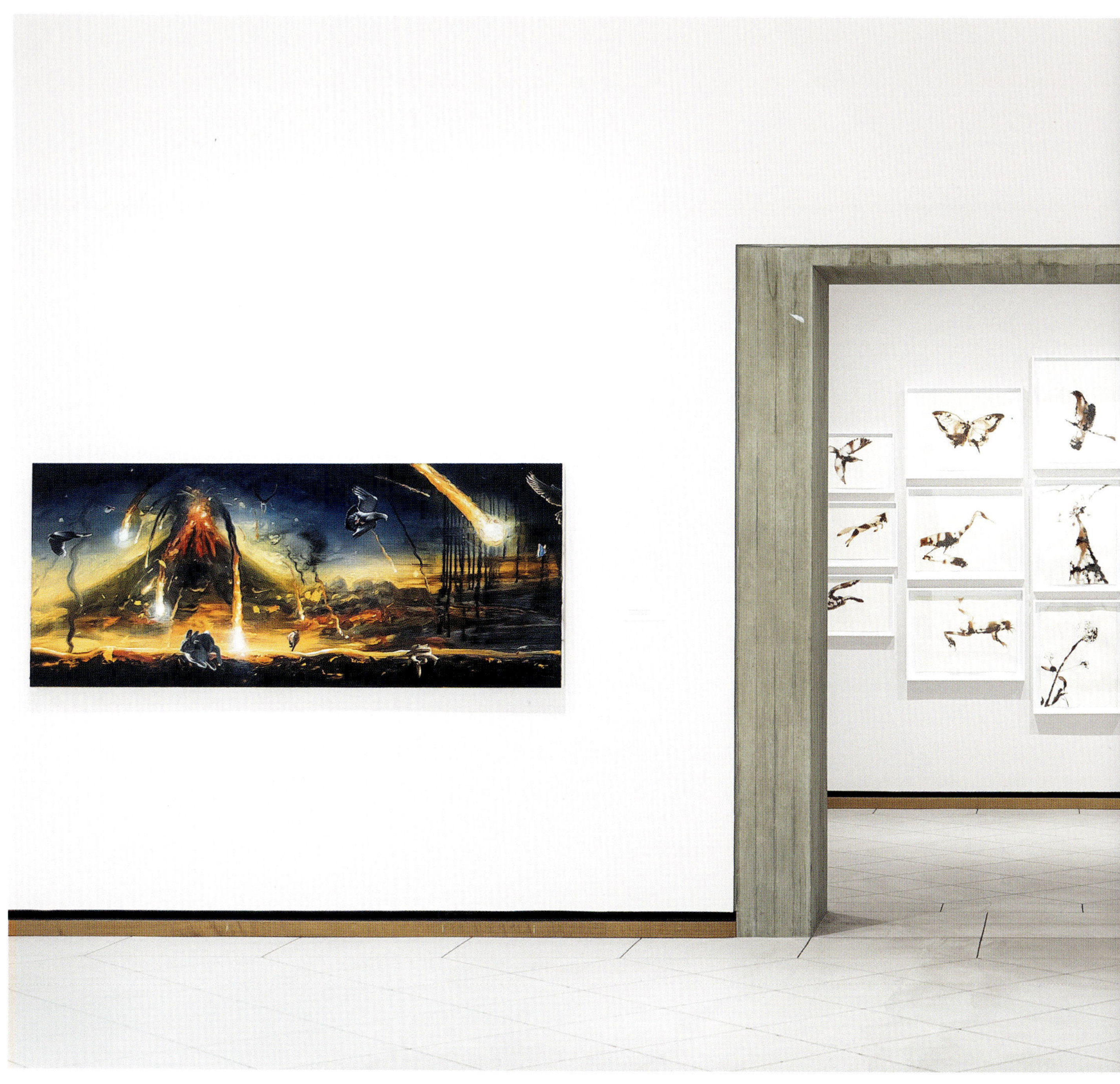

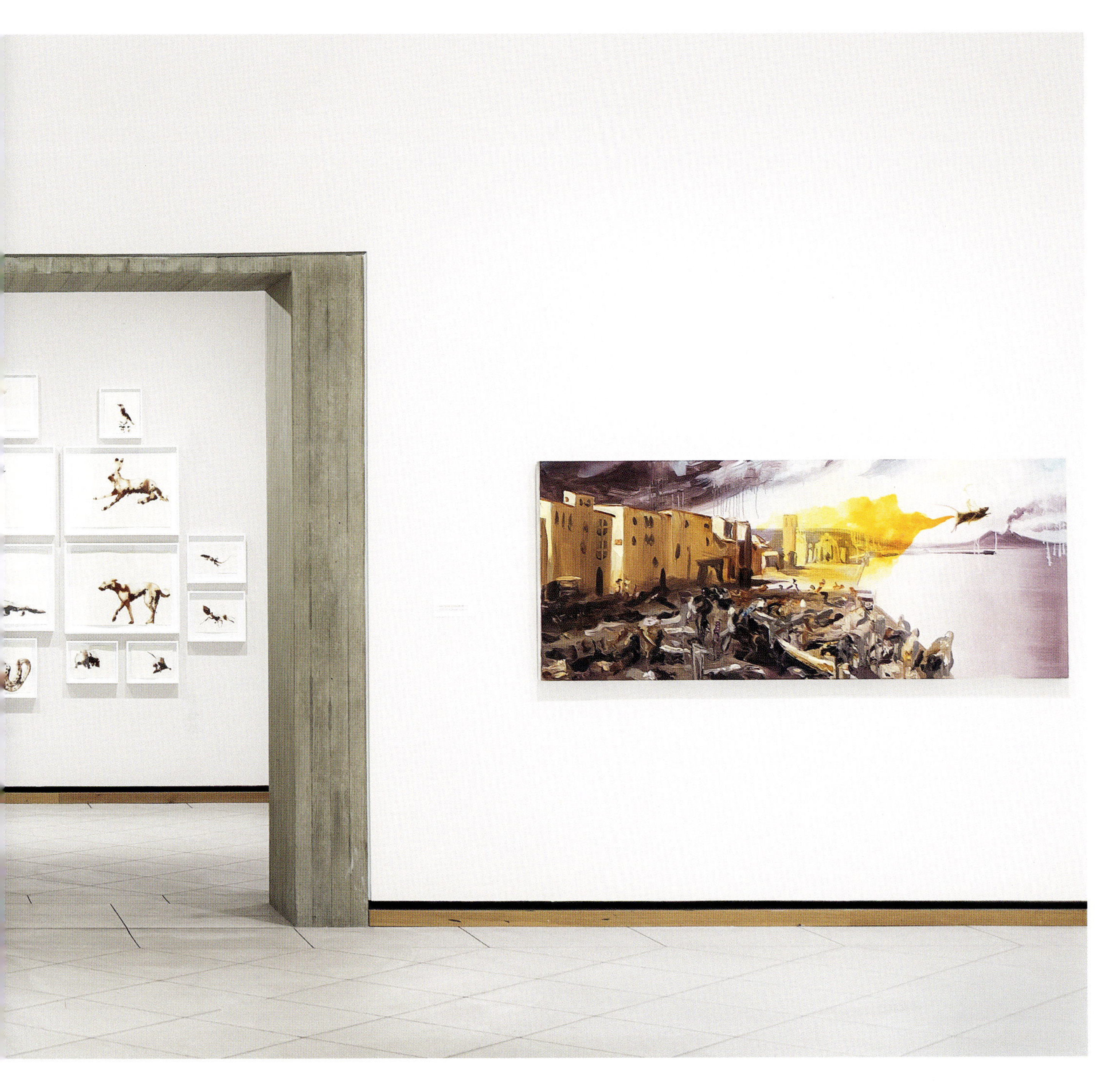

Alexis Rockman, Naples: Course of Empire
Installation view, Herbert F. Johnson Museum of Art, Cornell University, Ithaca, NY, January, 2026

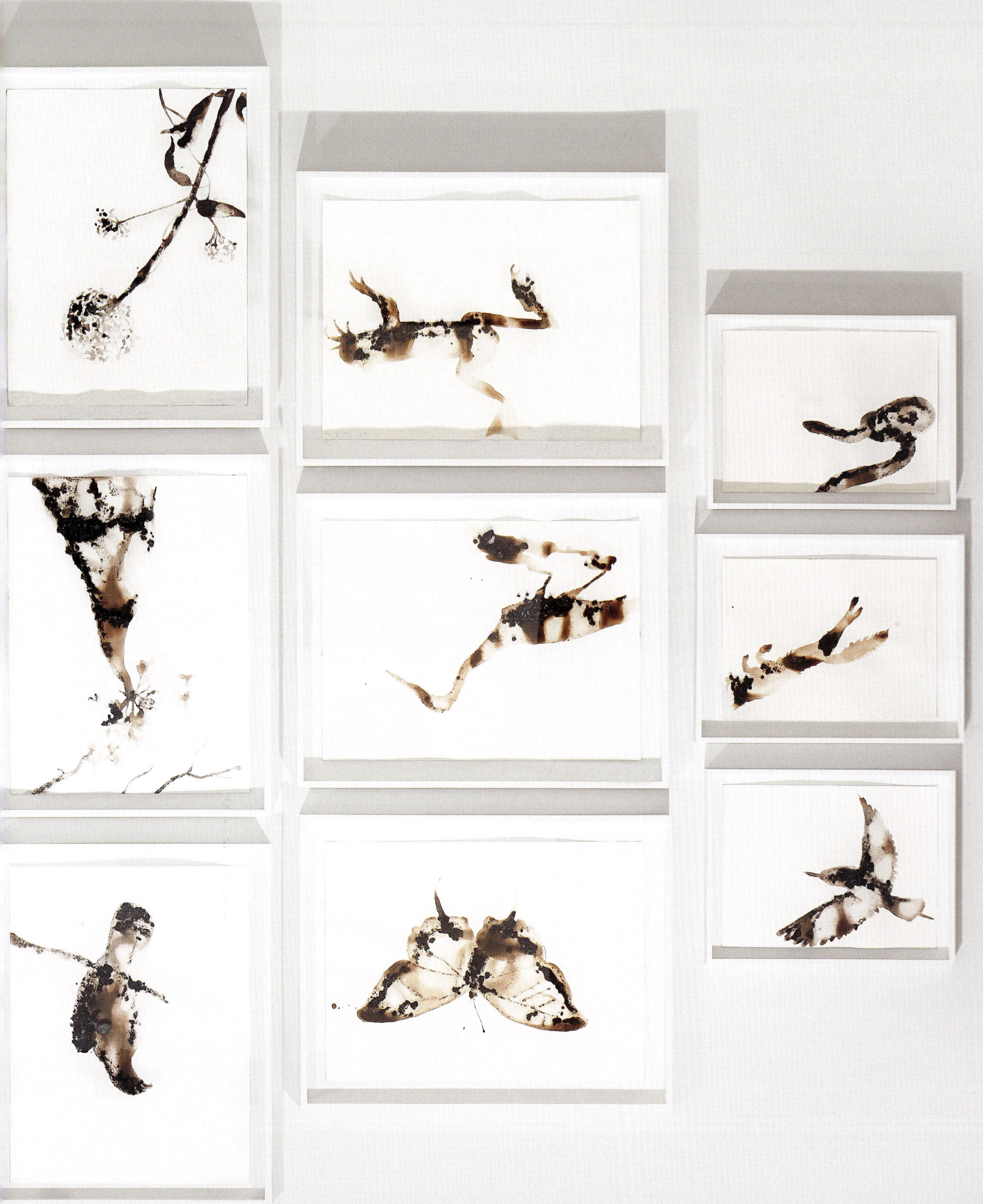

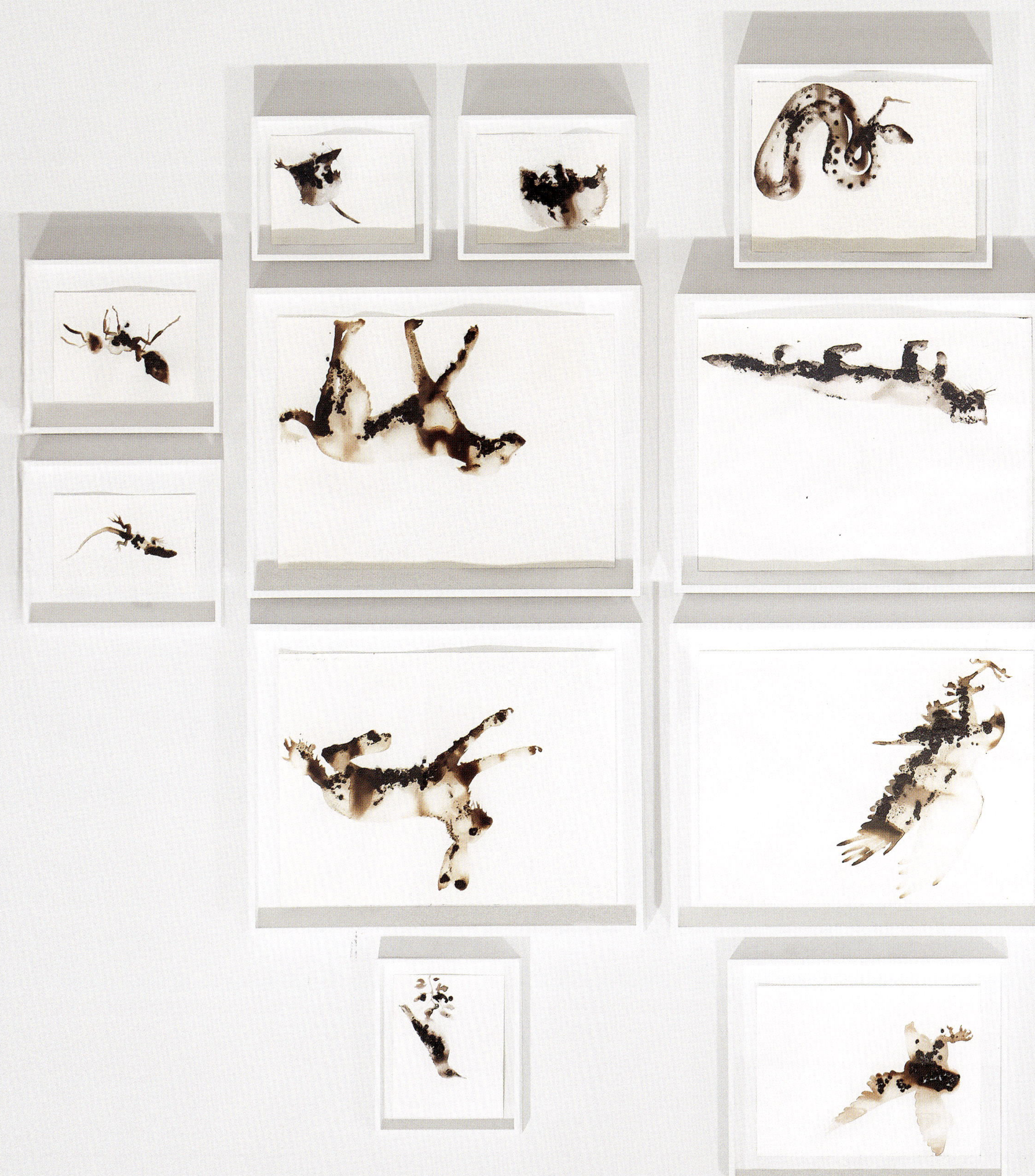

Vesuvius Field Drawings

Alexis Rockman's *Field Drawings* are an ongoing and key aspect of his work, produced concurrently with many of his site-specific projects. The gestural, monochromatic drawings typically depict animal and plant life utilizing a base combination of organic materials and acrylic polymer on paper. Although the *Field Drawings* employ a technical and graphic prowess present across Rockman's practice as a whole, the drawings are distinct in their instinctive execution and unpredictable process.

Rockman's first *Field Drawings* were an unexpected result of his 1994 trip to the rainforests of Guyana. After his only pencil was reduced to a nub, Rockman, provoked by a joke by fellow traveler Mark Dion about the mud drawings of British artist Richard Long, decided to create works using the only materials he had on hand — mud from the banks of the Essequibo River, the surrounding soil, and water.

Rockman has said of these early attempts: "*The first ones were made with just mud and water, and after they dried the mud flaked off the paper. I had some matte acrylic medium that I mixed in with the mud, and that worked to hold the pigment to the paper. I made a drawing of a mosquito and I liked the way it looked. I could see the possibilities — and also the prohibition — of using an earth art strategy to make a pictorial image. To me this gave a fresh, new meaning to the idea of earth art.*"

In his recent projects, Rockman has expanded the types of organic materials used in the *Field Drawings* to include a spectacular array of branches, cactuses, clay, fossils, leaves, mulch, pine needles, and sand, as well as more exotic materials like purple hematite, wombat fecal matter, the artist's blood, ground insects, and even trash from a traffic island on Bruckner Boulevard in the Bronx.

In the *Vesuvius Field Drawings*, Rockman utilized lava, molten rock, and ash from the slopes of Vesuvius to depict the landmark's local plants and animals, whose destiny is bound to the uncertain fate of the volcano's eruption.

All field drawings are lava, molten rock and ash from Mt. Vesuvius and acrylic polymer on paper

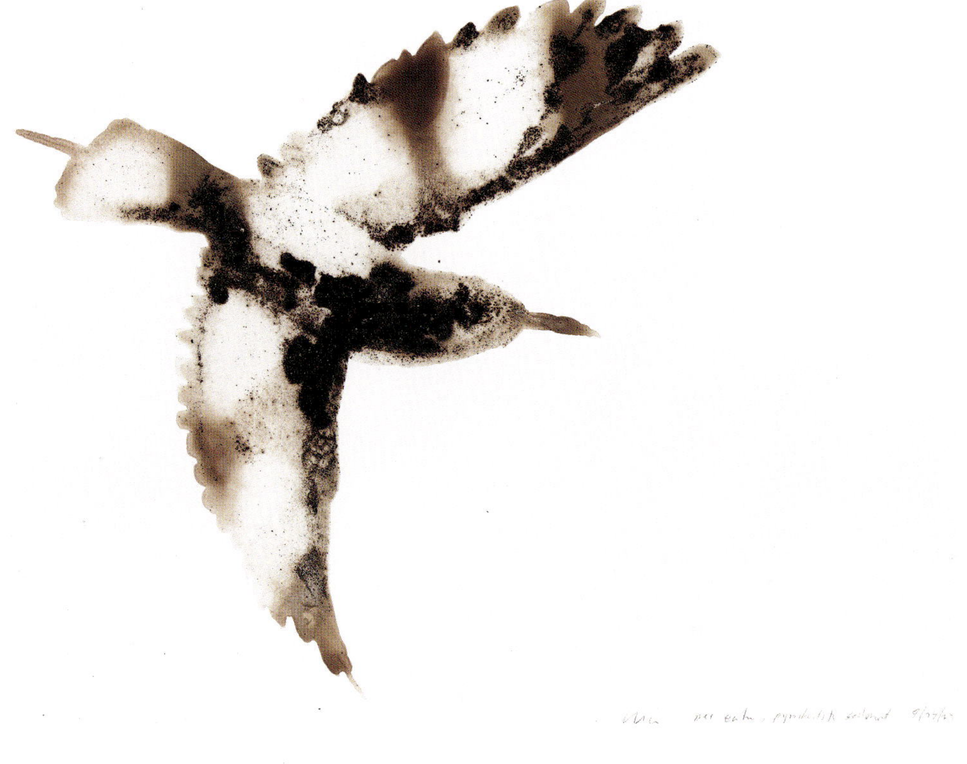

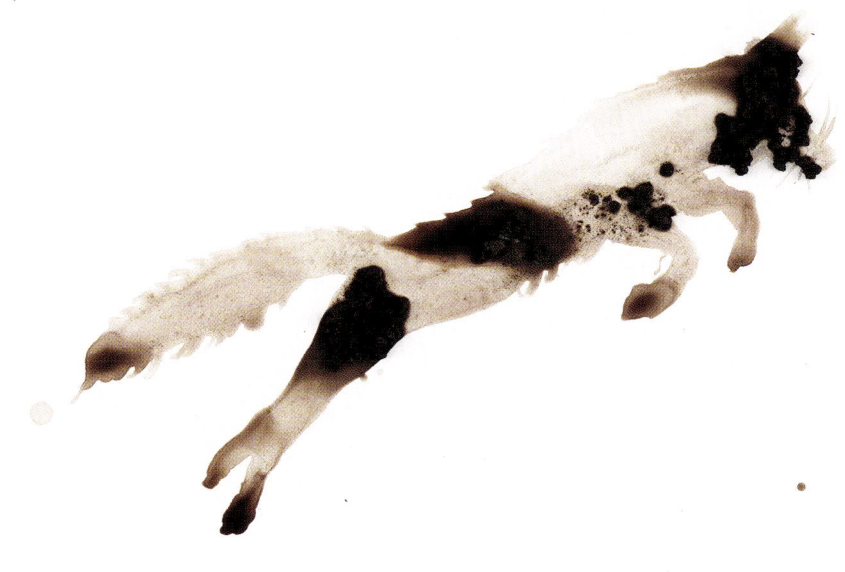

Bee-Eater [Merops apiaster], 2024. 12¼ × 16¼ inches (31.1 × 41.3 cm)
European Red Fox [Vulpes vulpes], 2024. 12¼ × 16¼ inches (31.1 × 41.3 cm)

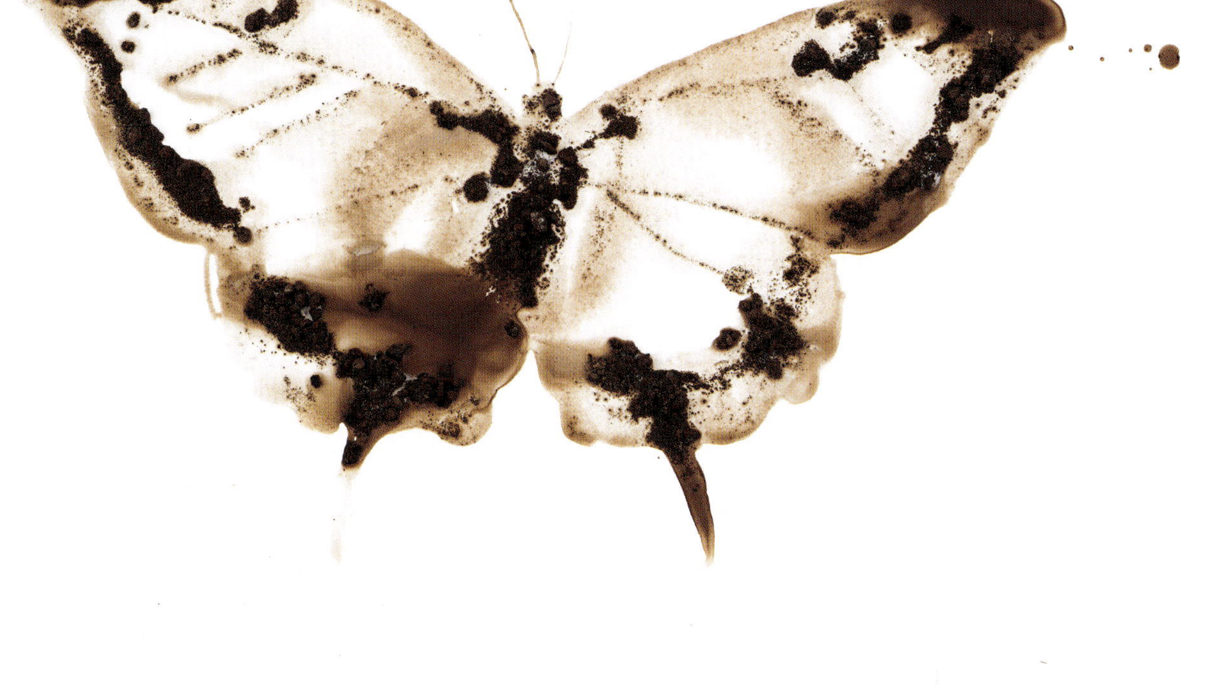

Old World Swallowtail [Papilio machaon], 2024. 18 × 24 inches (45.7 × 61 cm)

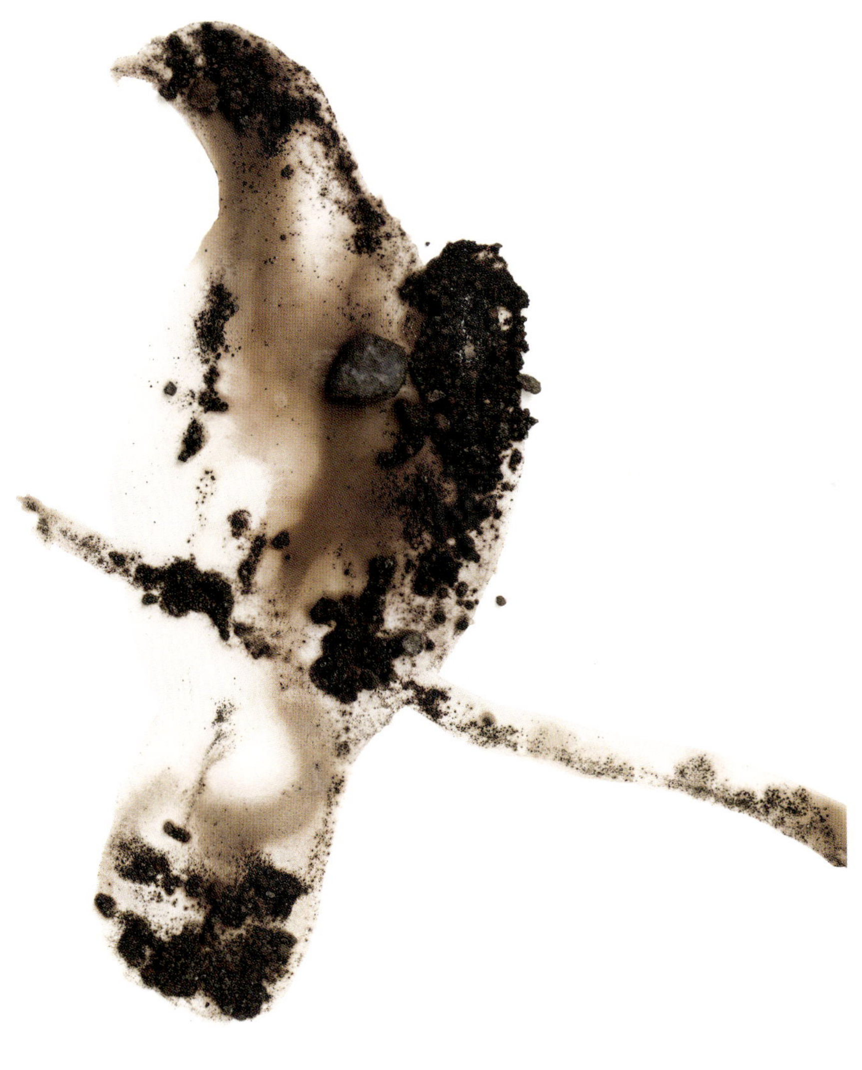

European Honey Buzzard [Pernis apivorus], 2024. 24 × 18 inches (61 × 45.7 cm)

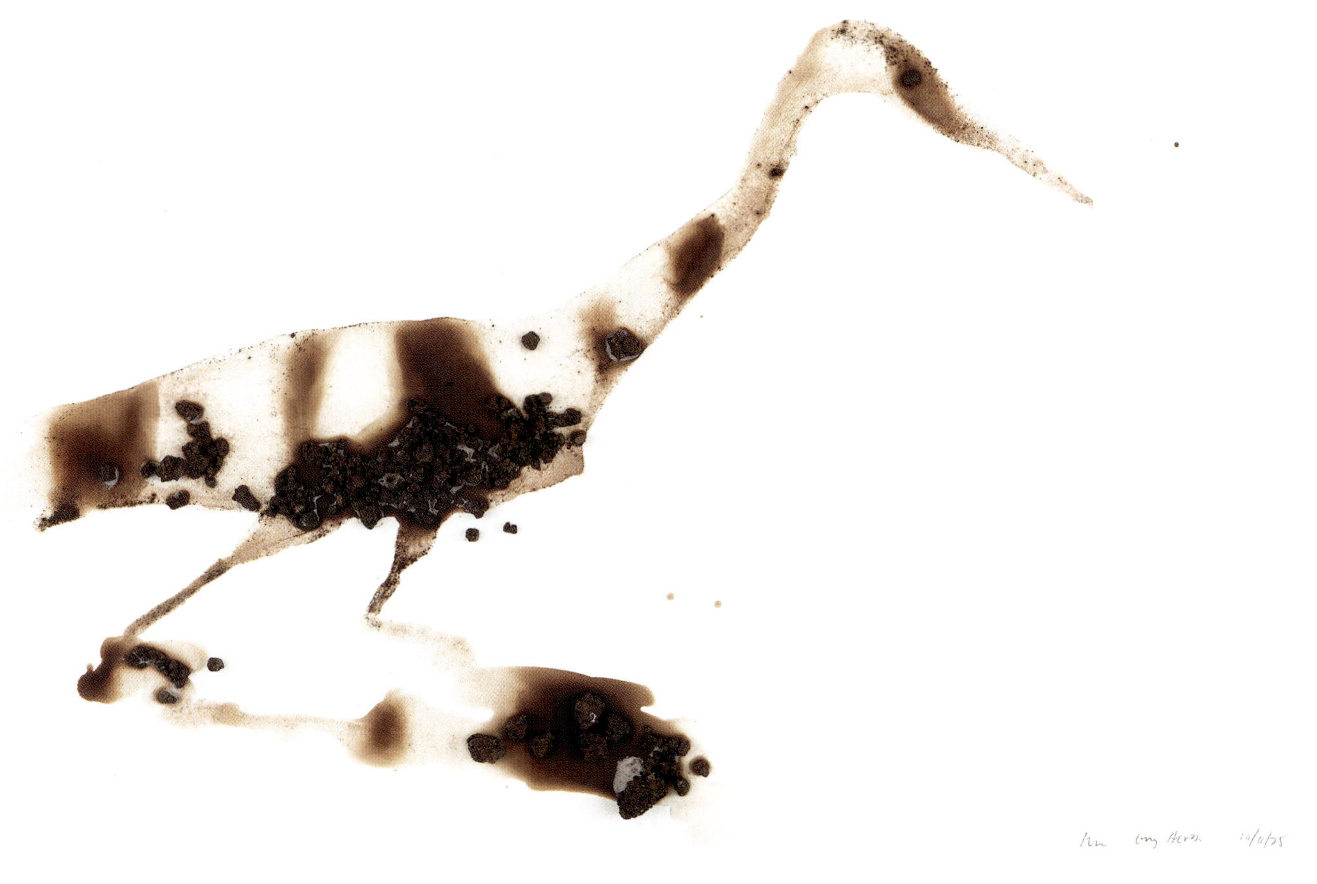

Grey Heron [Ardea cinerea], 2024. 18 × 24 inches (45.7 × 61 cm)

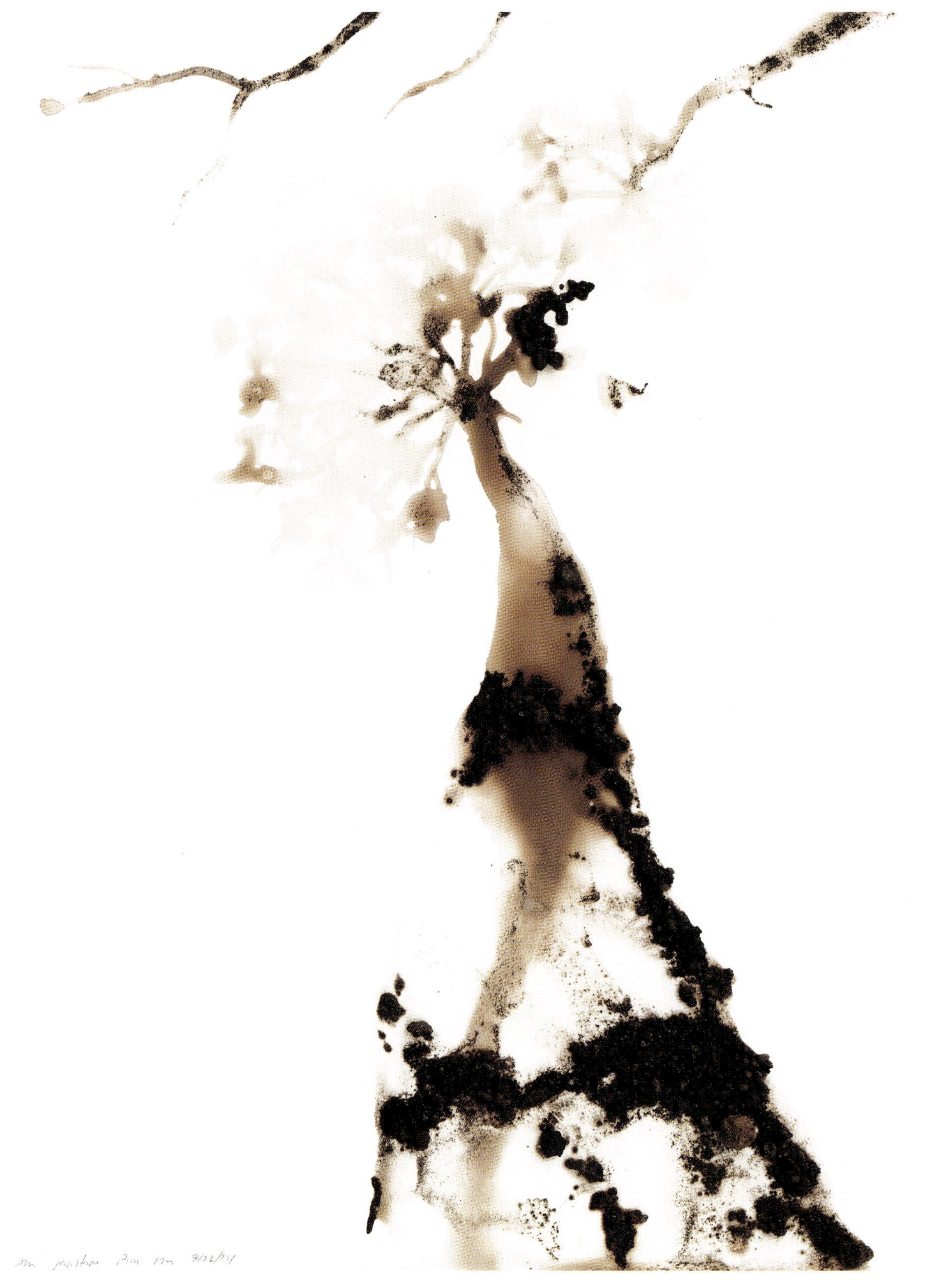

Maritime Pine [Pinus pinaster], 2024. 24 × 18 inches (61 × 45.7 cm)

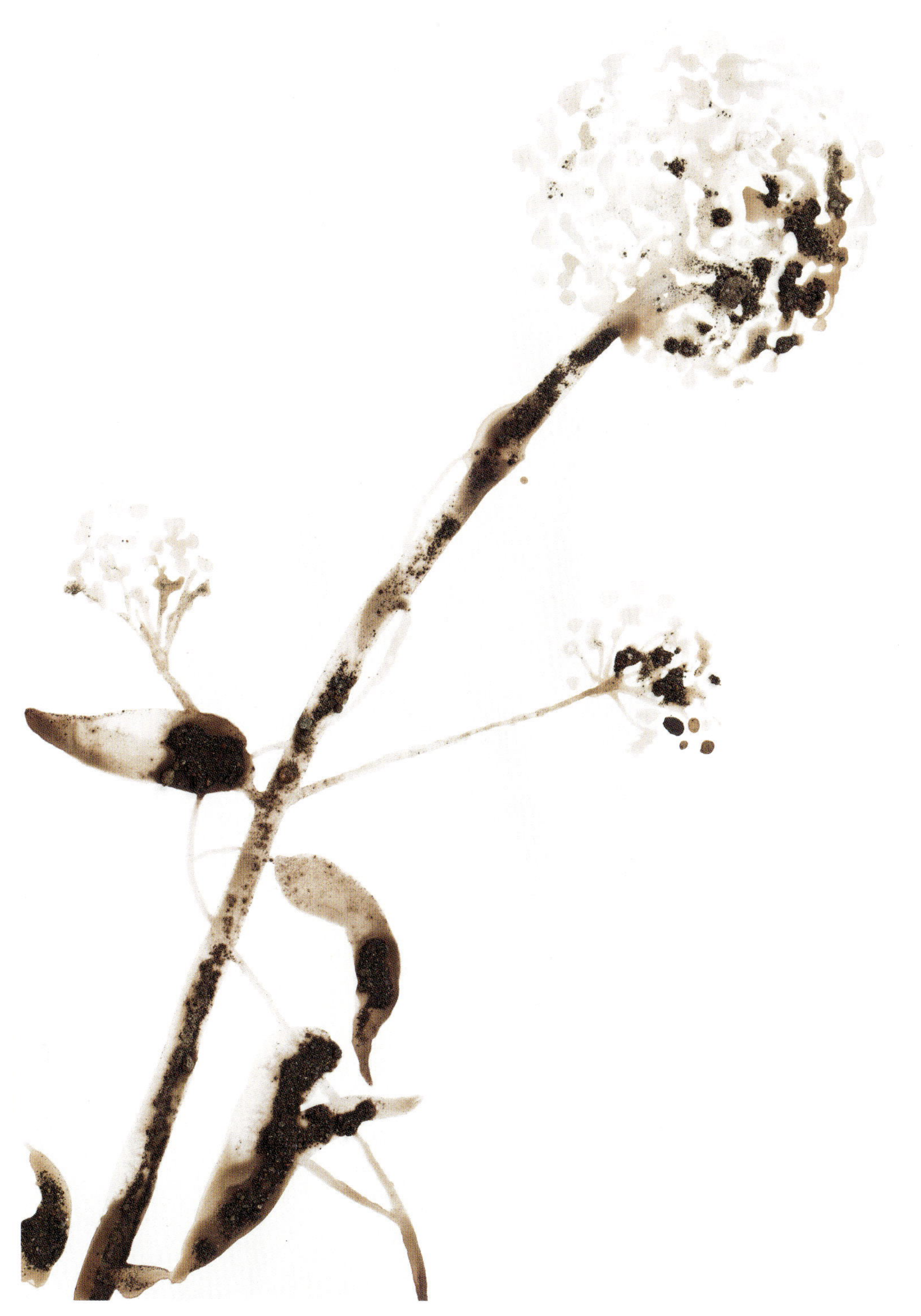

Red Valerian [Centranthus ruber], 2024. 24 × 18 inches (61 × 45.7 cm)

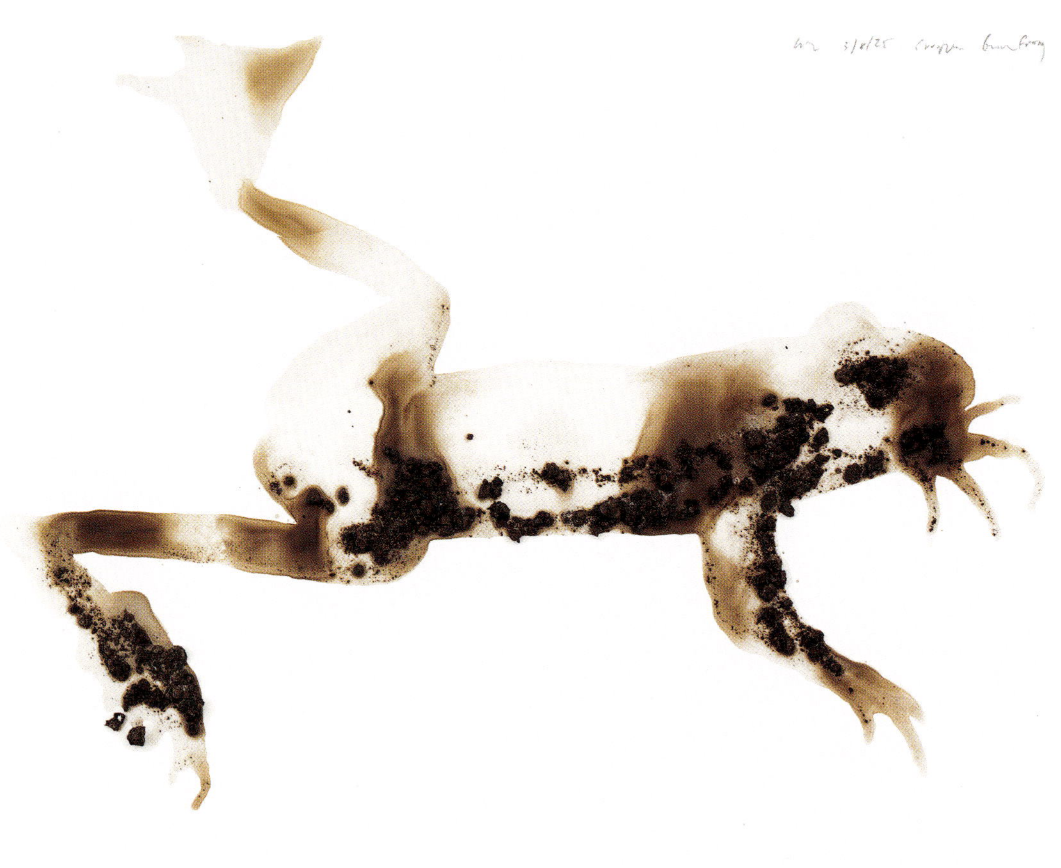

Pool Frog [Pelophylax lessonae], 2024. 18 × 24 inches (45.7 × 61 cm)

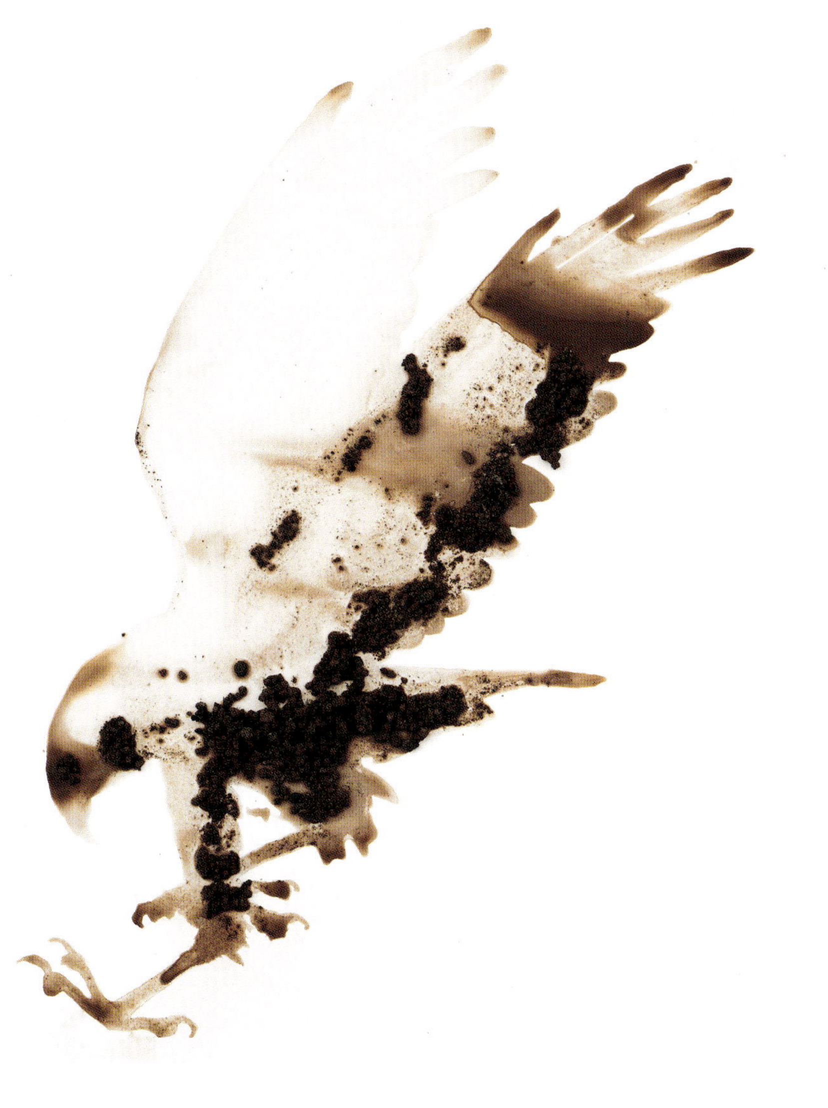

Western Marsh Harrier [Circus aeruginosus], 2024. 18 × 24 inches (45.7 × 61 cm)

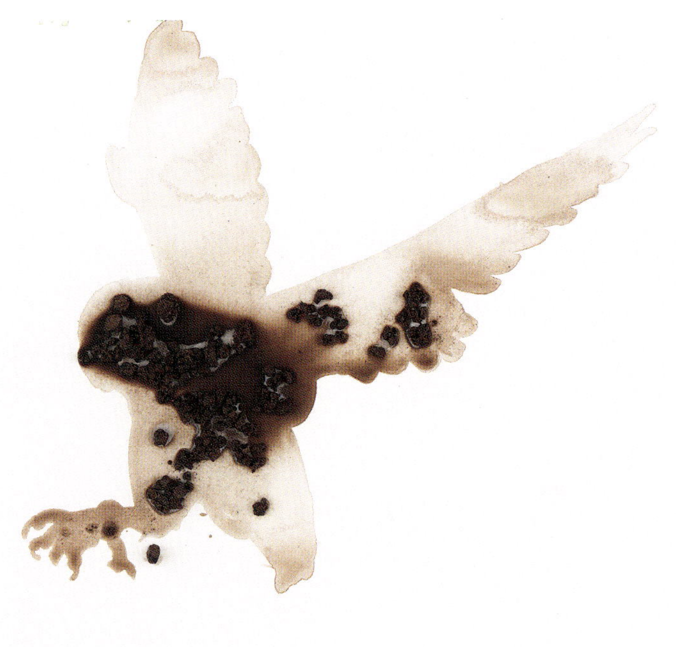

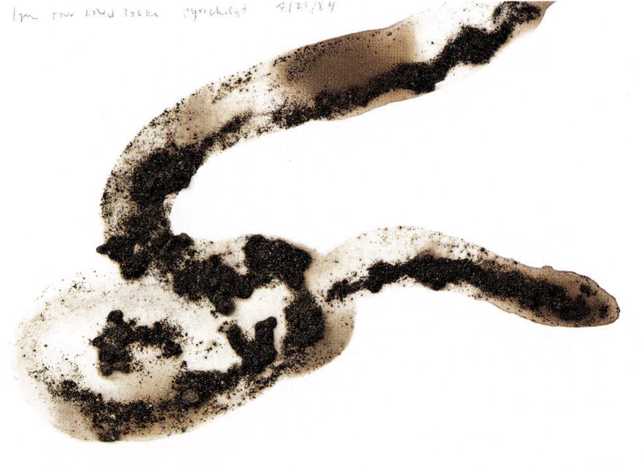

Barn Owl [Tyto alba], 2024. 12¼ × 16¼ inches (31.1 × 41.3 cm)
Four-Lined Snake [Elaphe quatuorlineata], 2024. 12¼ × 16¼ inches (31.1 × 41.3 cm)

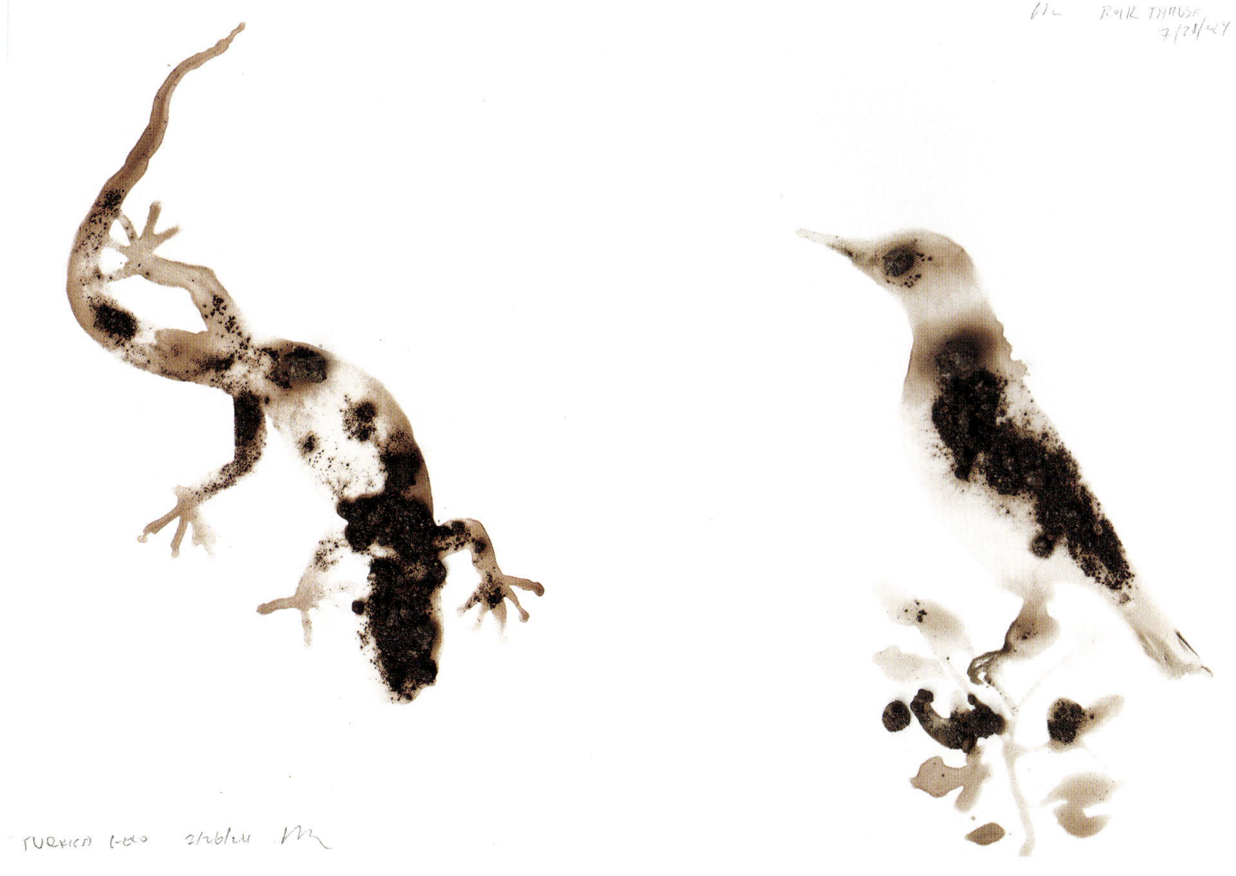

Turkish Gecko [Hemidactylus turcicus], 2024. 10¼ × 7 inches (26 × 17.8 cm)
Rufous-Tailed Rock-Thrush [Monticola saxatiliss], 2024. 10⅝ × 7⅝ inches (26 × 19.4 cm)

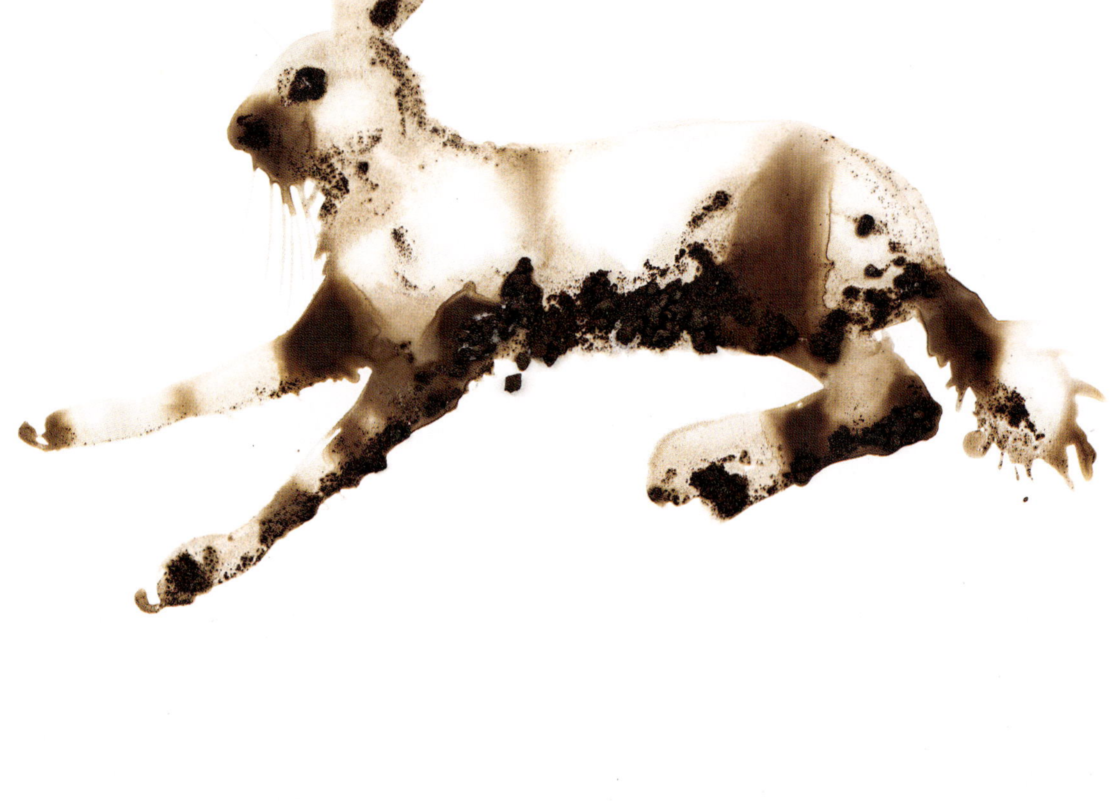

European Hare [Lepus europaeus], 2024. 18 × 24 inches (45.7 × 61 cm)

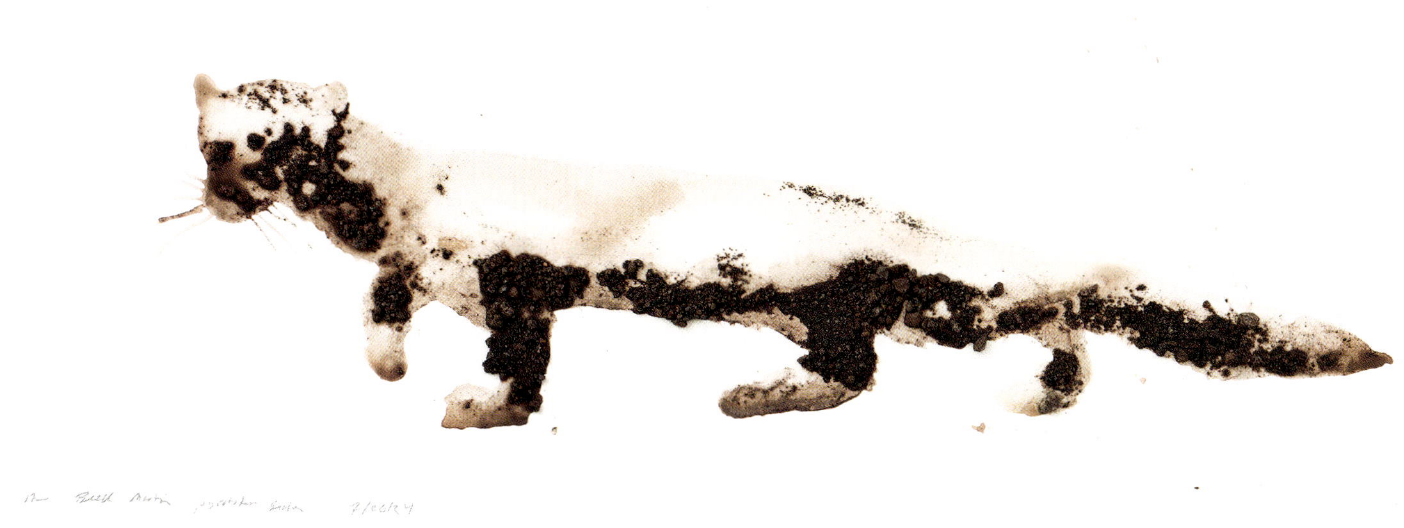

Beech Marten [Martes foina], 2024. 18 × 24 inches (45.7 × 61 cm)

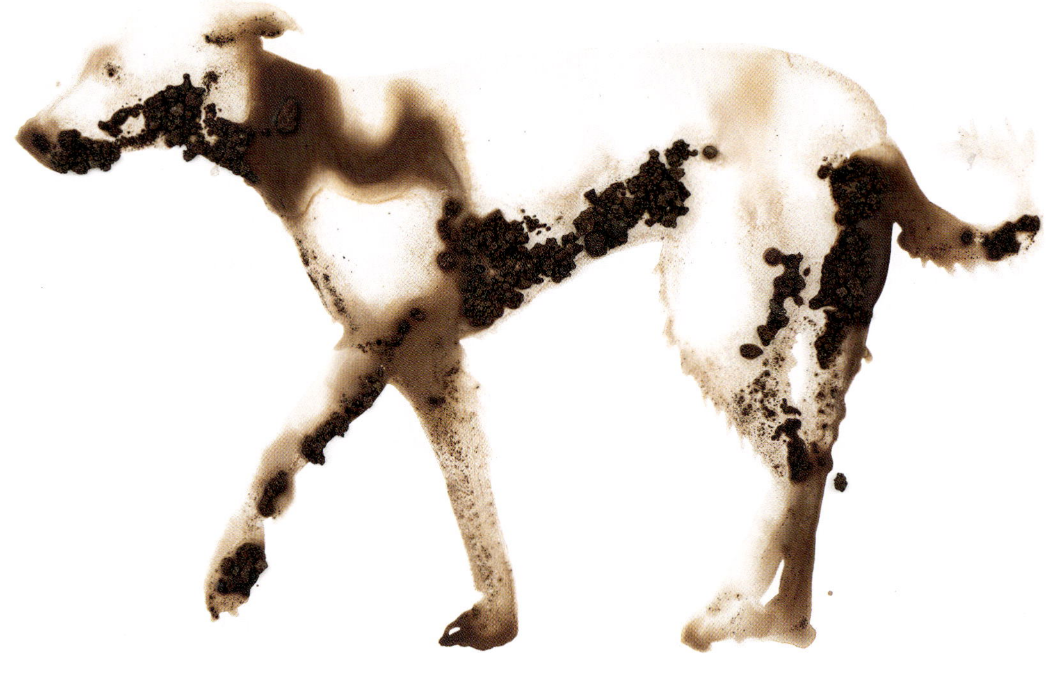

Dog III [Canus familiarus], 2024. 18 × 24 inches (45.7 × 61 cm)

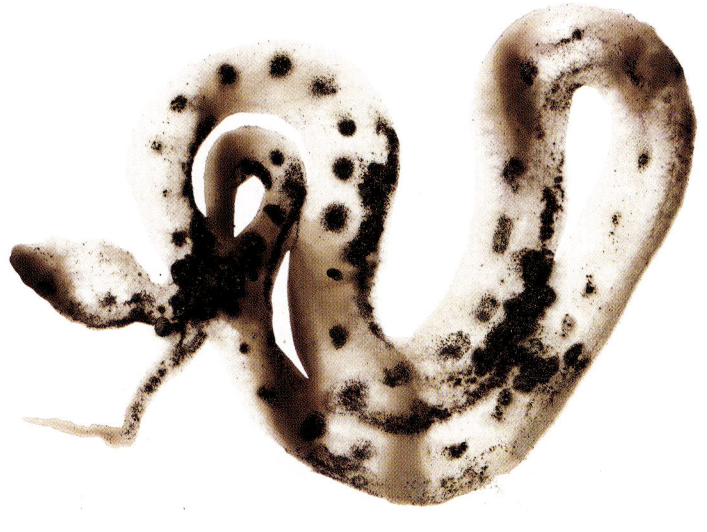

European Asp [Vipera aspis], 2024. 12¼ × 16¼ inches (31.1 × 41.3 cm)

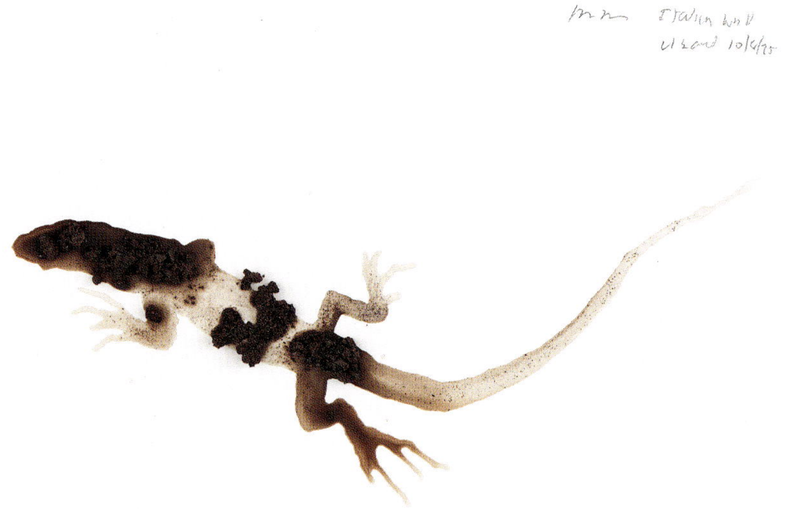

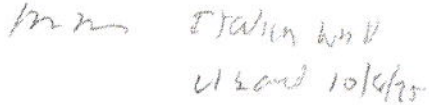

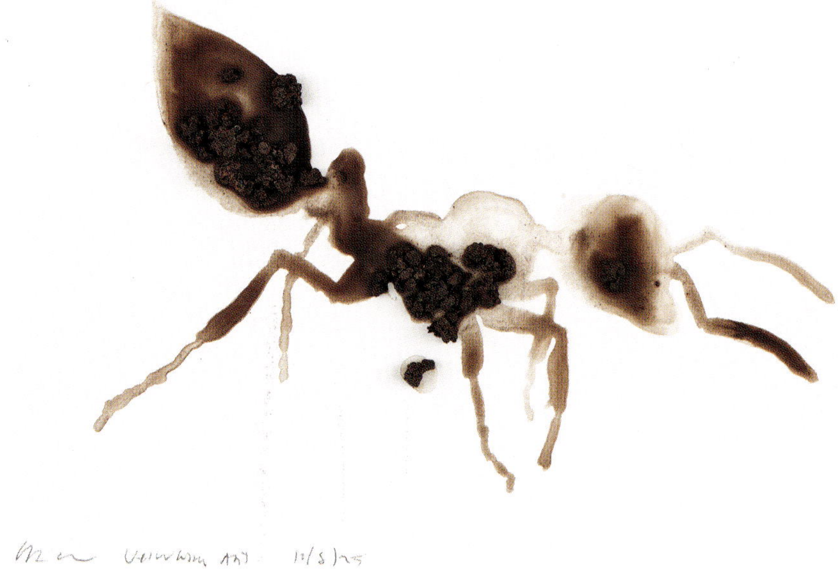

Italian Wall Lizard [Podarcis siculus], 2024. 7 × 10¼ inches (17.8 × 26 cm)
Vesuvius Ant [Crematogaster scutellaris], 2024. 8 × 10¼ inches (20.3 × 26 cm)

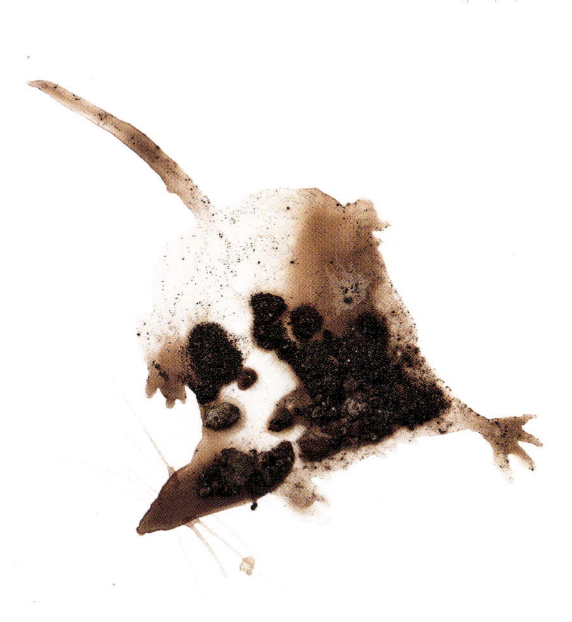

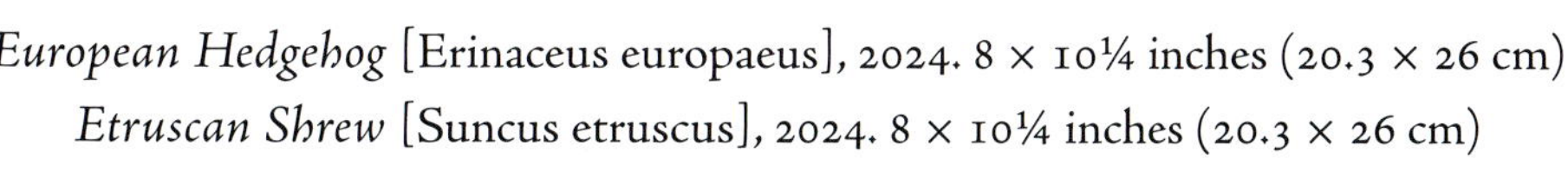

European Hedgehog [Erinaceus europaeus], 2024. 8 × 10¼ inches (20.3 × 26 cm)
Etruscan Shrew [Suncus etruscus], 2024. 8 × 10¼ inches (20.3 × 26 cm)

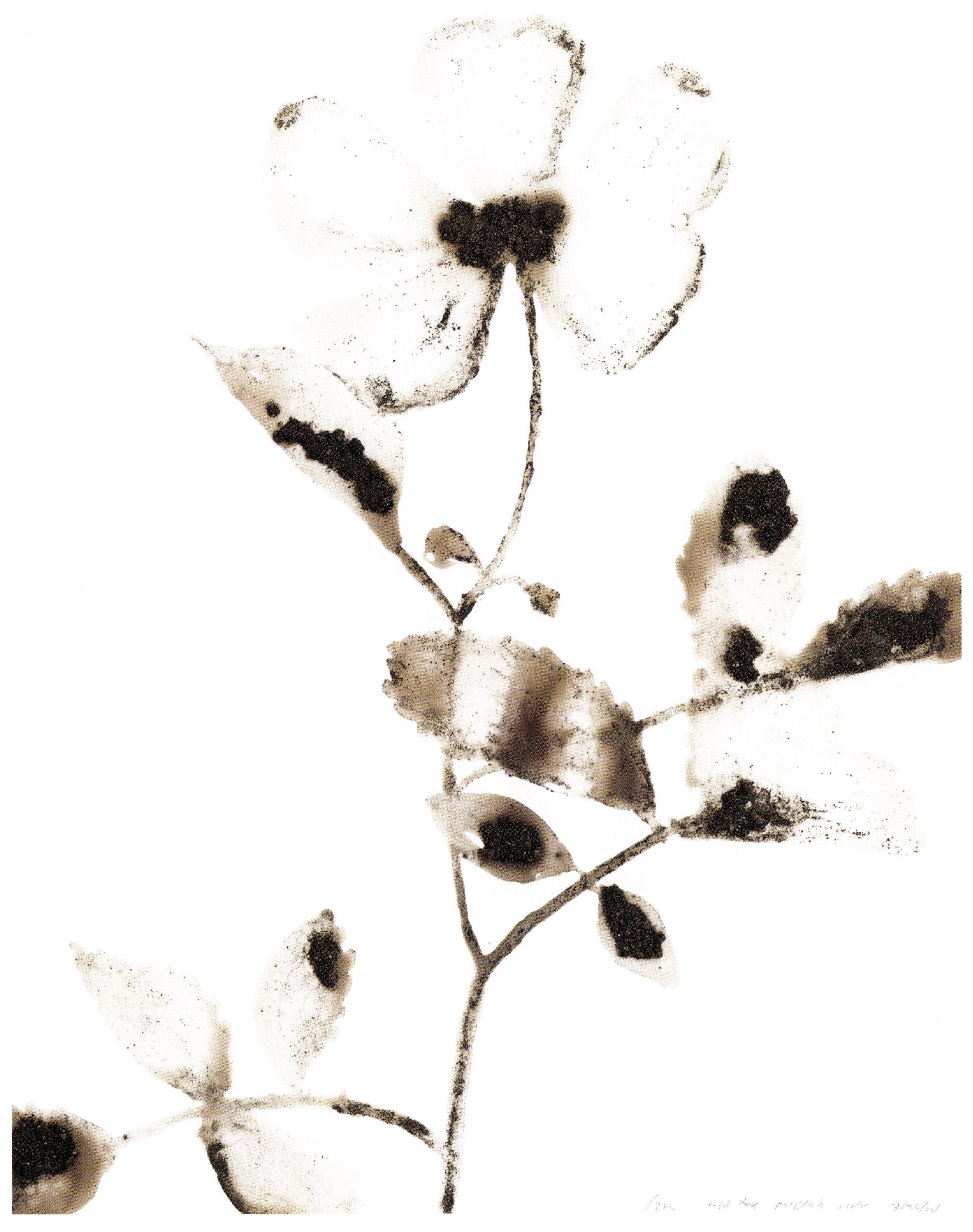

Wild Rose [Rosa sempervirens], 2024. 24 × 18 inches (61 × 45.7 cm)

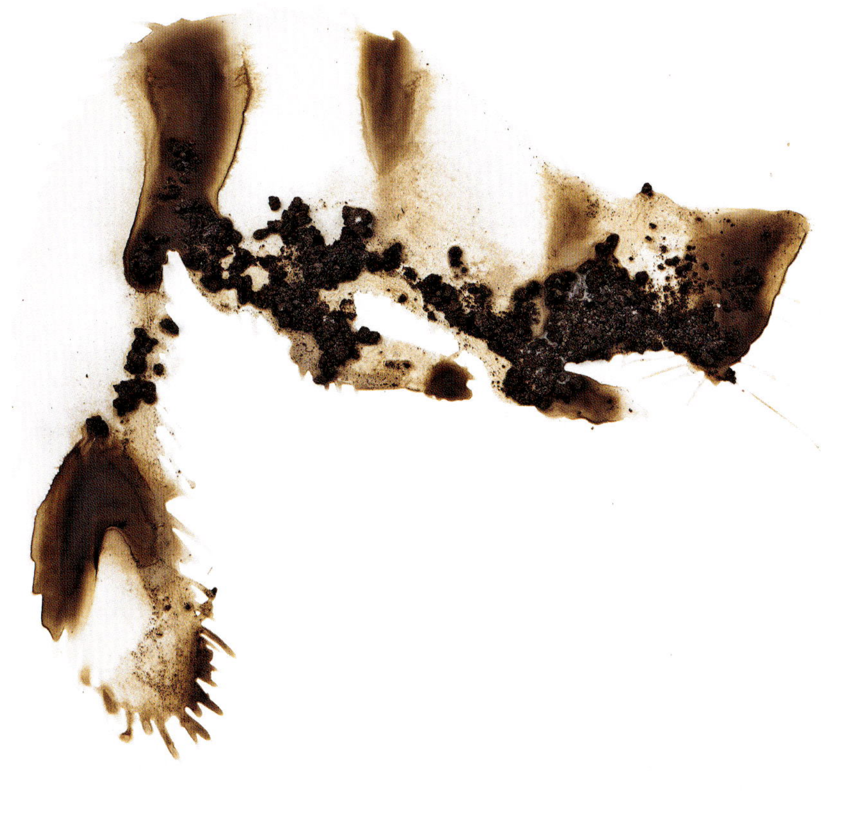

Beech Marten [Martes foina], 2024. 18 × 24 inches (45.7 × 61 cm)

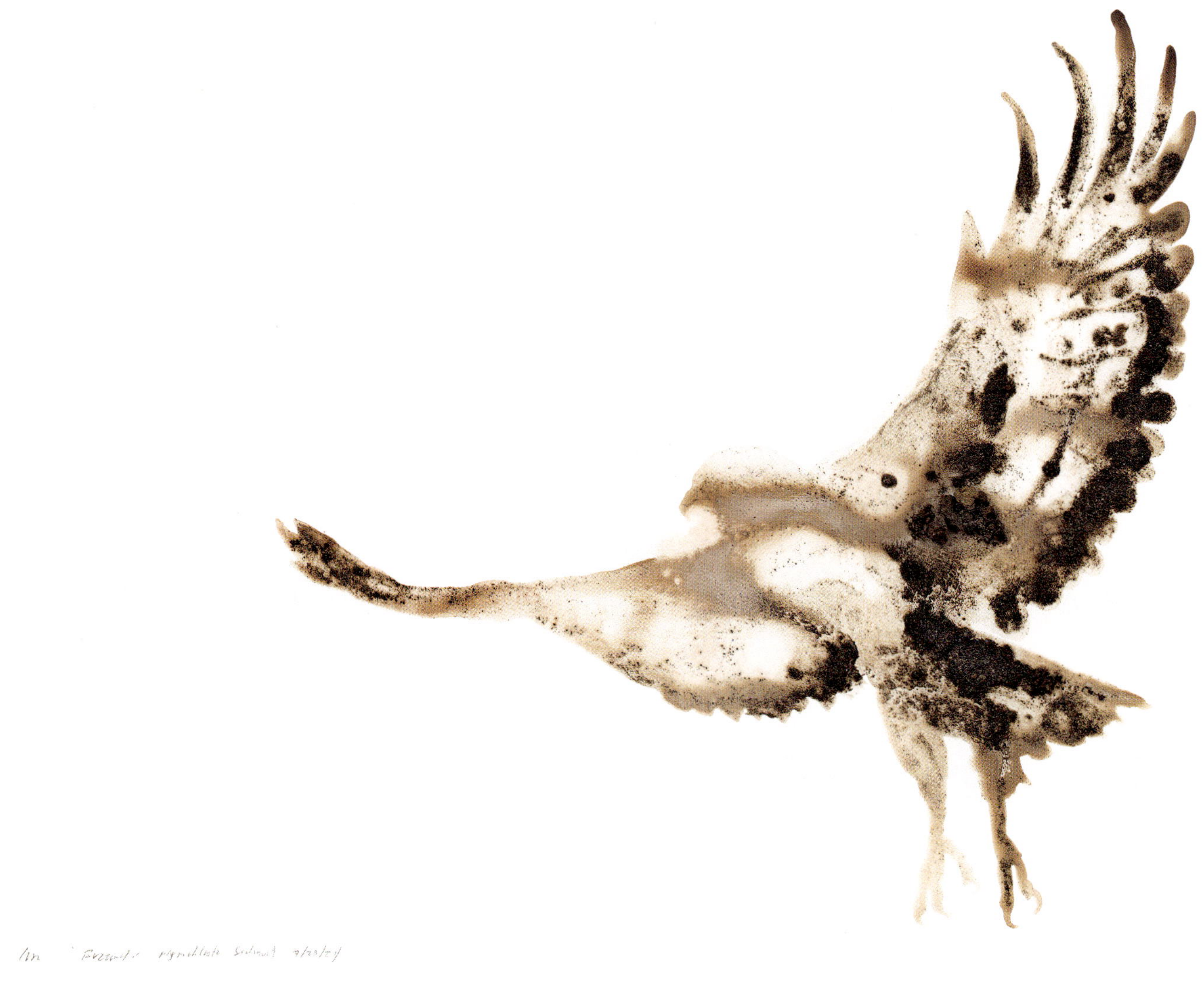

Buzzard [Buteo buteo], 2024. 18 × 24 inches (45.7 × 61 cm)

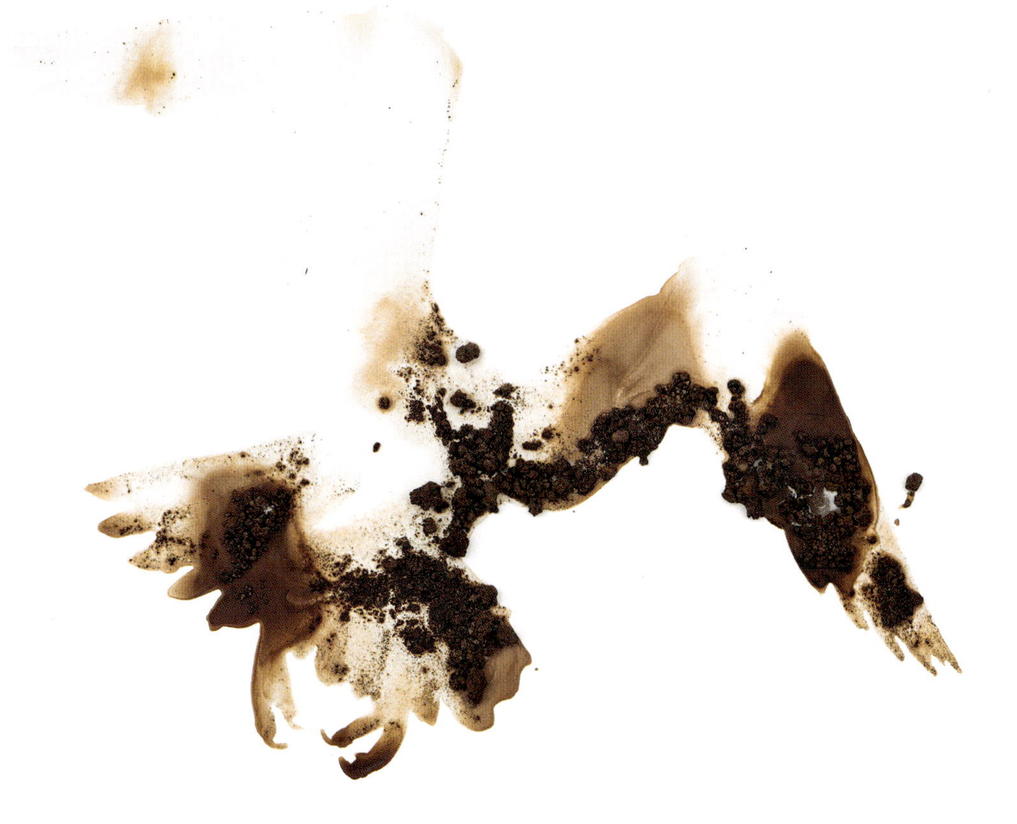

Peregrine Falcon [Falco peregrinus], 2024. 18 × 24 inches (45.7 × 61 cm). Private collection

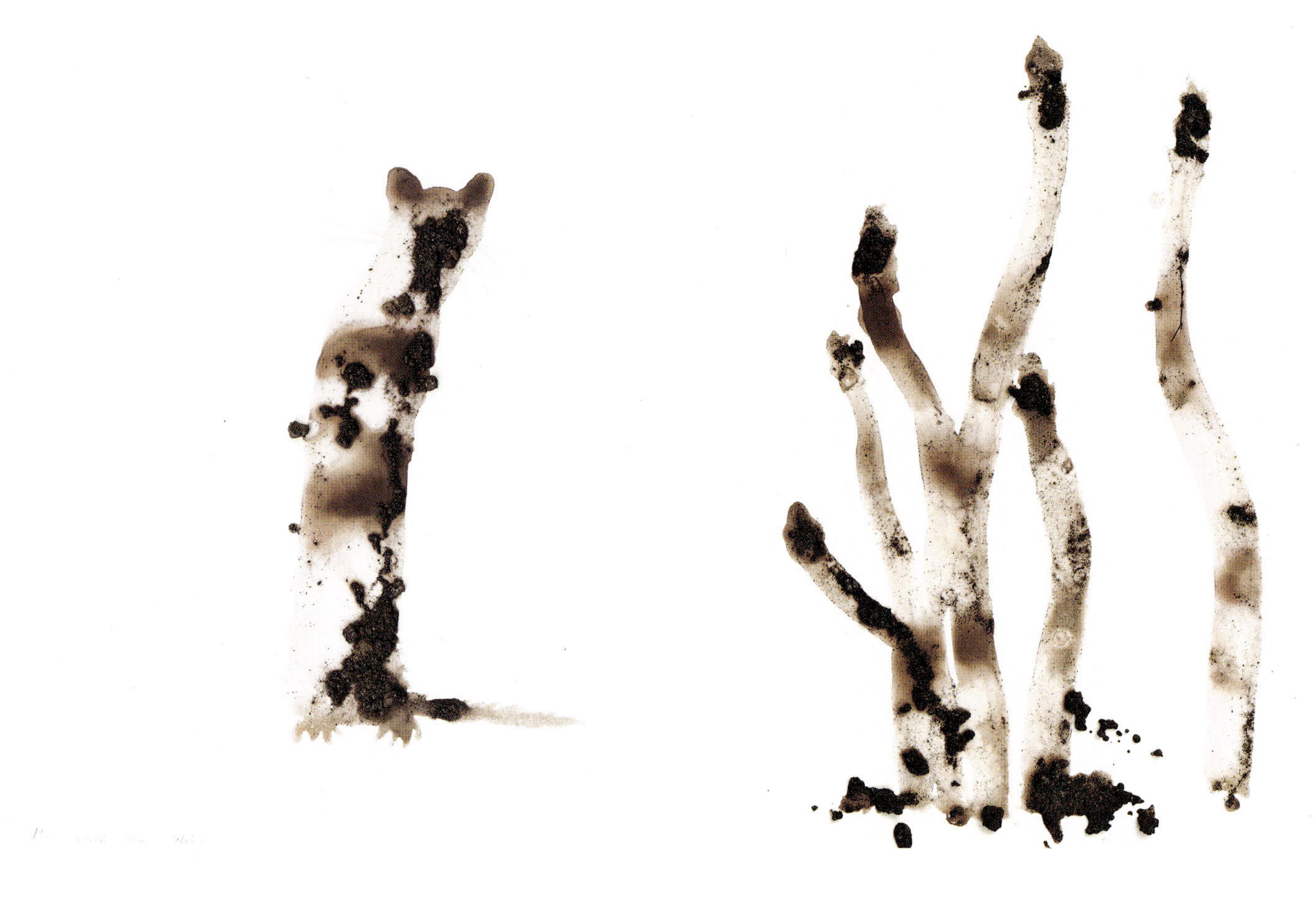

Weasel [Mustela nivalis], 2024. 16¼ × 12¼ inches (41.3 × 31.1 cm)
Wild Asparagus [Asparagus acutifolius], 2024. 16¼ × 12¼ inches (41.3 × 31.1 cm)

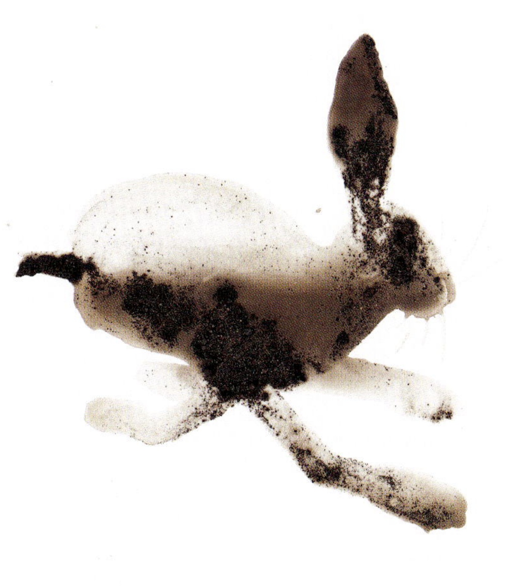

European Hare [Lepus europaeus], 2024. 16¼ × 12¼ inches (41.3 × 31.1 cm)

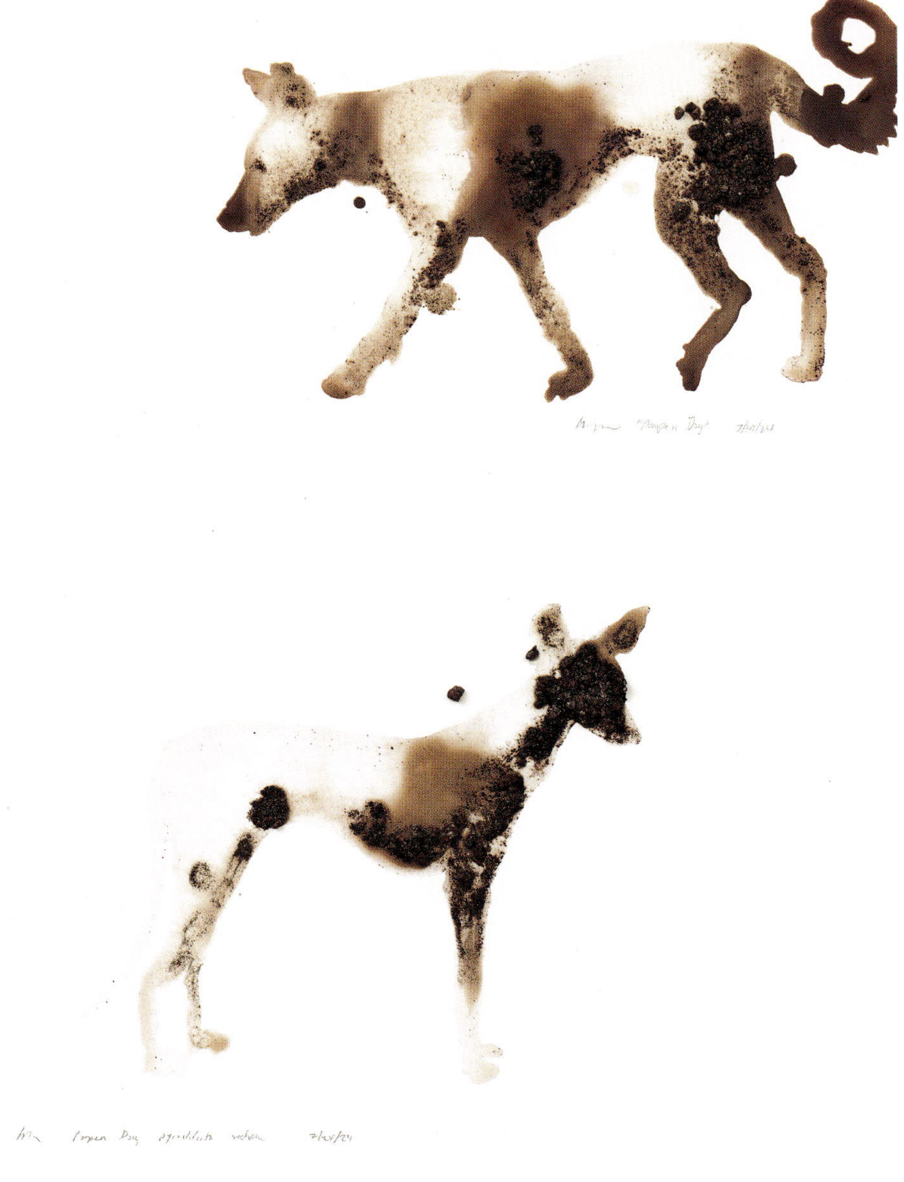

Domestic Dog [Canis familiaris], 2024. 12¼ × 16¼ inches (31.1 × 41.3 cm)
Domestic Dog II [Canis familiaris], 2024. 12¼ × 16¼ inches (31.1 × 41.3 cm)

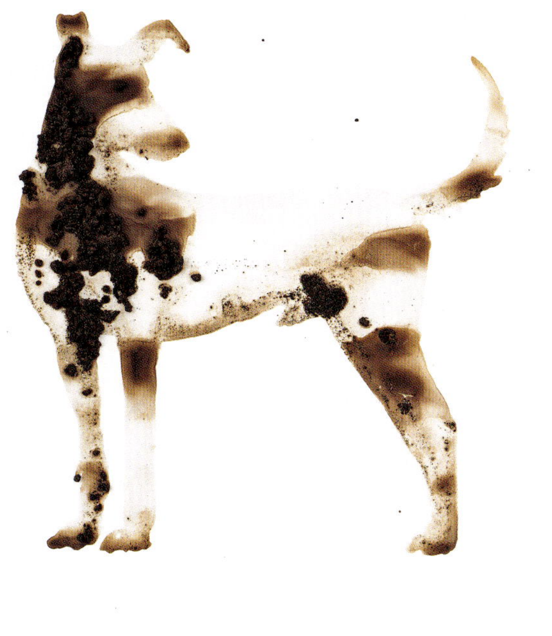

Dog IV [Canis familiaris], 2024. 12¼ × 16¼ inches (31.1 × 41.3 cm). Private collection
Emerald Toad [Bufotes viridis], 2024. 10¼ × 8 inches (26 × 20.3 cm)

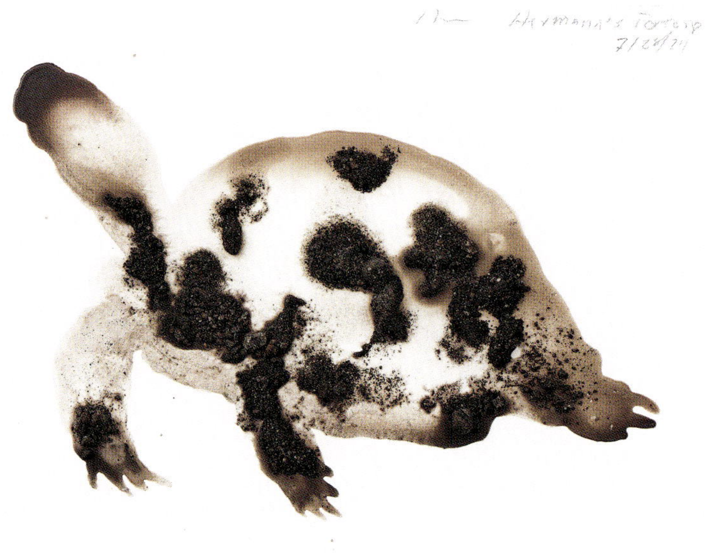

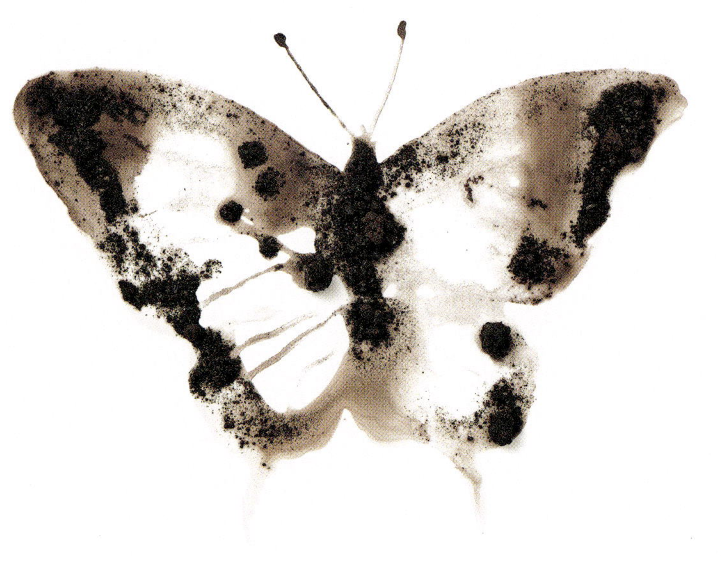

Hermann's Tortoise [Testudo hermanni], 2024. 7 × 10¼ inches (17.8 × 26 cm)
Old World Swallowtail [Papilio machaon], 2024. 8 × 10¼ inches (20.3 × 26 cm)

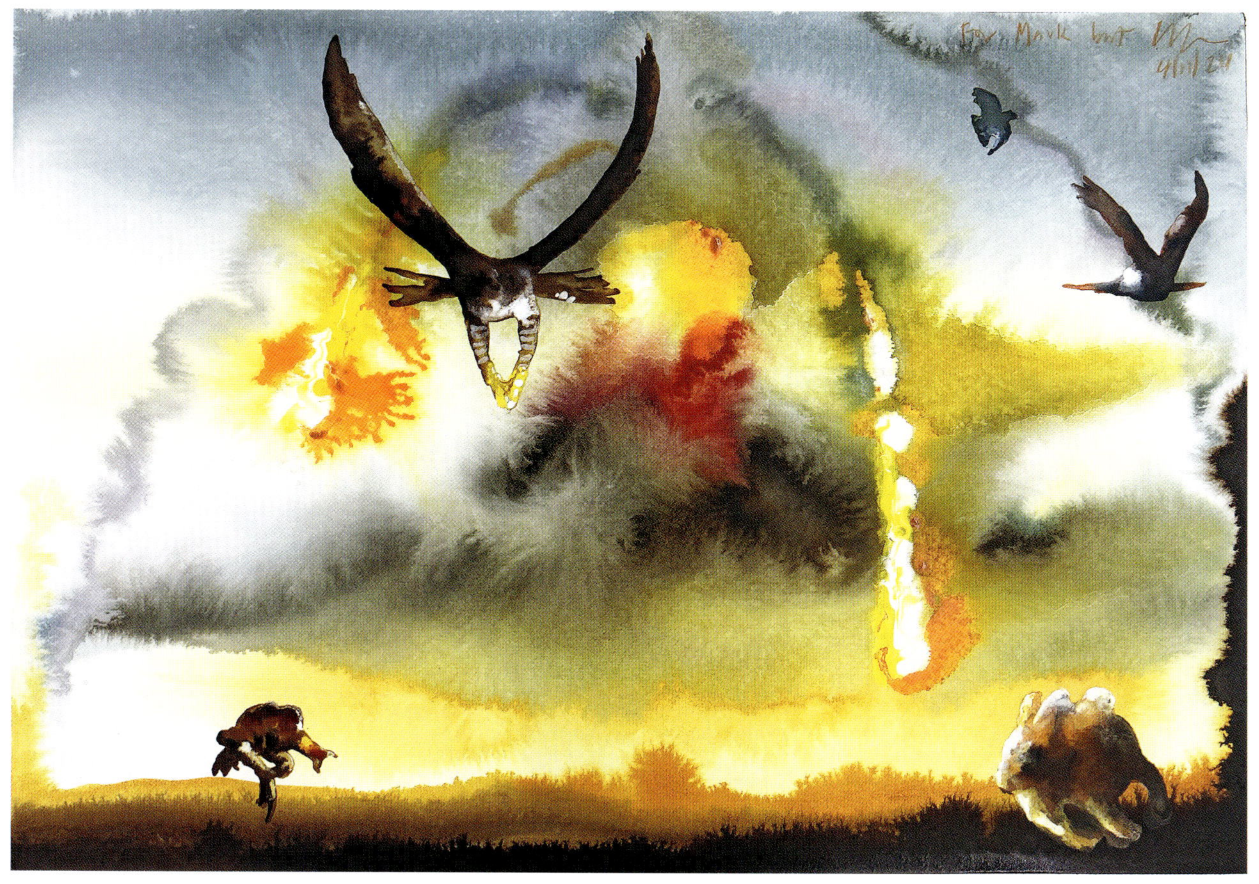

Mt. Vesuvius, Autumn, 79 AD, 2024
Watercolor and acrylic on paper, 14 × 20 inches (35.5 × 50.8 cm)

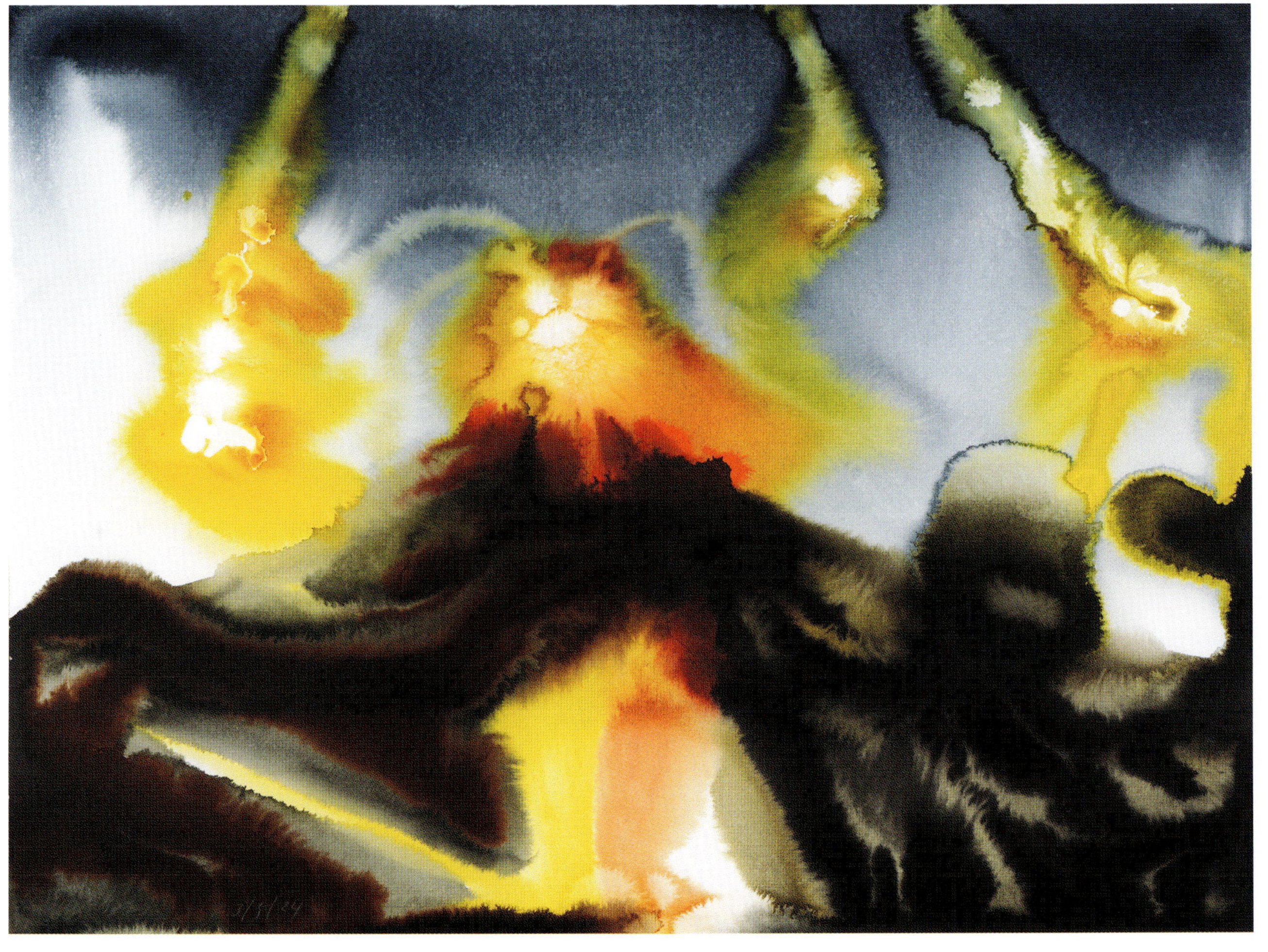

The Avellino Eruption of Mount Vesuvius, 1995 BCE, 2025
Watercolor and acrylic on paper, 18 × 24 inches (45.7 × 60.9 cm)

Pompeii Amphitheatre, 2026
Oil and cold wax on wood, 40 × 48 inches (101.6 × 121.9 cm)
Collection of Bram and Lara Hechtkopf

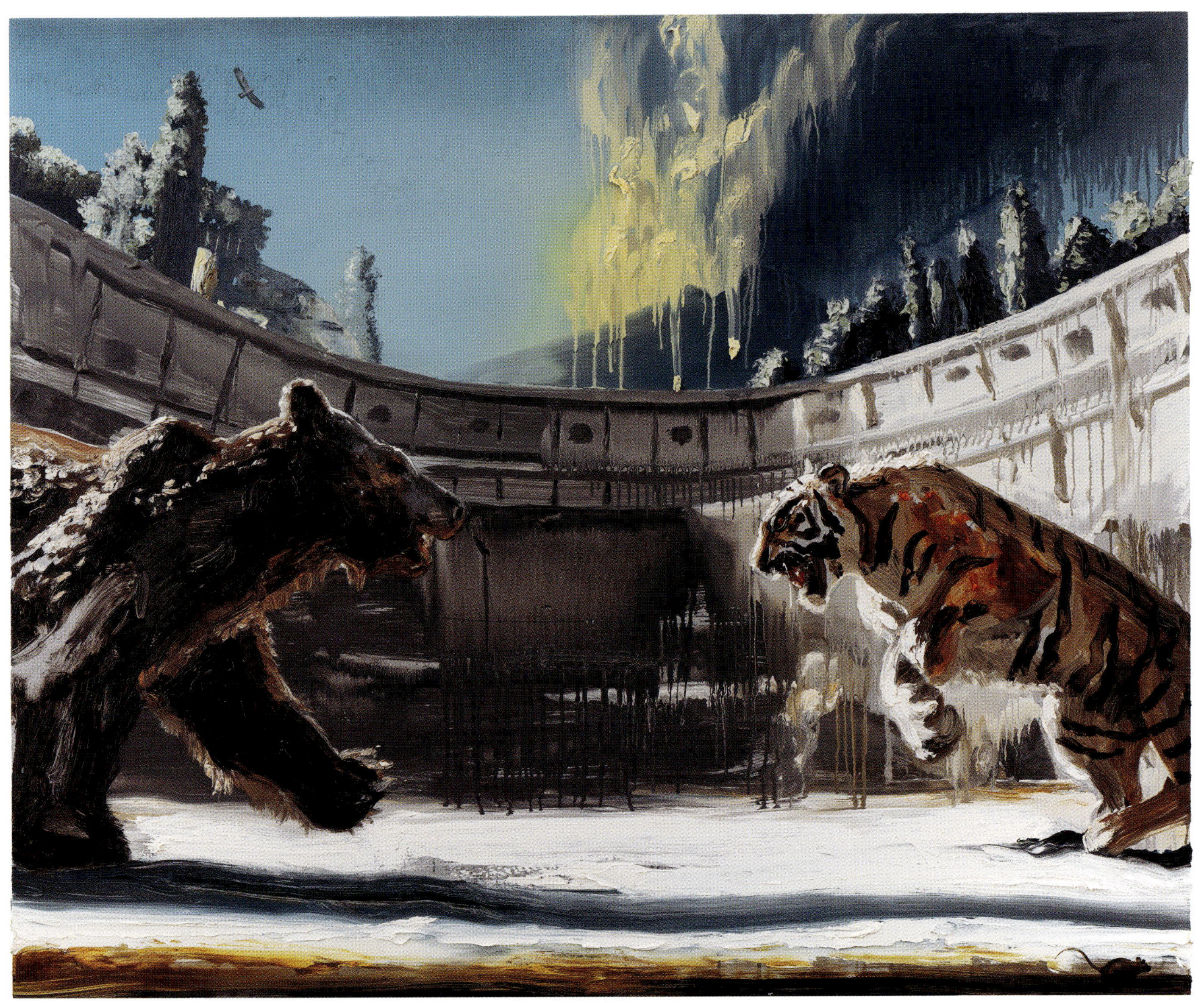

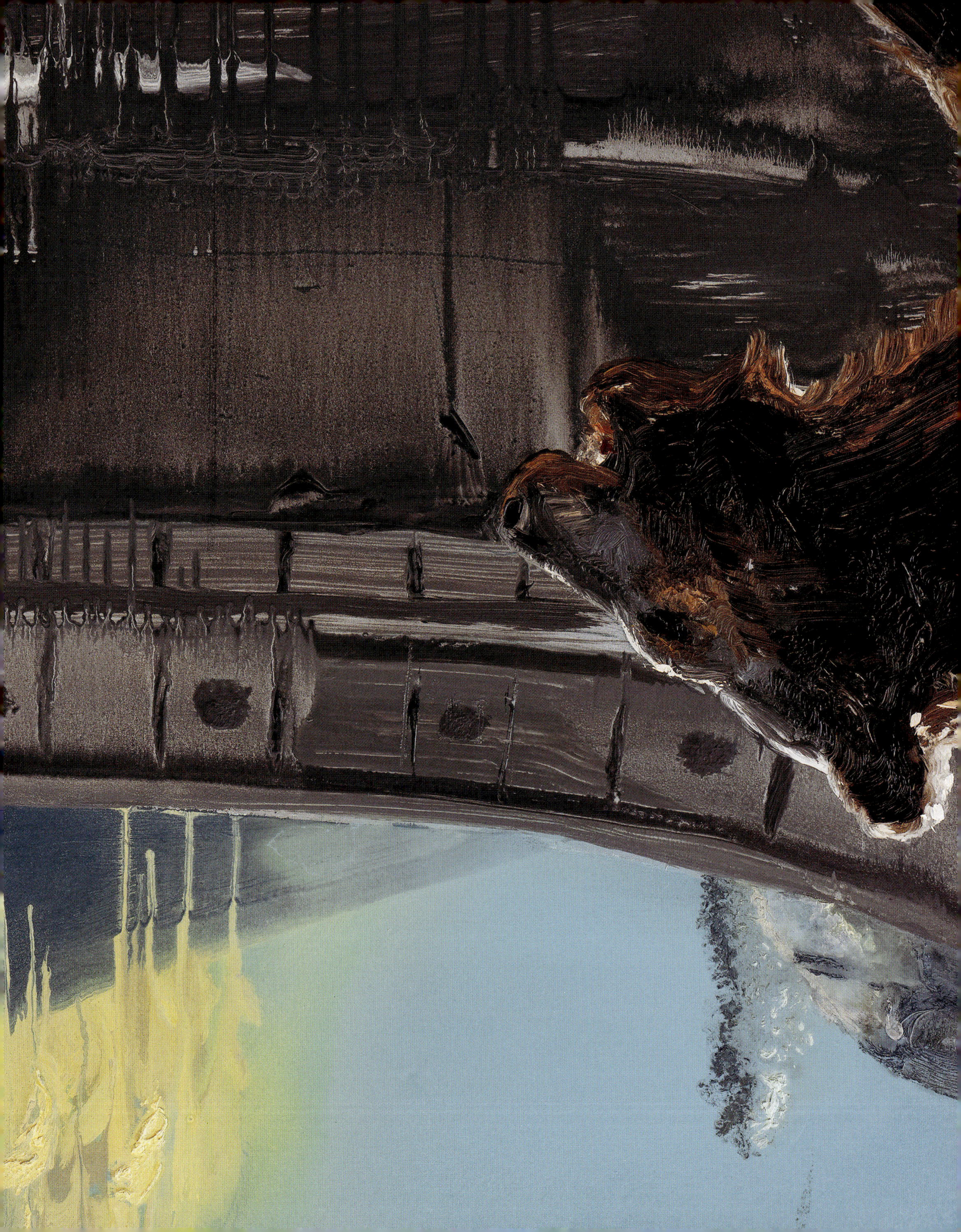

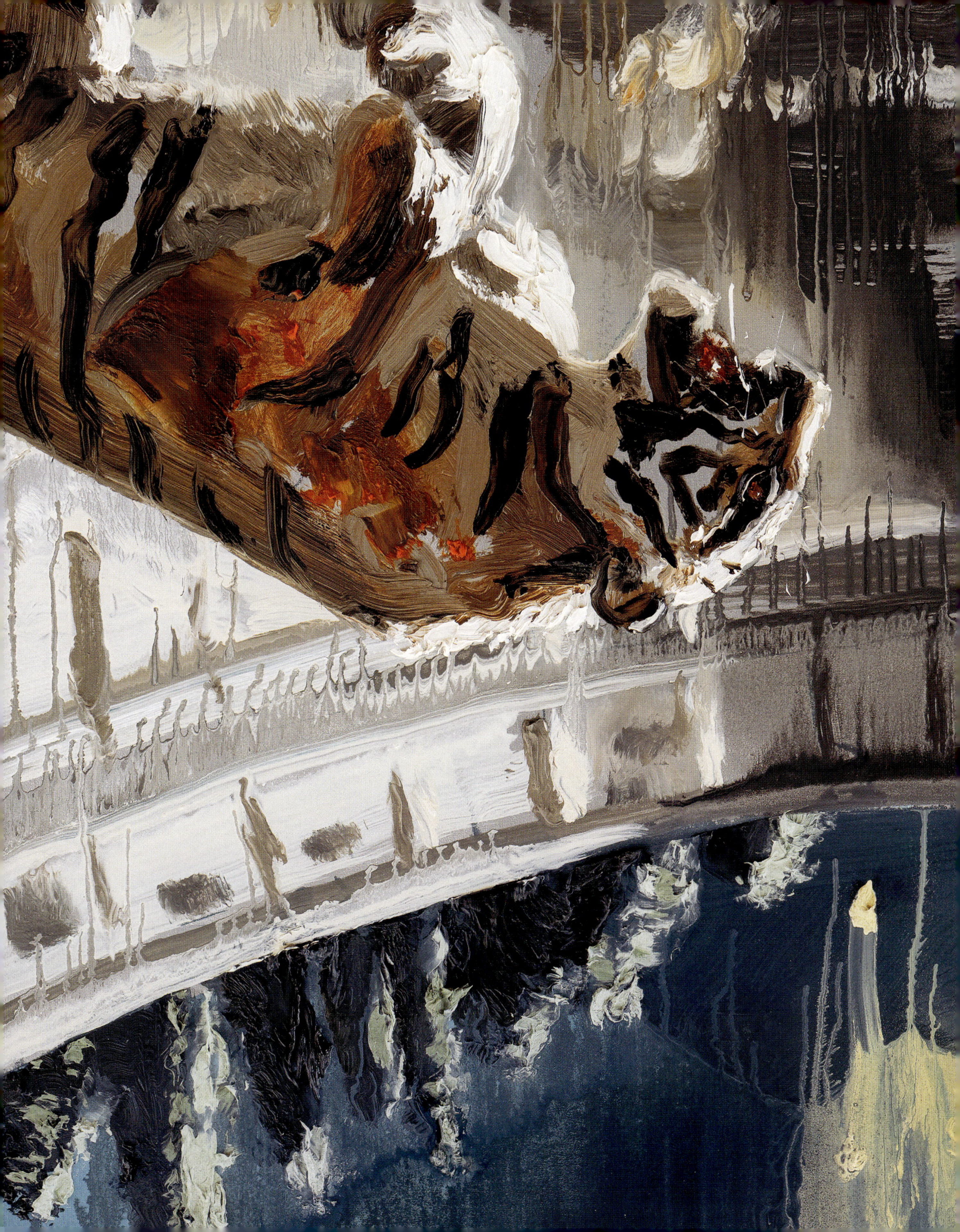

The Fossil Record: Tethys Sea, page 28

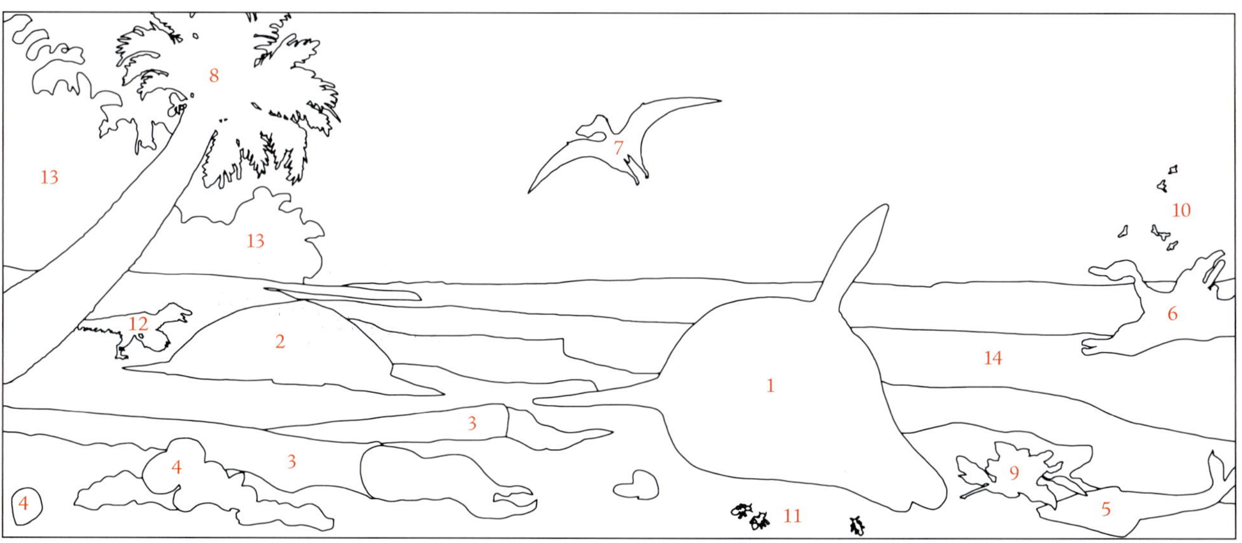

1. Ichthyosaur (*Ophthalmosaurus*)
2. Protostegid sea turtle (*Rhinochelys nammourensis*)
3. Belemnite (*Megateuthis sp.*)
4. Clams (*Inoceramus sp.*)
5. Guitarfish (*Spathobatis sp.*)
6. Hadrosaur (*Tethyshadros insularis*)
7. Pterosaur (*Anhanguera sp.*)
8. Cycad (*Pseudoctenis sp.*)
9. Magnolia (*sp.*)
10. Brachycera flies (*Nemestrinidae sp.*)
11. Ants (*Haidomyrmodes*)
12. Raptor (*Pyroraptor olympius*)
13. Bennettitales tree (*sp.*)
14. Tethys Sea coastline

Grotte di Pertosa, page 34

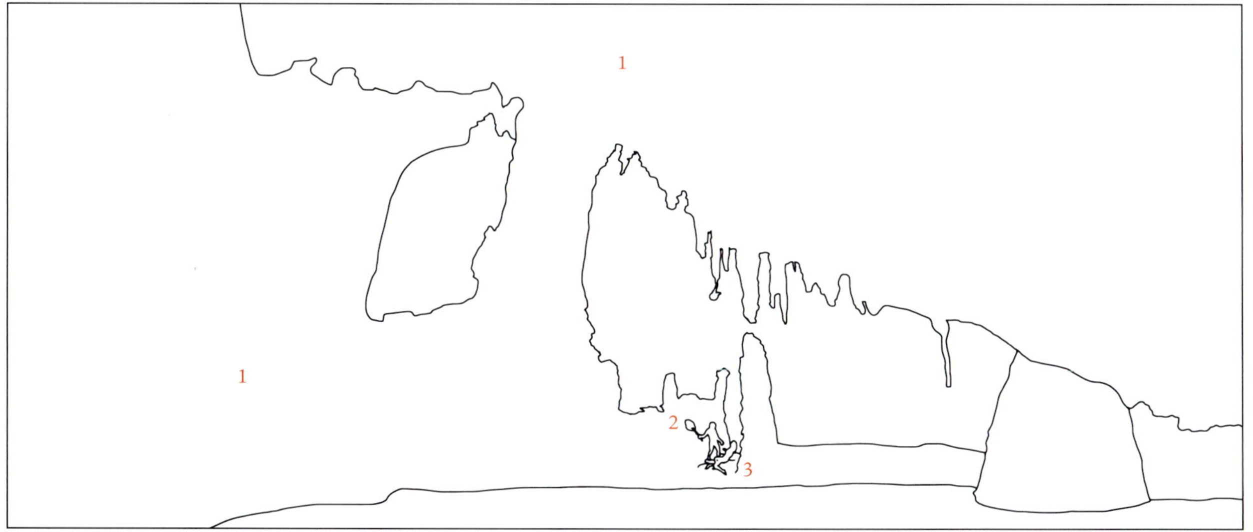

1. Grotte di Pertosa
2. Neanderthal (*Homo neanderthalensis*)
3. Human (*Homo sapiens*)

Mt. Vesuvius, Autumn, 79 AD, page 40

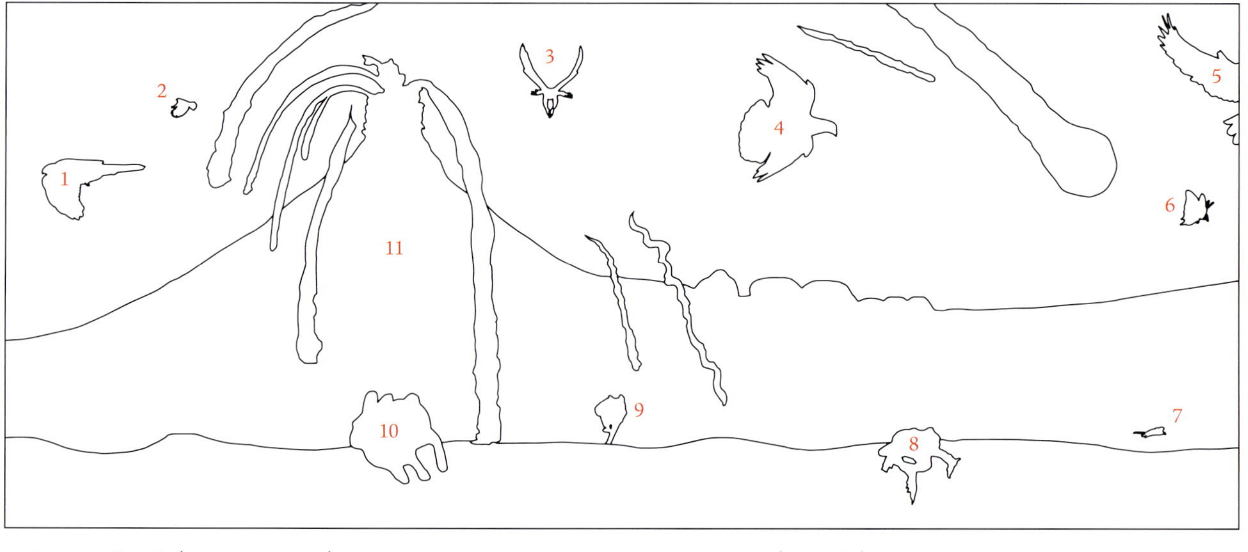

1. Sparrowhawk (*Accipiter nisus*)
2. Common redstart (*Phoenicurus phoenicurus*)
3. Peregrine falcon (*Falco peregrinus*)
4. Common pigeon (*Columba livia*)
5. Kestrel (*Falco tinnunculus*)
6. Two-tailed pasha (*Charaxes jasius*)
7. Dormouse (*Glis glis*)
8. European toad (*Bufo bufo*)
9. Red fox (*Vulpes vulpes*)
10. Wild rabbit (*Oryctolagus cuniculus*)
11. Mount Vesuvius

Plague in the Kingdom of Naples, 1656–1658, page 46

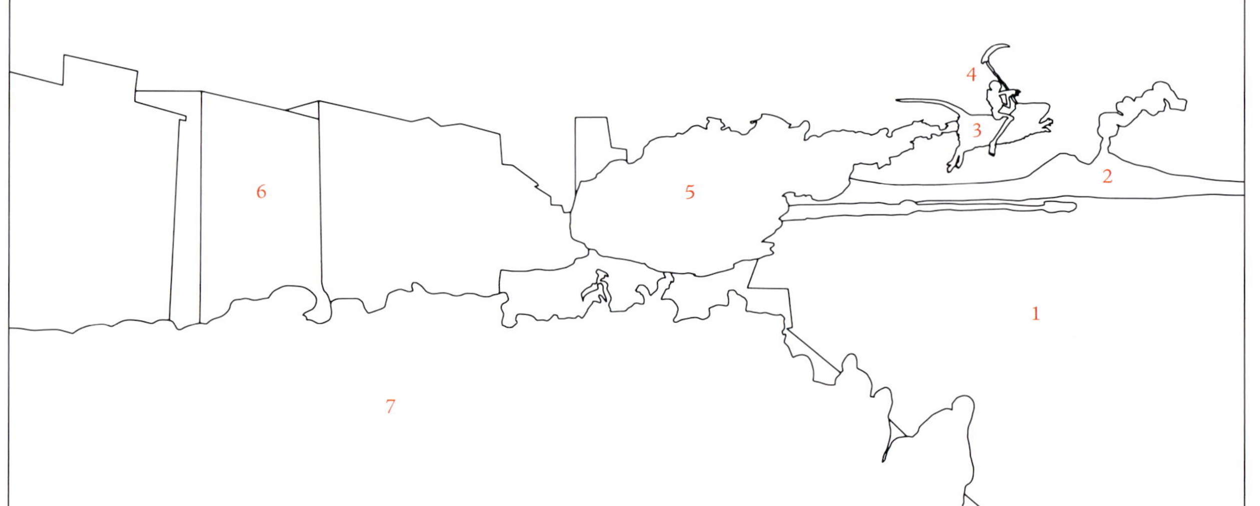

1. The Bay of Naples
2. Mount Vesuvius
3. Norway rat (*Rattus norvegicus*)
4. Allegory of Death
5. Bubonic plague
6. Naples
7. Local population

The Departed, page 52

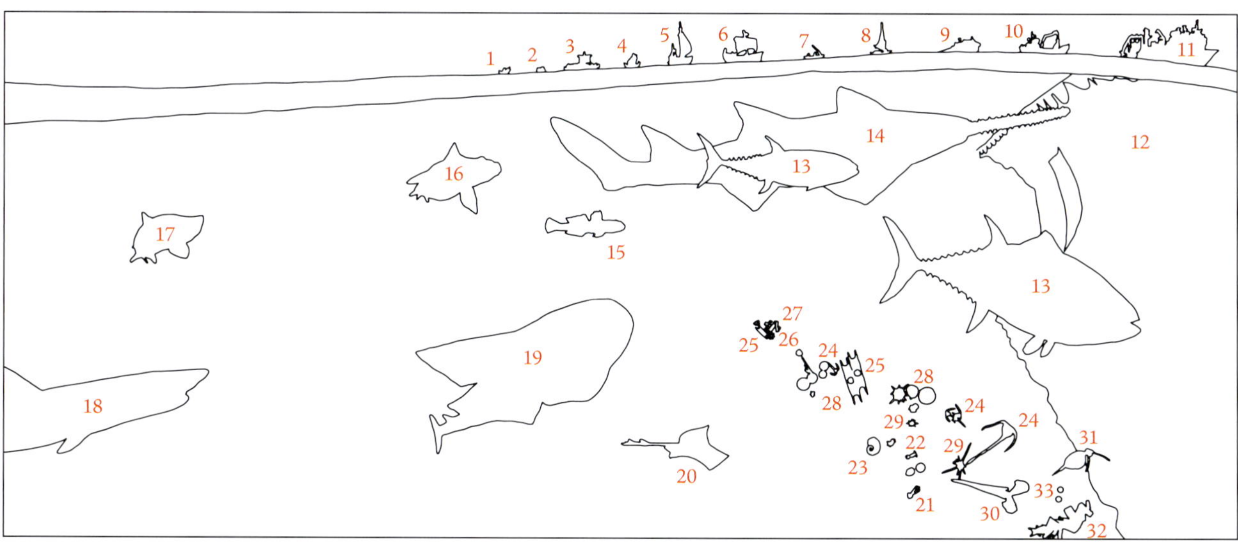

1. Indigenous Arctic qajaq (kayak, 2000 yrs old)
2. Coracle (2500 yrs old)
3. Marmotta canoe (7000 yrs old)
4. Reed boat (7000 yrs old)
5. Phoenician (3000 yrs old)
6. Kyrenian (2500 yrs old)
7. Roman ship (2000 yrs old)
8. Felucca (1000 yrs old)
9. Greek fishing boat (1970s)
10. Almadraba (Spanish tuna fishing vessel)
11. Minerva (Italian commercial fishing vessel, 2003)
12. Commercial gillnet
13. Atlantic bluefin tuna (*Thunnus thynnus*)
14. Smalltooth sawfish (*Pristis pectinata*)
15. Common goby (*Pomatoschistus microps*)
16. Angular roughshark (*Oxynotus centrina*)
17. Sand tiger shark (*Carcharias taurus*)
18. Shortfin mako shark (*Isurus oxyrinchus*)
19. Smoothback angelshark (*Squatina oculata*)
20. Bottlenose skate (*Rostroraja alba*)
21. Oweniid worm larva (*Owenia fusiformis*)
22. Copepod with egg sac (*Acartia enzoi*)
23. Heteropoda sea snail (*Atlanta sp.*)
24. Dinoflagellate (*Tripos macroceros*)
25. Diatom (*Odontella sp.*)
26. Diatom (*Asterionella formosa*)
27. Diatom (*Thalassiosira sp.*)
28. Green diatom (*Phaeocystis globosa*)
29. Radiolaria (*sp.*)
30. Pteropod (*Creseis virgula*)
31. Copepod (*Metridia longa*)
32. Brine shrimp (*Artemia salina*)
33. Diatom (*Coscinodiscus sp.*)

Acquario di Napoli - Stazione Zoologica Anton Dohrn, page 58

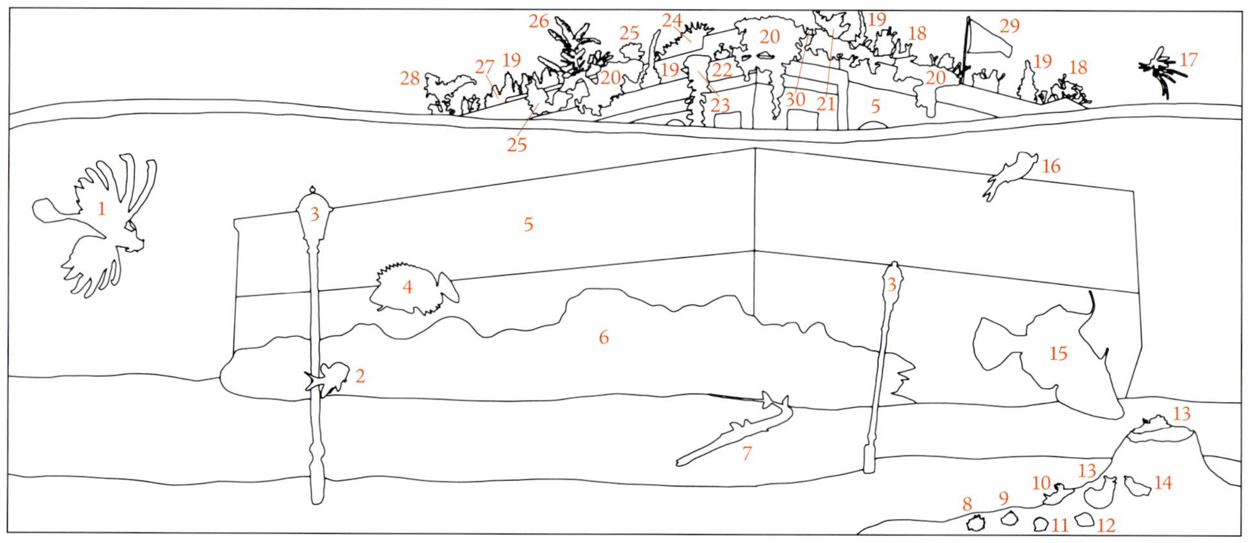

1. Lionfish (*Pterois miles*)
2. Redcoat (*Sargocentron rubrum*)
3. Lamposts (1870s)
4. Dusky spinefoot (*Siganus luridus*)
5. Stazione Zoologica Anton Dohrn
6. *Caulerpa taxifolia*
7. Bluespotted cornetfish (*Fistularia commersonii*)
8. Ragged sea hare (*Bursatella leachii*)
9. Spiny oyster (*Spondylus spinosus*)
10. Willan's chromodoris (*Chromodoris willani*)
11. Atlantic pearl oyster (*Pinctada radiata*)
12. Asian rapa whelk (*Rapana venosa*)
13. Spotted sea hare (*Aplysia dactylomela*)
14. Sea slug (*Haminoea cyanomarginata*)
15. Reticulated leatherjacket (*Stephanolepis diaspros*)
16. Bigfin reef squid (*Sepioteuthis lessoniana*)
17. Asian tiger mosquito (*Aedes albopictus*)
18. Cotton-batting plant (*Pseudognaphalium stramineum*)
19. Common mullein (*Verbascum thapsus*)
20. English ivy (*Hedera helix*)
21. Common buttonbush (*Cephalanthus occidentalis*)
22. Dandelion (*Taraxacum officinale*)
23. Poison ivy (*Toxicodendron radicans*)
24. Needle bush (*Hakea sericea*)
25. Bushy needlewood (*Baccharis halimifolia*)
26. Tree-of-Heaven (*Ailanthus altissima*)
27. Pokeweed (*Phytolacca americana*)
28. Chinese tallow (*Triadica sebifera*)
29. Flag of Naples
30. Domestic cat (*Felis catus*)

Post Human: Palazzo Donn'Anna, page 64

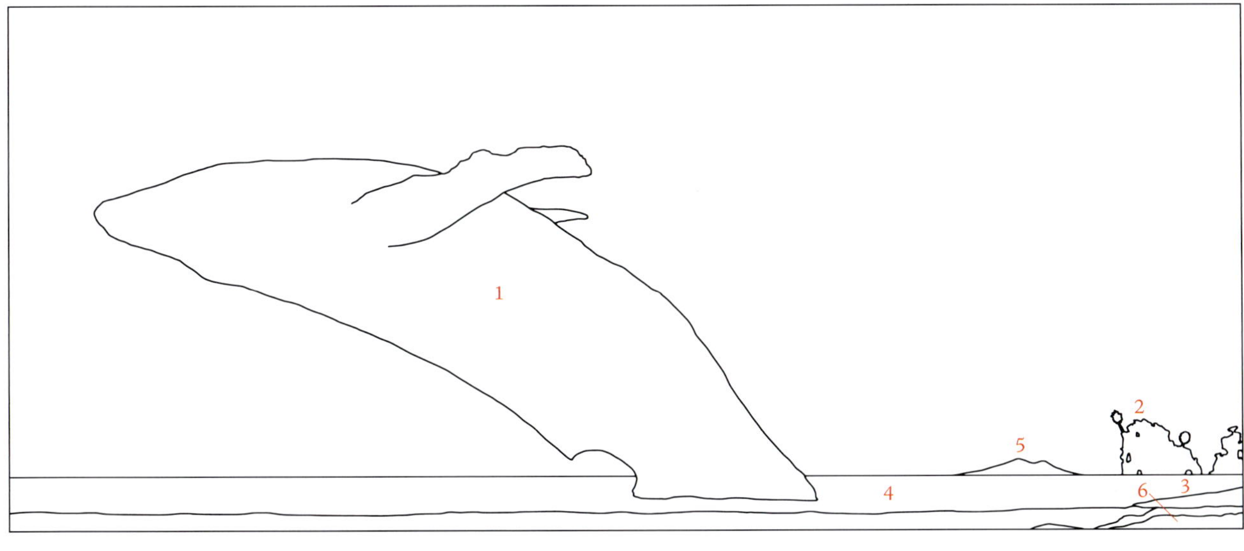

1. Humpback whale (*Megaptera novaeangliae*)
2. Palazzo Donn'Anna, Via Posillipo, 16c, 80123 Napoli NA, Italy
3. Largo Donn'Anna
4. Bay of Naples
5. Mount Vesuvius
6. Landfill

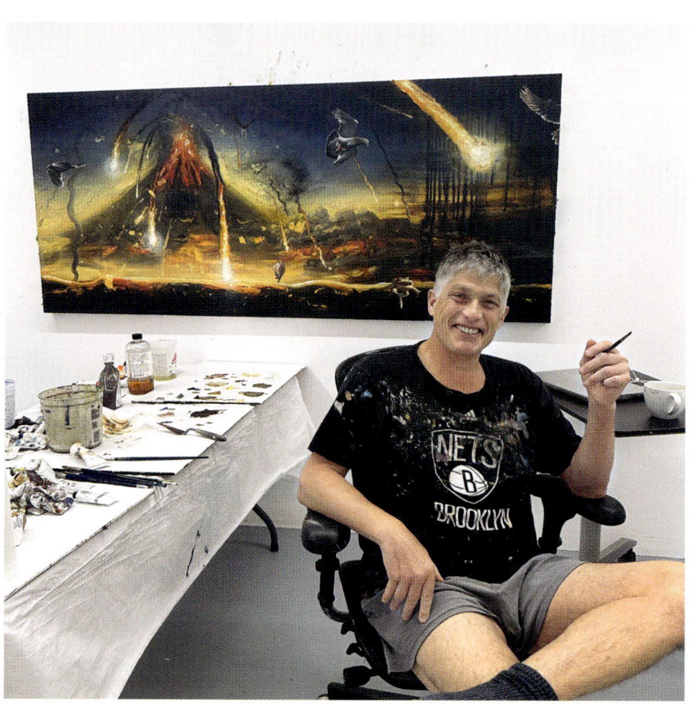

Alexis Rockman wishes to acknowledge:

Alja Zoe Freier, Jonas Abro, Olivia Smith, Chris Dorland, and David Deutsch, Magenta Plains, New York

Maurizio Morra Greco, Giulia Pollicita, Fondazione Morra Greco

Ferdinando Boero, Emeritus Professor of Zoology, Università del Salento;
Chair Stazione Zoologica Anton Dohrn; University of Naples Federico II

Michele Papa, Chief Curator, The Anatomy Museum of the University of Naples Federico II

Laura Massetti, Professor, Naples National Archaeological Museum

Piergiulio Cappelletti, Professor, Royal Mineralogy Museum Center of Natural Sciences

Andrea Inselmann, Gale and Ira Drukier Curator of Modern and Contemporary Art,
Herbert F. Johnson Museum of Art, Cornell University

Bram and Lara Hechtkopf

Gerard and Ilaria Viganò-Francis

Elisabeth Rochau-Shalem, Senior Editor, Hirmer Publishers

Tony Morgan, Alexander Winch (for his tireless research and help), and Adam Reich

Mark Dion, Dana Sherwood, Trey Abdula, Kiki Jai Raj,
and especially Dorothy Spears

Graphic design and typesetting: Tony Morgan/Step Graphics
Senior Editor Hirmer Publishers: Elisabeth Rochau-Shalem
Project management Hirmer Publishers: Rainer Arnold

Prepress: Reproline mediateam GmbH&Co. KG, Unterföhring

Paper: GardaMatt Art 150 g/m2
Typeface: Adobe Jenson Pro
Printing and binding: Printer Trento S.p.A.

Printed in Italy

Bibliographic information published by the Deutsche Nationalbibliothek
The Deutsche Nationalbibliothek lists this publication in the Deutsche Nationalbibliografie; detailed bibliographic data is available on the Internet at https://www.dnb.de.

Alexis Rockman images courtesy of the Artist and Magenta Plains, New York.
Plate photography by Adam Reich, except installation photography, pp. 22–27 by Object Studies, courtesy of Magenta Plains, New York; and pp. 70–73 by David O. Brown, courtesy of the Herbert F. Johnson Museum of Art, Cornell University.
Other photography: Dorothy Spears (pp. 7, 12, 16, 17 top right, 18, 111); Alexis Rockman (pp. 9, 10, 17 middle left); Giulia Pollicita (p. 17 top left, lower right); Mark Dion (pp. 17 lower left, 20); Dana Sherwood (p. 19).

ISBN 978-3-7774-4786-5

Hirmer Publishers (Hirmer Verlag GmbH)
Managing Director: Kerstin Ludolph
Bayerstraße 57–59, 80335 Munich, Germany
www.hirmerpublishers.com

Magenta Plains
149 Canal Street, New York, NY 10002
www. magentaplains.com

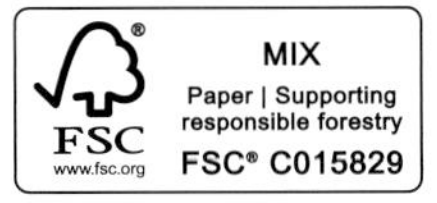

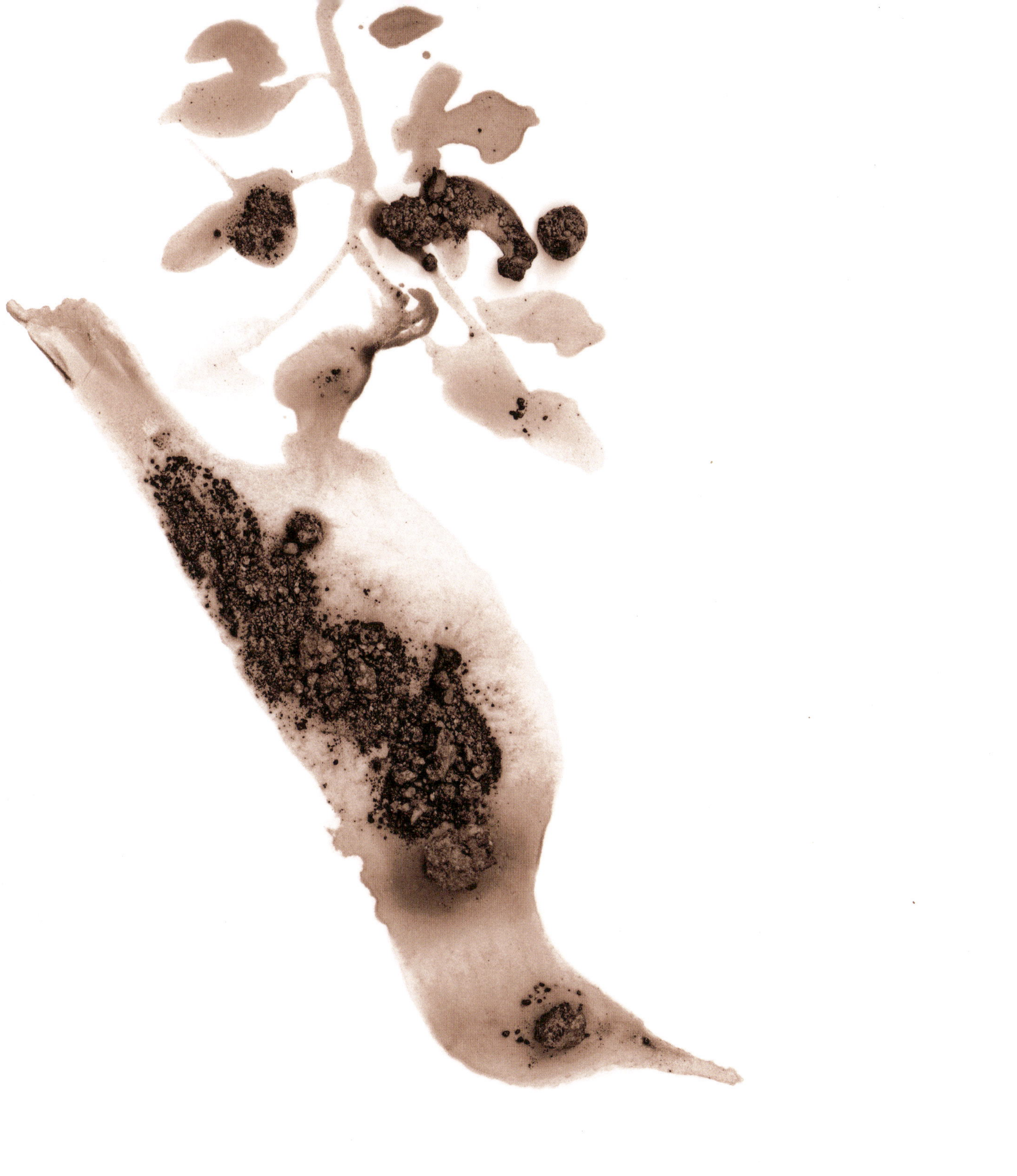

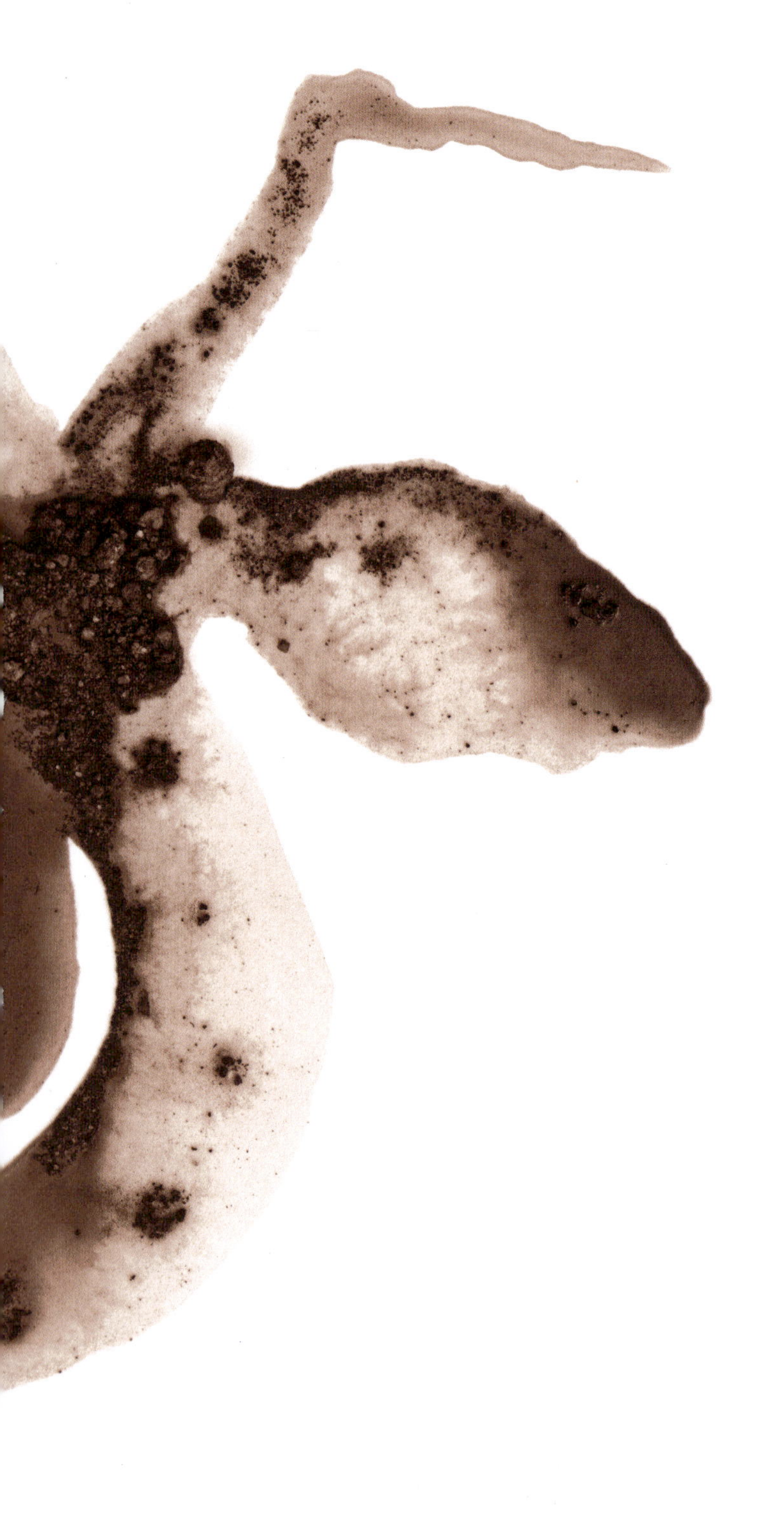